On the Edge of Human Technology

GÖTE NYMAN

DEDICATION

This book does not directly deal with peace but I dedicate its best thoughts to the peace work with human technology where 'human' comes before 'technology', the way we have learned and studied it at Peace Innovation lab, Stanford.

CONTENTS

ACKNOWLEDGMENTS

I've been blessed with the encouraging and human attitude of my HUVA, Human Beings in the Sixth Wave –project friends and colleagues Ossi Kuittinen, Chair at SimAnalytics Ltd and Markku Wilenius, Professor of Future Studies. Especially the section 'Humanification of AI', on human AI is an outcome of our numerous discussions and collaboration with Ossi. My colleagues and friends Mark Nelson, Co-Director from Stanford Peace Innovation lab and Takashi Kawai, Professor from Waseda University have always inspired me to bravely introduce my thoughts on human technology topics and now in writing. It has been amazing to notice how often our thoughts with Professor Takashi Kawai, with our own personal touches and directions, have progressed along similar routes. Having a punching bag at home was no surprise. Over several conversations, Mika Pantzar, Professor at University of Helsinki has motivated me (without perhaps knowing it) to write this book, being a wonderful critical colleague with a lively academic stance, something that a writer must be prepared to take and cherish, especially in the case of an essay.

Many of my lessons described here have their origins in the collaboration with my POEM teams at UH working with M-real Ltd, e.g. Henrik Damen and Esa Torniainen, and the camera team at Nokia with e.g. Joni Oja and Tero Vuori, to mention only some of these wonderful world-class professionals and people; I cannot list all the influential and amazing people I have met and listened to during my work. Some of them and their roles are introduced in the text. Working with Dr. Jukka Häkkinen I've learned about human 3D vision and seen the human-technological knowledge demands for the design of future VR, AR devices and apps. Insights from game experience research originate from the work with Dr. Jari Takatalo, now at Rovio. I want to mention two specific occasions that have had an unusual influence on my thinking about 'humanification of technology'. The first one is due to the fondness and companionship I experienced with the FIND team during our collaboration in Nagoya, Japan and then another similar atmosphere I met with SimAnalytics people in Finland, when working with some of the most fascinating, AI-related challenges of human technology design and implementation. With Hannu Tuomisaari I learned a lot on formulating the concept of Internet of behaviors and various ways to consider its implementation.

I'm grateful to Muzaffer Topdagi, for the friendship and his amazing, open-minded and highly professional work in implementing the idea of situational intelligence in our common projects and sw products where the concept of internet of behaviors has found its first tangible form.

I could not have a better coach, supporter and advisor than my dear wife Kiisa Hulkko-Nyman, who has helped me immensely – not only with this book – to find trust in what and how I write and how to find ever better modes of writing.

Finally, most of the ideas presented here are constrained by my own biases. This is a very personal and in that sense limited essay. I happily carry the responsibility for possible neglects, repetitions, mistakes and misunderstandings. I've felt it worthwhile to take the risk and explain my thoughts in writing.

About this book

I decided to write a spontaneous, but empirically grounded, personal essay on a wide spectrum of human-technology topics that extend from e.g. visual to organizational perception and from human centered design to human AI and the Internet of behaviors. The excuse for such a diverse, general – and partly speculative - approach is that I wanted to collect and formulate the thoughts and ideas from my practical and theoretical encounters with the edges of human, especially digital technologies. It would have been too much to put all this into a form of a detailed literature review and references.

I don't have a coherent 'theory' of human technology to suggest and defend, but some elements for theory building are embedded in the text. Hence the personal essay, which I hope can serve as inspiration if it is not muted by sharp academic critic. Most of the concepts I introduce have been part of successful and long-term research and development work, on real technology and media markets while some of the ideas introduced are still novel, even imagination and reach beyond UI and HCI. The story is a logical-conceptual one, with the aim to describe the underlying thinking while trying to clarify my own mind as well. I have tried to refer to relevant sources so that they are easy to find, even with Google which I think is still a primitive tool for this very human purpose. I will prepare a document of sources in my blog and will not include them in the book. I have not worked alone as the references tell.

My motivation

I chose to call my essay *On the Edge of Human Technology*. The title emerged from the observations on how difficult it is to get contextually relevant advice to ambitious human technology problems by searching advice and help from systematic academic treatments on human-technology-media relationships and HCI. Often there is a lack of realistic feel of what it means to work with human tech and convince the engineers and publishers designing their products on the radical value and potential of ambitious human factors.

After 40 ears of surfing on this enchanting edge and having followed it wobble and move, I have realized that my take on some of these phenomena is somewhat original – in good or in bad, I cannot say. Writing a book about it did not feel silly and it became an invitation to test and see my own thinking. I can see now that the story is not a straight lane of thoughts at all but rather what I love to characterize as a reflection of the persistent chaotic attractors in my thinking and life with human technology.

I start with a rather extensive, free-wheeling series of critical thoughts and observations to convince the reader on the relevance of these views and explain the critical stance to what I see as modern, especially digital technologies as we use and talk about them and in fact, are forced to use them daily – to organize our inner and physical life around them. To avoid falling into philosophical bemoaning and despair I take up two simple everyday case examples (from Facebook and Google) and use them as proof of their earned criticism. I only suggest some technically simple solutions, but they are conceptually transformational improvements to some of the basic human- and social-technological practices of today.

The ideas may be primitive in nature, but provide a deeper human design perspective, in the way we look at human users of any digital service. To put it briefly: I believe in future 'bottom-up technologies' that give or return the individual the initiative, respect the context of his or her life and personal situations, and protect her from technological tyranny. This is in sharp contrast to the 'top-down', AI and ML-based, analytic and manipulative operations on which we typically rely today and which many believe will dominate our future life with their ever better 'intelligent' services. I believe in the value of human situational intelligence of future technologies where 'human situation' has its deepest meaning and which can be impossible for any technological service to recognize without human help.

I'm not a technology-philosopher and often I wonder if I'm a psychologist either. A large part of the book is devoted to practical approaches and methods that originate from our studies on image quality, reader experiences, communication, network collaboration, university-business collaboration, AI implementation, and gaming, for example. The earliest ones of these may appear as distant fields of study and r&d but looking at them now, after some years, they share the same human-centered approach we have followed for almost four decades already – and my ex-team continues some of it, with its own spices and orientation. I also present a general essay on a wider topic, touching the developments of current technologies, as related to infrastructure, human motivation and organizational strategy management.

I have remained critical about the practical potential of current brain research to help in building human technologies for everyday use. Consequently, I have not dealt with the brain recordings work, single cell studies, I conducted with Dr. Lea Leinonen at Professor Juhani Hyvärinen's lab. They would have offered a lot of energy for speculation about the 'intelligent brain' having its ways of interpreting the word, the way it becomes visible already at single cell level.

At the end of the book I describe my personal history and explain the views and ways to think about HCI and some aspects of media and organizational life. I've been rather extensive in using this opportunity to thank some of my early colleagues with whom I learned so much.

Following the avalanche of digital tools, platforms and applications it is crystal-clear that these developments will repeatedly surprise us. It is impossible to write a book that would cover them all but I believe there is a place for a conceptual approach, and that was my motivation to take up this task. Finally, I've tried to build a healthy workplace during my whole career and saw this as a proper place to be explicit with this endeavor. I believe these thoughts are not irrelevant in the work with human technology.

Ideas … Speculation

In the conceptually innovative but rather speculative parts, I introduce some thoughts on the relationship between the Internet and behavior by describing a compelling but somewhat controversial bottom-up approach. The idea of the *Internet of Behaviors* (IoB) is outlined, an analog to IoT but with the difference that IoB addresses human, occurring or planned behaviors or situations instead of addressing artificial objects like IoT does. Its purpose is to address behaviors so that people's identities can be kept unknown and their privacy secured. There is no need to explain here why this separation between behavior and identity is a significant step. Further, I want to emphasize that by 'behavior' I mean both internal (in the mind) and external behavior.

Quite a few conceptual application examples are introduced here in a very primitive form, but I hope they serve as inspiration for further human technology thinking.

I introduce the most speculative idea I have ever written about technology, that is, how to improve the current network models and their representations of human behavior and connectivity. It is very general description and based on the concepts – as an analogy - derived from the string theory in physics. It is not only about network representations but about ways to formally represent complex, multi-dimensional, interacting and interdependent human behaviors and life processes in general.

An unusual decision was to include the IoB idea in my fiction novel *Perceptions of (the) Les Demoiselles d'Avignon* which I have now finished and try to get published soon. There I have used imagination to see how the IoB concept could live and benefit mankind – without the hard, practical limitations of getting technology on real markets. It is highly conceptual - so far.

Finally, I explain the problems I have met in trying to offer a human-centered approach in technology and business settings. Again, this is not to frustrate the reader but to introduce ways of thinking about these very common problems, which are often silenced, but that every HCI professional meets. It is an organizational innovation challenge itself, to find ways to create demand for serious human-technology solutions and then find people and firms willing to invest in it, on the hard and skeptical business-technology markets.

1 THE ORIGINAL SINS OF HCI

1. Towards humanification of HCI

The evolution of human-computer interaction (HCI) has been consistent, but conceptually not very fast since 1970s. In 1980s it was guided by the belief that an effective user interface makes us all masters of digital technology. Today, we can only guess what this interaction will be like with the best AR, VR, AI and Machine Learning systems of the next decades. There is a rush of unfounded and wild rumors about brain-technology interfaces. While various means are used to record the eeg and eye movements for controlling devices, even building UIs, there are significant problems preventing them from becoming useful everyday tools. To name one: the knowledge of the signal base for abstract thoughts, thinking and planning is very primitive. A further note has a place here on my critical stance towards the brain-computer interface speculations.

As a young psychologist, I worked with brain damaged people. Among many of them, their families and children, I remember a young mother, who had an anatomically minor trauma in her *gyrus angularis* (in the parietal lobe) and because of that she had completely lost her sense of direction and ability to do simple multiplications and divisions. It destroyed her job as a waitress and made her life otherwise extremely difficult. Some patients had similar 'small' lesions in other parts of the brain like in Broca's or Wernice's areas with devastating impact on speech. The brain is an extremely sensitive, interconnected system and anyone imagining processor implants and other artificial devices in the brain for normal healthy people must think twice. In patient work and in case of severe neurological problems, the needs are different as is known from the technological treatment of Parkinsonism, for example.

Forgetting these, it is nevertheless likely that we will see a massive renovation of current user interfaces and in our ways of interacting with intelligent devices and systems. During my 'expert visit' to Toyota Nagoya in Japan, I was inspired by the strong human insight there, leading to their honestly human approach in car-HCI and the way it is demonstrated in their visionary concept car. This direction of human-technology evolution is not only about emotional design, which is aimed at improving the traditional, cold-cognitive ones; there is a deeper, progressive undercurrent, which I like to call *humanification of HCI*. It is getting momentum with high-quality speech recognition and synthesis systems and with AI in general.

A major breakthrough in HCI took place at around 1980 - 1990 when graphic user interfaces (GUI), spread from Xerox PARC, and started invading pc:s and other devices, relieving people from learning what many then experienced as cryptic versions of computer command languages. I had my role in introducing such concepts to the mobile phones of Nokia (it was Mobira then) in the late 1980s.

Knowing the 'use languages' was the key to power. This situation has not changed much, only the languages are changing. The dark side of the *ease of use* meant that computer users gave away the command and control of their personal computers and the inbuilt software functions: we started trusting the easy-to-use *direct access* symbols like icons and click buttons to command our devices. Most users adopted new graphical mental-conceptual images of their systems and about the services they were using; these views, the mental models of 'computers', became increasingly distant from the actual computer, its components, programs, algorithms, and the operating system. This could have been useful and even somewhat amusing if it were not so alarming to realize that *the term 'direct access', in fact meant 99% indirect actions*. The only direct action provided was the touching of the screen and the triggering of a set of unknown operations, some of them extremely malicious to the systems of today, even global ones – and to the person using them. Current Facebook and other apps lure people to this and we know what has happened to our personal data. The click paradigm emerged and became dominant.

In an abstract and 'democratic' sense, we as citizens gained a higher amateur skill-level in the use of computers and happily gave away some of the technical, system-related and administrator rights and responsibilities concerning our computers. As a result, 'selecting an icon' in a personal device can now launch practically anything within the sw system and its network without the standard user knowing or understanding at all what is going on at that moment and especially as an indirect consequence of it.

The mishaps and misunderstanding of direct access are not limited to pure ict systems only. In 2017 U.S.S. John S. McCain and an oil tanker collided when the sailors lost control of the ship, which resulted in the death of 10 people and many more injured. The National Transportation Safety Board found problems in the use of the multi-functional touchscreen-based control of navigation and then for some ships, the Navy decided to use traditional mechanical knobs and other controls. The accident was not a simple UI hazard; education and training problems were included (see "Navy ditches touchscreens for knobs and dials after fatal crash", TechCrunch 2019).

Graphical User Interface (GUI) was the first major step in opening the devices to the world, allowing personal computers and later also other digital devices to conquer our private life, in stealth mode, invisible and unknown to the user who did not see or understand the commands and traffic generated by icon touches. With an increasing artificial intelligence, learning, intimacy and connectivity of computers and everyday devices, this 'direct manipulation' has had alarming consequences and any behavior can today become a trigger to unknown program operations.

This was unnatural: think about life in general and how we typically see what follows from our actions and how we learn to control and use our limbs, senses, and actions. Only in accidents it can happen that we touch something that has unfortunate consequences. Non-professional users learned quickly to overlook the risks and when the first serious security issues like viruses appeared and multiplied, it was already too late. The control of the computer as a system had become too difficult for standard users. Of course, this is nothing new in technology, similar evolution has been observed for cars which are practically impossible to service without professional tools and computer systems. But the difference is that people use computers to manage their life, practically every aspect of it.

2. A new burden

The responsibility of using the net and mobile services has been forced on us as consumers and citizens while the scope of damages can be unlimited. A successful attack on our personal ict systems can destroy our life, even our friends' lives, and economy in a second and the responsibility lies on us, not on the banks, device designers or the operators who sell us their services. The no-brainer explanation, of course, is that the operating systems and even the dominating processors like Intel can have unexpected vulnerabilities so that hackers and spies can use them. This is the most astonishing, harmful development in the HCI realm, impossible to understand how it has come about and has not been stopped in time.

No doubt, we will face similar problems of responsibility when AI becomes an intimate part of our life. We, as users have learned to be helpless with the pathologies of technology and rely on the available external security services to defend us, when in fact it should be the responsibility of the device and system designers and the firms selling their devices and services to us. The security situation with pc:s and mobile phones reminds more of a state of war than that of peace. Some are waiting for the block chain technology to come and save us, but the coming of the amazing, powerful quantum computing is already in the horizon.

The spread of false news, falsified audio and video, combination of any signals to generate illusory people acting or talking is no more science fiction and we will meet their unforeseen consequences, perhaps already at the time this book is published and read. Games could become a new test bed for such phenomena. Hence, it is no surprise that the ethics of AI has become a globally popular topic. Unfortunately, it often misses the practical circumstances where 'AI ethics happens', as an outcome of technological, managerial and work-related practices and decisions

Empirical studies on human-agent interaction and common decision making are needed for finding ground for the designs of AI-technology uses. An excellent recent example of such empirical work, using self-driving car simulation is the doctoral thesis by Dave Miller from Stanford having the title "Human-computer moral conflicts".

The problems with technology are not personal only; a seizure of techno-pathology can scare a nation. The incidence in Hawaii, January 2018 showed how a false alarm via tv, radio and cell phones forced the whole population of a state to live under the fear that they are under a nuclear attack – for 38 minutes!

The missile alert was a scary example of pathological adaptation to bad design:

"BALLISTIC MISSILE THREAT INBOUND TO HAWAII. SEEK IMMEDIATE SHELTER. THIS IS NOT A DRILL."

The first explanation after the incident was that it was a human error and even photographs of 'the responsible person' were distributed. A rare voice of reason, Don Norman was quick to respond to this with his analysis and comment:

"How do false alerts happen? As soon as I read about the false alert of a missile attack on Hawaii I knew who would be blamed: some poor, innocent person. Human error, would be the explanation. But it would be wrong. The real culprit is poor design: poor, bad, incompetent."
(Fastcompany).

Unfortunately, Norman's voice did not carry far and the employee was probably fired or punished, together with some of his colleagues.

Quite recently, a similar 'human error' launched a massive false alarm of an air-traffic accident at Helsinki-Vantaa Airport in Finland. The faults in human-technology design in critical places and situations serve as perfect examples and proof on how adaptive we have become and how institutions use the technology: we have adapted to the worst of circumstances. Sometimes we wake up, like when Steve Jobs showed us better alternatives to ict use experiences. His message was simply about human-centric technology. However, the answer to the question 'What is human', changes all the time with technology and what Jobs offered to us then is now a core ingredient in many human-technology designs, with their problems; we must prepare for and design the next generation of *humanification of HCI.*

There is a serious asymmetry problem, with no cure visible: users have gained extensive functionality and services but paid the price of losing control of their personal data and security. Ask any computer user, how the system state and configuration of his computer or mobile device have been modified, let's say within a day or two, and what kind of data is being exchanged between his system and unknown external actors, and you will receive puzzled looks. If the same number of strangers and aliens were moving around at our homes, peeking through our windows, visiting our bedrooms, ringing the doorbell at any time of the day, stealing stuff, and even talking to us, every minute, we would be seriously alarmed and tried to do something about it, run away or fight.

We have been taught to remain ignorant to the issues of technologically induced asymmetry and most of us can only trust updates and digital security services. We suffer from a helplessness syndrome, *a pathological form of technology acceptance.* An intense global debate and actions especially in Europe (e.g. GDPR), however, have been launched concerning the regulations for managing and controlling this asymmetry and the way the platform giants treat our data and make fortunes with it. The question arises, do we need better and more regulation, better system architecture or transformative innovations? The simple answer is 'yes'.

3.   Blind spot in the net: asymmetric human data markets

In 2001 the Nobel prize for economics was awarded to George Akerlof, Michael Spence and Joseph Stiglitz for their research and findings on the "Markets with asymmetric information." To quote the news of the prize from The Royal Swedish Academy of Sciences:

"Many markets are characterized by asymmetric information: actors on one side of the market have much better information than those on the other."

The news explained the asymmetries occurring between borrowers vs. lenders, managers vs. shareholders, prospective clients vs. insurance companies. However, the data collected of us vs. the data we own, as citizens were not included in this remarkable list.

Today the balance between the information we have and what outsider agents have on us is shifting, fast. An increasingly large part of the total information intake originates from us, from our actions, habits, preferences, personality traits, locations, interests, genes, and even of our breathing, pulse and other physiological states. The temporal, spatial and situational accuracy of the intelligent sensor systems improve and speed up the widening of this asymmetry gap: what is collected today ends up in the hands of the operator-emperors, their partners and beyond. This data is meant to be theirs forever and it is their most powerful asset without which they would be nothing. When someone then uses this data against us, we carry the responsibility to pay the price, defend ourselves and survive.

Examples of data asymmetry:

- Someone has data about the places we have visited (location spying).
- We cannot know what kind of machine learning (ML) models have been applied to our personal data.
- Somewhere there is knowledge on our relationships with other people but we don't know where this data is and who has it.
- There is data about me that only its current owner (who stole it from me) knows about.
- There is legally obtained data that can harm me but I cannot know how it could do that, directly or indirectly.
- We don't know who is responsible if harm is done to us, directly or indirectly, through the net services we have paid for.

Some of these issues have been touched by the GPDR regulation but most of the problems remain outside its reach. Many continue to worry that we are heading towards a dystopia where the giants will maintain their power over us, more than any Government can ever do and we will lose the vital control of our life and living: the 'platform giants' will guide us and charge for our everyday living, health and even death – avoiding their responsibility for consequences.

With the latest tools, like the Google assistant, the asymmetry is more likely to increase than decrease. The Google assistant can - if it does what it was promised to do contact anyone, arrange things for its user and communicate in an expressive tone in natural language. In addition to the help it provides, intimate personal matters can be left for systems like it to deal with – and the data related to this. Leaving intimate, human data for a robot to handle does not mean that it will be handled in a human way.

The data flow from us to 'them' is not symmetric with the data flow from 'them' to us: my data has specific value to the operators, either as data about an individual or as data about a member of a cluster or community of people. As data targets, we typically receive transformed, tuned, or hidden data and it is impossible for us to see what kind of data and algorithms have been used before the transformation and before it has been sent to us as an offer, persuasive act or any kind of service or data. It forces us to react to it in one way or another; often we try to defend ourselves against these persuasive acts and avoid any potential harm, but we have no way of knowing what exactly the persuasive algorithms are and what is the psychology behind their design.

Hence, it is not only a matter of asymmetry in the ownership of the data but also in the quality and nature of transactions. The cost of data takes a strange turn. First we give our data about location and activities, for example, for free or as a form of 'subjectively beneficial transaction', and in return we receive informed messages or services on something the operators have guessed could be relevant to us. Next the operator combines, correlates and uses any other available data and calculations to increase the value of our data to make profit by selling it to third and fourth and fifth parties who are economically or otherwise motivated to approach us or help other agents to do that. In its dynamics, this complex process and the underlying architecture is not much different from the tax-haven architectures and tax-avoidance models used by the big companies and criminals, but it's in reverse.

We do not know what is going on with our data and where it takes place and who directly or indirectly benefits from its value increase. By giving away our data we become members of communities having access to services, public and private, and can enjoy the benefits of social connectivity, offers, help, encouragement and other rewards that condition us to the use of the services: we live under continuous, modern and high-level form of operant conditioning.

The direction of the socio-technological development is clear: unless we agree to pay for the data and services we receive, in one way or another, we do not get the best available knowledge of ourselves and can become poor laggards; it is a continuously evolving data and service ecosystem. When we accept the technologist's lure we are rewarded like the Pavlovian dog for complying and have already learned to enjoy it: instead of a sip of juice or a candy – like experimental animals get - we get our daily delightful moments from using Facebook, Google, and Instagram. Often, however, we don't have the money or any other valuable assets to offer in exchange, to get access to the most valuable knowledge we need. We have learned to live both on the negative and positive, asymmetric edge of technology.

4.   The hidden human asset – the subject-person

The future of human and social data markets is alarming; there are no effective forces capable of opposing the asymmetric development; regulations are slow to follow and cover the emerging problems and threats. However, we do have a private, largely forgotten asset, which we daily control and manage - the extremely special, personal, human data which has mostly remained untouchable. Only we have the possession of it and we are its masters: what we are as cultural human beings, in our real-time, creative and colorful, personal mind spaces, with our intentions and interpretations of our realities, our love and care – towards our internal-mental and external-action spaces alike. It is our subjective self, with which we live from moment to moment. These private mental, experiential and intention data and other forms of subjective knowledge have remained the most underestimated aspects of human knowledge that make the world happen, every minute.

Knowing the moment-to-moment intentions of the North Korean President, or other leading characters in power, we would be wiser, or at least know more, for good and bad. Often the value of human intention knowledge is underestimated and it has not yet interested the data market operators who rely on their ML and AI based guesses of the next moves of their target audiences. They prefer to guess. With the current operant conditioning model imposed on us by the giants, we are losing the chances for free subjective living, something that relies on our spontaneous, personal and dynamic interpretations, experiences and creative intentions: market push and operant conditioning aim at defining us and our behaviors. By conditioning us, the AI and ML algorithms get better in guessing our behaviors.

However, by looking at our external behavior, using the best big data, ML and data collection methods, the operators can observe only the projection of our individual, internal worlds on their technical spaces. As human beings, we are 'the mother of all inverse problems' and as a community of people we can do, say, think of things that from the outset may look the same but occur for totally different - individual, biological, social, situational and cultural - reasons. The operators are, of course, getting better every day at guessing our internal states and manipulating us accordingly but they cannot avoid the inverse problem.

5. Do they know us as human beings, do they care?

Only a couple of decades ago it was still natural to think that even and especially without technology we can learn to know more about ourselves, our psychological essence the subconscious included, than any agent outside us can ever do.

A common belief and a fear now is that the emperors, Alibaba, Amazon, Facebook, Google and their likes will soon, if not already now, know us in relevant detail: our interests, preferences, personality, values, moves, and everyday habits at work and at home, even our emerging love affairs, and why not, our moment of death. One would be tempted to assume, looking at the profiles the knowledge operators have of us, that they already know our psychology better than any therapist can find out, perhaps even better than we know ourselves.

A personal story on algorithmic guessing. In July 2019 I received the usual 'memory post' from Facebook that reminded me of something I had reported on 11th July 2017. The idea was nice, but they never asked me what was significant to me at that time, thinking about it now, and that has ever since changed my whole life: they could not guess (or even try it in this case, I assume) if something important had happened to me *after* that. I was close to having a serious brain damage just a week after that 'memory post'.

Curious enough and unlike many seem to think, the psychology of human behavior and mind has never been so profoundly underestimated in its richness, multi-dimensionality, depth, spirituality, and mysteries, misunderstood in its situational, delicate and colorful complexities as is happening today. What is it – to know someone, a person in her whole life context and even after life? The latest psychologically tuned apps and the psychological logic behind them try to dwarf the ideas of the pragmatic William James, one of the founding fathers of psychology, on what psychology is about: "Psychology is the science of *mental* life". Will the platform giants know our mental life in the very near future? They barely know the surface of our minds and spiritual landscapes.

The inspiration to write a book originated from these insights on how much overlook and false beliefs about practical (often disguised as popular academic paradigms) psychology exist today. This is especially true within the HCI contexts, organizational discourses, app businesses, where technologists and firms make fortunes with their persuasive and addictive services. Similar views occur among popular brain studies and speculations. If the Pavlovian and instrumental or operational conditioning were the only psychological mechanisms driving human behavior, experiences and mental life, there would be no need to write this book.

No doubt, primitive and effective methods do condition us every day at work, at home, in sickness and in health, simply because they have a history on markets and in the society and they are easy to design and control; they work; with them our external behaviors and feelings can be modified, guided and reinforced daily. Nevertheless, it is only surface like human walking – all kinds of practices and industries can be built around it but it is still only walking. We change our behavior due to persuasion and conditioning, and react emotionally, but this is not the whole truth of our private mental spaces, not even close. Most 'human' models underlying modern technologies are mindless, but luckily fresh exceptions emerge, trying to help us to learn and grow physically and spiritually.

The dominating operators lack true human interest. Their current business-technological models work top-down, using the available, superficial big data while neglecting our private mental worlds, their complexities, our intentions and psychic, constructive-interpretative processes, which are directed both outwards and inwards, in time and space. For big data masters, a sudden change of attitude and motivation, unexpected thoughts and actions, creativity, are noise, outlier behavior and a source of errors in the analysis while for us humans, it's about the most essential, personal content and style of everyday life. There is more to us as creative humans than the big data eyes and the conditioning apparatuses can see.

Ironic enough the 'problem of the mind' is familiar to machine and algorithm designers, especially in deep learning and artificial networks: quite recently, the researchers have realized how important it would be for the engineers to communicate with the 'artificial mental world' of the learning networks, and to understand their inner workings when the systems end up producing important, perhaps even fatal AI decisions.

Engineers working with deep learning deal with huge artificial systems and computations taking place in the masses of artificial synapses where machine learning happens. There is no well-defined model or protocol by which such networks should communicate about their internal and learning states with their users. Hence, the users remain uncertain about what might be going on in their 'minds' and how to be in touch with them as collaborating partners. Some may think that the deep learning systems will soon be like the human brain, there are programs already aiming at that. However, it is not a problem of small scale. Funny enough, it seems possible that technologists will be the first ones to get theoretically serious about the scope of the human mind: the number of synapses in all the brains of mankind is larger than the estimated number of stars in the known universe. Any artificial system is still a dwarf compared against the living and interacting brains and minds on the earth.

The engineers have realized the depth and complexity of the problem of the *'machine mind' and* are looking for ways to 'understand' the unpredictability of AI, its (un)explainability and incomprehensibility. AI may not be able to express all its functioning and even when it can do it, there is a challenge for humans to understand it (see eg. Yampolskiy, 2019). DARPA (Explainable AI, xAI) and Google (Explainable AI) have launched extensive projects to deal with this relatively new problem and the first steps seem to suggest they look for strong, technologically orientated solutions although some signs of cognitive-human aspects have already occurred. My educated guess is, there will be demand for solutions that touch the whole implementation process (we have named it the Triad of AI implementation and describe it here later). No doubt, this problem will be repeatedly reformulated in the very near future.

The deep-learning networks are relatively complex input-output machines and their users should know what, exactly, the systems have learned, how and what they have *not* learned and how they might behave in front of any possible, exceptional situation and external (human or artificial) pressure. A pre-school child facing a new problem knows when to say: "I don't understand that" or "I cannot handle that", "Help me!" We can imagine what kind of problems will result from the activities of ignorant machine learning systems having poor meta-skills and facing unusual, but critical situations. Like humans, they are not perfect, but their imperfection can be dangerous. To fail gracefully is an amazing human and social skill.

6.   Accurate predictions do not imply understanding

There is an invisible vicious cycle in how the Internet
giants try to learn to know us and how they make us behave
within the constraints of their inbuilt models derived from this
learning. Their predictions of our behaviors improve, but what
does it mean?

Consider the following. Based on the earlier games of *Los
Angeles Rams* and *New England Patriots* and their recent game
performances many could have made the correct prediction of
the winner in 2019: New England Patriots. Some even
commented that it was the most boring Super Bowl game ever,
which probably meant that the result and the game itself were
highly predictable. However, any amateur understands that it is
impossible to know exactly what went on in the minds of the
players and their coaches during the heated game, so many
variables and complexities, including the audience, individual
motivations and fears, integrated together with the emerging
situations, make it an impossible task to know the true life of
the game. However, predictions of the game outcomes can be
surprisingly accurate and in case of betting, for example, it is
sufficient. Nevertheless, big data and brain sciences are rather
helpless in explaining the soul of the game - who indeed would
hire even a top-class brain scientist to coach the teams? The
owners would never do that because they know that modeling,
predicting and understanding do not yet live on the same
planet with our minds.

In June 2018 Goldman Sachs used some form of 'AI' to
publicly predict the world champion in Football 2018 in
Moscow. The games had just started:

*"The final, Goldman Sachs predicts - and would be a highly charged
game, if true - would be played between former winner, Germany and
Brazil. Brazil is expected to win the match to lift their sixth World
Cup. "* (Business Today, 2018).

Well, the final was played by *France* and *Croatia*. More seriously, as football enthusiasts know, there was an intense discussion on what on earth had happened to these great teams, Germany and Brazil, and their players. In other words, what had happened in their minds (and bodies) and why?

Facebook and Google record our every possible act in virtual and physical worlds. A massive data pool is generated, fed to machine learning and an implied model (typically it is not explicitly expressed) of us is constructed – the *Image of Man*, if you like, of you and me. The *Image of Man* model is then used in predicting (guessing) our behavior and interests and to manipulate us in various synchronous ways, with selective feeds, targeted ads and news and of course, running a series of asynchronous or synchronous luring campaigns. By using the model and selective persuasive acts it supports, we are being pushed towards specific behaviors and attitudes and then observed how we react to the lure. Data is then again recorded and collected and used for learning more. The vicious cycle has taken a full cycle when the operators are finally ready to assume they have learned enough of us to guide us in what we do – when we agree to live within the technological realms they offer and use the tools they force on us. We are the Pavlovian dogs, adopting the only tools offered to us, with nowhere to run. There is a risk that we, as humans, come to accept that model as a correct or relevant one to represent us. When using simple everyday services this might not hurt us, but we know the risks.

Often the giants are successful but major failures are frequent and occur in the form of irrelevant offerings, disturbing sites popping up, spread of fake news, and bad timing of ads. This will continue in the foreseeable future and beyond. For many, their economically successful mass performance has created an illusion of service quality and of freedom to choose what we want when in fact we are constrained by the technologies we have adopted and have agreed to live within the domains defined by them. From the perspective of the giants, we behave like the model Man they have created of us, but it is only a model.

The human and spiritual consequences of the manipulative cycle have remained stealth and mostly overlooked: many of us believe that we behave as our true, independent selves and that the best technologies do good work and help us in this. There hides the underlying wish or fear, depending on the perspective, that technological services can 'see' through us and one day, they will objectively know what is happening in our brains even before we become aware of it. (Which phenomenon itself, is not surprising at all, our bodies are crowded with physiological activities which lead to behaviors we cannot accurately know or predict; 'predictive brain waves and signals' have been known for decades, but they are primitive).

It is not rare to read – at least between the lines of the futuristic, speculative texts – that within the visible future, it becomes possible to perfectly record and read our brains and we become 100% transparent, so much that what way say or think does not matter. 'Brain dump' is not an infrequent term used in these wild speculations, referring to the possibility to copy our brain contents to artificial storages and back.

No surprise then, that it is already commonplace to think – you can see it in basic research and market research discourses – that we should not trust what people say and explain because, firstly, it is claimed that people are biased and even lie or fabricate their stories, and secondly, people simply cannot explain everything about their thoughts, motives, and preferences accurately. Funny enough, the researchers claiming this, assume that we have no reason to doubt what *they* tell us, when they 'explain' how various physiological recordings will replace human communication. Perhaps we should record their brains, stop listening and wait for the enlightening?

Following these futuristic thoughts, we can imagine an Internet of Brains, where every human brain is represented and shared and served all over the world. Perhaps, as an added value, unlike in expensive psychoanalysis, the future technology promises to help us and save the therapy costs if only we agree to be monitored and accept the technological support and therapy as a service – and whatever is necessary in the business models its operators follow. This may sound like an insane joke, but reading about some futurist visions it is exactly what is expected to happen in not so distant future, perhaps within the next 50 to 100 years. Some probably think this is a pessimistic time constant.

In the public media and discourse, there is a peculiar cultural ingredient in the way human beings are considered. Quite a few seem to think about the functioning of the human mind (without being explicit about it), according to the classic Freudian legacy and the psychoanalytical model of man, i.e. there is the dark side in all of us, the invisible subconscious with its dangerous and fascinating forces, operating in a continuous, inaccessible mode, and only rarely, due to therapy, significant life events, and perhaps with the help of amazing future technologies we can become aware of the impact our subconscious has on the 'conscious, behaving me'.

A colleague of mine, once argued that even Freud's model of the human mind reflects the then available technologies and is a simple analogue model, derived from the dominant technology at the birth of psychoanalysis: the pneumatic model of man, including a chamber, its dynamic valves, and pistons as a metaphor. Insert a pressure by pushing a piston towards the chamber and the pressure must come out through the valves or the other pistons. There is no other alternative – within this technology. Once you accept the hydraulic pump model of the human mind, the technology as a reference, there is not much you can do to understand other viewpoints. Freud did not have operating systems. Not much has changed since then.

You might think that taking up Freud and the psychoanalytic Image of Man in the context of modern technology is a far-fetched idea. However, some of the core ideas in Freud's teachings were how we, as human beings and individuals, due to the psychodynamic forces that govern out mental life, learn to see and experience the world, ourselves, and our close ones. Freud explained, how we gain self-awareness, and especially how we can be relieved from the damaging effects of the traumas we have faced. A most intriguing aspect of Freud's ideas concerned the role of the unconscious and repression of socially unacceptable needs and drives that originate from the hidden *id*, which as Freud saw it, are the permanent components of human personality and which – if not controlled – aim at pleasures and immediate satisfaction of any, especially sexual urges.

Due to modern technology, everything we have learned, over generations, to suppress and hide, is now openly available to us in the net, from extreme aggression and murders to any possible form of sexual behavior. Hence, whatever the social norms and teachings may be, technology has opened the door to what used to be hidden and secretive. For some, it has become a means to conduct, record and socially share insane deeds. There are ways to prevent children from watching harmful tv and network material, but they cannot stop a teen-ager. What would have been Freud's reaction to the situation like this is an intriguing question to ponder.

7. Can the net cure: healing by spying?

There looms the idea that by facing the evil, we can be relieved from the bad and its effects on us. I assume Wikileaks as a product of digitalization and the net believes in this. While it has predecessors in the world of journalism and activism, digitalization has been its true source of power, both in acquiring knowledge, distributing it and launching reactions to it. The situation being like this, it is somewhat astonishing how little public discussion there is about the ways Wikileaks connects with people, organizations and nations and how it works now and in the future. After all, it takes its data from individuals, or uses them, and then delivers it to various stakeholders and to other individuals or institutes. It is unclear how much development has occurred in its way to use the available human-technology potential in its operations.

The hate and love felt by citizens and public organization representatives for *Wikileaks* bears an astonishing resemblance to the hate and love affair that many psychological, medical, and social science professionals have with psychoanalysis. In the deepest sense, both Wikileaks and psychoanalysis deal with the Dark (evil) and Bright (good) side of knowledge supposed to exist in our minds, in societies and in social media discourses. Their distant relatives are the open source, open innovation, open science movements and the growing spectrum of open X.

Innovations are expected to deal with Dark and Bright knowledge: better understanding of the knowledge creation processes, secure storage strategies, re-thinking ownership and ipr of data, responsibility in data ownership, innovative broadcasting models, relevant sharing platforms, sustainable use cultures, and finally – ways of leaking Dark knowledge, data and their sources when necessary. But that is not all: there are serious motivations to build an open X environment that is healthy for individuals, communities and the society in the long run. So far, their success has been meager; negative incidences have increased and become more serious as shown by the impact of fake news, Hawaii incident, crypto currency frauds, shooting down of the passenger plane in Ukraine, and the hacker interferences in elections.

Since childhood we are all taught, in one way or another, the division between good and evil knowledge, and we learn to hide our Dark data or keep it and its use in decent control: in our social contexts we have learned proper manners and ways of protecting ourselves and others. It is possible that the revelations of Dark data a'la Wikileaks become more difficult if not impossible when organizations learn to use best practices and technologies to hide their critical Dark data: as a society, we will learn new ways to hide sensitive data, just like we learn already as children; we can behave like our powerful leaders behave daily although the scale is different. Blockchain will probably speed up this development for a while.

Personal information management will improve as it has always done to feed and protect knowledge assets. An optimistic guess is that new business (grass roots) models will replace the existing models that still rely on top-down, big data and push approaches. If these initiatives succeed the existing models will be moved aside by human-centric ones and be replaced by MyData (https://mydata.org) kind of approaches aiming at human-centric data markets. A major friction factor in this is, however, the huge amount of money and power the giants have gained. On the other hand, they have become prisoners, too. I remember an old Swedish proverb from school, more than 60 years ago, which reminds of this: "Gyllene bojor äro också bojor", that is, "Golden chains are chains, too."

8.   Revelations as a form of societal therapy?

Wikileaks (W) home page has changed over the years but still some years ago (2011) we could read the following and I assume that these early statements reflect their overall thinking:

"We provide an innovative, secure and anonymous way for independent sources around the world to leak information to our journalists. We publish material of ethical, political and historical significance while keeping the identity of our sources anonymous, thus providing a universal way for the revealing of suppressed and censored injustices."

Accordingly, their role is to leak information to journalists who are presumably taken as 'trusted' parties, or who represent what W characterized as "A *healthy, vibrant and inquisitive journalistic media.*" This is hoped to be for the good of global society.

Journalists carry out tasks similar or analogous to those of the therapists who help patients by bringing unconscious, problematic information to consciousness and make the audience (the patient) aware of it. However, journalists and the publicity-hungry media do not act like therapists, and they do not have the same mission and responsibility. A journalist can have the role of an investigator, a participant, a spy, a constructionist, or a businessperson, for example. Therapeutically motivated journalist roles are exceptions. Hence, anything can happen in their hands to the 'patient', especially if the journalistic target has done something that is believed to be wrong, and straightforward journalistic ethics are followed: offering facts. The responsibility lies elsewhere, on the shoulders of people and organizations, which we, or the journalists don't usually know.

The aim of W is to disclose *"suppressed and censored injustices"*. This is a very practical aim and we can compare it against the mission of psychoanalysis. The concepts of 'suppression', 'censorship', 'injustice' indeed are part of the everyday language of psychoanalysis. On the home page of the American Psychoanalytical Association APsaA we could read (from 2011):

"The purpose of psychoanalytic treatment is to help people change and progress in their lives. The development of self-awareness/insight is a step in achieving that progress.

People make the best choices they can, given the limitations of their assumptions about themselves and their circumstances.

Psychoanalytic treatment gives patients the opportunity to examine these assumptions, understand their origins in their lives, modify them if necessary, and make better choices for themselves."

Wikileaks and psychoanalysis: parallel beliefs. APsaA explains that psychoanalysis wants to "help people change and progress in their lives" and that this can happen by developing their self-awareness/insight and that the psychoanalytical process (therapy) allows the patients to observe and analyze important aspects of their lives, for their own good.

In summary, Wikileaks and psychoanalysis have at least the following beliefs in common, what they believe in:

- The healing power of increasing self-awareness (individuals, society),
- The positive value of better self-perception (individuals, society),
- The necessity of protecting the anonymity of their sources, and
- Their own role in providing conditions of better self-perception, awareness and health.

Wikileaks and therapists both face serious problems. During psychoanalytic therapy process, for example, it is not easy to protect the patient from her/his personal (primary) data related to the Dark and Bright aspects of the unconscious. When a patient encounters valuable personal knowledge during the process, the experience becomes attached to other, specific persons like father, mother or a loved one or to some other significant person or even a community. After the therapy sessions, these relationships have changed. Not quite unlike this, Wikileaks failed to protect one of its major sources in US and who faced terrible consequences because of that. People involved in the leaked cases in general cannot be perfectly protected. The possibilities for responsible compensations remain open in cases of serious damage to individuals.

A therapist must try to protect the real person-source and her close ones, if possible. However, often it is not possible to do it, even with the highest ethical standards, since patients will inevitably carry their personal therapy experiences to everyday life and family context in the form of changed attitudes, ways of talking, fears, preferences, and interpretations. The consequences are complex and can sometimes be devastating as the examples of false memories evoked in therapy sessions (non-psychoanalytical) have shown (see the work by Elisabeth Loftus, for example, Scientific Am., 1997). No doubt, Wikileaks suffers from analogous problematic side effects that their data may cause in different contexts to people and communities who have been only indirectly involved in e.g. hiding important data.

9. The right to interfere - professionalism and care

In psychoanalysis like in other forms of care, the motivation to interfere with patient's private life rests on the assumption, belief and wish that the patient will benefit from the sometimes painful and burdensome process. I'm not a psychoanalysis specialists but it is my personal observation from some patients I have known to undergo such a therapy that psychoanalytical treatment can lead to a (temporarily) strong individualistic life style, for example.

W lacks the compassionate understanding of its 'patients' that would be similar or analogous to what is described by APasA: "People make the best choices they can, given the limitations of their assumptions about themselves and their circumstances." W does not entertain this understanding or mercy: it explicitly wants to reveal the suppression, hiding of critical data or other – from W perspective – repressive behavior that has taken place, whatever the local source conditions might have been (which remain often unknown). It wants to reveal these evil deeds. In this sense, it is a form of brutal therapy believed and hoped to save the patient - the society, its institutions or the communities suffering from mistreatment. Wikileaks wants to help correct evident injustices through journalistic processes.

10. Unavoidable injustice in life

In psychoanalysis, almost always, the therapy process touches personal knowledge that is a consequence of unavoidable injustices, occurring in many layers of our lives: difficult parent histories, tragic life and family experiences or just random disastrous events that have changed either our own or our parents' or spouse's life. Such things just happen, despite the explicit aims and claims by the parents, for example, of doing their best. The injustices cannot be avoided and often they cannot be mended or corrected, their factual causes may have disappeared already and even the people involved might have died. Still the patient can be helped to live with these subjective forces and to understand their role in his/her life.

Wikileaks could benefit from an exchange of ideas with open-minded psychoanalysts. It could even lead to specific Wikileaks *modes* of dealing with its original sources of Dark knowledge by compassionate understanding of the conditions of these human sources and in this way, perhaps, encourage secure revelation of sensitive and ethically sustainable data. Technology can provide options for contributing to this.

When people hide information and knowledge, their individual reasons to do so vary even for identical data and circumstances. So, when their secret data becomes exposed, the consequences are socially and personally variable. As Wikileaks surely has learned hundreds of times, every data has a history, a context, numerous owners, stakeholders, and they are dynamic in a very human and social sense. It is not a matter of truth or non-truth.

11. A theory of societal healing?

Analogies can be misleading, but there is an insightful parallel in these two separate worlds. Wikileaks acts as a forceful therapist who makes the 'patient society' – forces it to do so - to see the material in its hidden unconsciousness, to see it 'as it is'. W rests on a belief in the positive power of these activities and it sees itself explicitly as an organization that heals the society (http://wikileaks.org/About.html, (2011):

"Publishing improves transparency, and this transparency creates a better society for all people. Better scrutiny leads to reduced corruption and stronger democracies in all society's institutions, including government, corporations and other organisations. A healthy, vibrant and inquisitive journalistic media plays a vital role in achieving these goals. We are part of that media."

Opinions about the healing power of Wikileaks are divided, politically, economically and psychologically. What some consider as 'stolen' can be considered as 'liberating' and 'truthful' information that Wikileaks brings to the national and global consciousness. What a therapist might see as 'revelation of repressed knowledge' can be in e.g. a parent's eye a shame, a cause of conflict, and a disaster to the family.

While it can be argued that Wikileaks helps nations to heal themselves it is far from clear how this healing process might or will take place. The same is true with the psychoanalytical process of healing: it is not known what exactly happens in the brain and the psychology of a healing person. There are reasons to believe that the healing process is not unique and that several different pathways to healing are possible. However, with the increasing power of the net, digitalization and AI it is not impossible to imagine that the massive media and political consequences of Wikileaks revelations can soon be followed, practically in real time.

An interesting counter example to the psychoanalytical and Wikileaks way of thinking about healing is provided by cognitive behavior therapy. Its aim is to change the patient's negative life- and thought patterns, models and reaction styles, the ways he or she thinks about certain aspects of life and personal experiences. The question of 'what is the objective content of a patient's unconsciousness' is not the most relevant issue then. There is a lot of scientific controversy about this topic among psychologists and surely Wikileaks facess the battle of opinions. But it is a genuinely fruitful question to ask: what are the alternative pathways to healing?

12. Primary data without a theory has no immediate value

"The end of theory!" wrote Chris Anderson in 2008 in Wired magazine, suggesting that big data, analytics, algorithms and all the tools of modern technology will offer new and better ways to know about the world. What does it mean?

Like a good therapist, Wikileaks (or the giants) could avoid directly touching or revealing the most devastating or 'dangerous' information that for some reason could be evil for the patient (the society, individuals) and for the healing process. However, for both Wikileaks and therapists it is impossible to know – without a reliable theory - what will follow for the patient from processing such difficult information. Hence, the therapists and other actors dealing with Dark and Bright knowledge need a theory, explicit or implicit, about the world in which we live. This theory should be openly available for testing and evaluation, and it must be relevant for all the technological platforms where people communicate and collaborate. There is some knowledge of the consequences of therapy processes but Wikileaks and its relatives are still too young. Furthermore, experiences from the impact studies of therapies show that it is far from a simple research problem. The knowledge of such theories is beyond my knowledge horizon here but I can see its importance to us all, people, citizens and our institutions.

Wikileaks should be able to argue for what they do, based on such a theory, model or framework. Not all actions, especially new and radical ones, can be based on evidence simply because such evidence does not exist, yet. From the history of science, we know how any simple primary data – an observation, record or a measurement can change the world. In empirical sciences this can be straightforward like when it was discovered that light rays bend in a gravitational field. However, without a theory related to the phenomenon studied, primary data has no meaning. Why would anyone care how the light rays behave or which object hit the ground first in Galilei's experiment – or did not hit – if these observations did not have any theoretical consequences?

A good question is, how to provide conditions for such a theoretical transparency? What happens to the patient or her close ones, when a therapist who collects data of a patient's history has no theory of the patient's psychodynamics or the impacts of the data on the patient's family? Can we simply assume that there can be strong enough reasons for Wikileaks or anyone of the giants to publish their observations or their derived meanings - without worrying (theorizing) about the diverse consequences? Perhaps, sometimes they just must and can publicize the data, even without a theory, but even this is a precondition to building one.

A therapist may or may not like the patient but the main mission of a committed therapist is to help the patient in all cases. Without that motivation and relevant skills, 'therapy' will turn into a game of intrusion and a means for attention catch, like the famous public presentations of hypnosis where people were and still are made to behave in ridiculous and shameful ways. There is a clear boundary separating these different interests, but not everyone is willing to respect it. Wikileaks and the giants of the net share an ethical problem.

13. Spying on the models of us

We have woken up to consider the consequences of the data collected from us, but before the European GDPR the legal conditions of these data processing operations were practically unknown to citizens and the users of apps and services. The platform giants have not been different from Wikileaks in how they deal with our data, by collecting, and sharing it. The difference is that the giants have shared it with unknown parties and sold it with the simple purpose of making money. Not so long ago, there was a popular, hidden belief that what is happening with our data would or could be beneficial for people and mankind. Underlying this optimistic thinking is the artificial model of man.

This is how I see it now:

The behaving actor (citizen, community member, client, user, victim) the giants now spy on, follow, profile and manipulate is not the person him or herself. It is only the model of a theoretical-virtual person living and following the roles defined and allowed by and within the existing technological platforms and chambers.

Anyone adopting modern digital services becomes engaged with the operators' networks, their representations of reality, their tools, and becomes a target of their manipulative cycles, algorithms, and actions. The operators define the world of technology, the *de facto living space* they offer for the users to habit and adopt various social and human practices: to see, live in and experience, to be prepared for its feeds and to act upon them, to see the world through these systems. The users are persuaded to behave within the pre-defined roles and the underlying (hidden) model of Man. Often we simply feel comfortable in these roles like someone addicted to games. The design of this artificial world aims at guiding and tunneling our behavior so that it can be measured and quantified as the operators see best for their business.

The simplest and most banal example of this forced, global role-playing game, accepted by billions of people, is *the thumb*. Indeed, the world lives the *era of the thumb*. It is more powerful, than any rational, well-grounded argumentations presented as serious texts in books, sites, social, digital or printed media. There is no escaping from this astounding artificial and computational thumb-reality yet. Many don't see this as strange at all and happily wave their thumbs, typically up. We could even choose to use more fingers, lips, toes or emojis and hope to escape the thumb-world, but even that is not enough to break out from the technological prison, the one-thumb world. It is the strongest sign in the world today, practically beating any religious symbols. At the writing of this, it was world-wide news that Facebook tested new strategies in publishing thumb-frequencies.

If this – the relationship between technology and human mind and being - were a research problem in quantum mechanics, no sane physicist would claim that the 'model of Man' built in this way would have much to do with the real object of interest, the person. They would warn us on how the data collecting process, the biased representation of reality, and the modeling and manipulating maneuvers can seriously disturb, even break the reality of the human mind – the actual object of observation.

Heisenberg would be happily confused. To recite the Schrödinger's cat metaphor, the giant operators seem to imply they can know what – their model Man - is in the box without opening it and seriously talking to the fellow inside. When, in rare cases, they peek into the box they find out that it is more like the famous Chinese box: in the box sits their model Man, translating every message and action the operators feed to the box and who then returns messages and acts by using the UI, carefully following a rule set which he has learned by living in the closed box. The poor chap does not resemble human beings at all: he is not allowed to express him or herself freely, make his own interpretations, have preferences, ask for help, or pray and change his mind; he must obey the rules he has been forced from the outside to learn. Some brain scientists claim to be opening the brain box, believing the human being sits there waiting.

For a mysterious reason, it seems that quantum physicists are more sensitive to interaction phenomena than many of the behavioral scientists and economists designing and running these systems with which we live. This said, of course the technological models work as any physical experiment works, in one way or another, they have always done so, since the dawn of technology, but there is a price to be paid: what is missed or lost remains invisible. This is far from conquering or even coming close to understanding the human mind and soul.

We could forget the invisible biases in the design of the model Man and take it as a plain and practical curiosity, of no real importance and consequences, if it did not seriously impact and distort the common beliefs of what we have about others, about us as human beings and citizens, and about the human nature and social communities in general. The artificial models feed the development and growth of individuals, from early childhood and education to adultness and they create community dynamics on a global scale, by guiding and constraining the life of billions of children. Present-day technologies have a strong impact on how we see ourselves and others; the services available lure us to think in simplistic psychological terms about the very complex and rich, even mysterious aspects of our minds and about the relationships with other people and citizens, different from us.

A curious example of the deep-reaching persuasion upon us are the 'personality tests' circulating in Facebook, which are not much different from standard psychological tests and are typically used as proof (without saying that explicitly) of the stability of our personalities. They invite people to try the tests and believe that personality is somehow an important success factor in life. With these apps we can measure what we are like by adopting the tools and their underlying assumptions; they look at how we behave and use our thumbs in Facebook. However, there is accumulating scientific evidence showing that the notion of personality is complex and it has very little if anything to offer in predicting the success of an individual in work life, for example and that personality even changes over time. Facebook especially is putting psychological methods at test and right now, psychology seems to be losing the game – it is too academic and slow to match the pace and popularity of the hungry and competent media.

14. Persuasion to comply

The models of man persuade us to comply, it is the price we pay to gain access to services which reward us with psychological, social and material benefits. It is no accident, that junk mail folders are full of announcements about 'Winning in a lottery', and that we receive invitations to join 'clubs' or get coupons offering amazing advantages and discounts as exchange. We are expected to behave like reward-seeking automats. At the writing of this, there is no doubt that this phenomenon or a movement – trying to get people hooked in any money-generating app, not unlike with drugs - is the strongest driving force guiding the development of human-technology relationships.

Bullying and technology. An alarming example of the way internet paves the way to serious, harmful behaviors and even psychologically boosts it, is bullying, which in its extreme form has led to teen-age suicides. It is not rare to read about comments where bullying is considered as a pathological form of latent human behavior which only waits for a chance to express itself and that the net and the social media environment only open the gates to this dormant, bad behavior. Technology, as it is seen in this view, is not directly causing, creating or generating the problem. Practically never is bullying seen as a direct outcome of bad and harmful human-technology design, which itself and directly generates and builds pathological relationships between and among people.

In everyday life, apps and services do keep people connected with their social networks and offer means to express themselves, but they also detach individuals from their natural, tangible and powerful social environments. By doing this, they give form, even engineer new kind of behaviors that would not otherwise have a chance to occur because they would be constrained or prevented by parents, relatives, friends, teachers, priests, public forums, and any healthy real-life spaces. Current technological platform-based services are extremely bad in supporting positive human growth and protecting the human mind. Consequently, anything that is possible in human thinking and behavior, with the new tools, has become possible to record, express, share and target. A massive human-technological design for new behaviors is happening and not all of it is good.

Aggressive behaviors in the net remind of Freud's ideas about the nature of human character: observing the worst forms of network behavior is like seeing the id and libido running free, having escaped any control, and guiding the most primitive human needs and desires, including sexuality and the search for massive and fast gratification. However, the net – the modern technology – has not only opened the social wormhole to these disastrous human behaviors, but it has itself built a world where such behaviors flourish, are fed, protected, and reinforced: inherent in this are the expressions, impulses, interaction and satisfaction of needs which have become possible in a more direct form than anywhere else, serious crimes and wars excluded. Sad enough, these harmful phenomena scale up and down. It is not about people and their bad motives only, it's about lack of seriously human technology design.

15. Positive persuasion

Active initiatives like the Peace Innovation Laboratory at Stanford, and some others have seen the potential of network and app technology to monitor and promote positive behaviors, peace, human well-being, education, and equality and to pro-actively and by design prevent or stop the darkest phenomena from occurring. You can think of them as organized forms of human self-defense if you like, but it is also possible to see them as an emerging design culture for positive behaviors in contrast to designs leading to platforms of potentially destructive behaviors; human-technological design matters. Even these positive initiatives need to know what there is to learn about the nature of the human being who lives and plays with the latest technology; she is a moving and adaptive target, as much as the fastest developing technology can ever be. Unfortunately, with few exceptions, psychologists are slow to introduce transformational and spiritually solid approaches to human-centered technology design. One possible reason to this is that research traditions and academic practices in psychology do not meet in this.

There is a peculiar parallel between traditional ways of measuring peace and evaluating the quality of human computer interfaces – by quantifying the lack of problems. The famous peace activist and researcher Johan Galtung noted in 1964 how peace measures typically look at the measures of war and conflicts, by taking the inverse of the measures like the number of war casualties, conflicts, and the amount of money spent on arms and using these as indexes of peace. The reason for this kind of development was probably clear to Galtung: it is difficult to quantify positive behaviors or at least there was no significant tradition of doing it. Hence, most peace indexes were based on negative measures and only recently positive indexes have emerged, for example, *The 2016 Positive Peace Report* which describers its aim at measuring positive peace: "latest research on the attitudes, institutions and structures that create and sustain peaceful societies."

Identifying and measuring the peace-contributing economical, human, social and technological factors, however, is not a straightforward task. Rosanna Guadagno, Mark Nelson and Laurence Lock Lee (2018) have introduced what they call "Peace data standard" to tackle these problems and suggest guidelines for collecting and using peace data in various big data contexts.

At the Peace Innovation Institute (https://www.peaceinnovation.com), the outcome of collaboration between Stanford University and the City of Hague, with the support from numerous engineering societies and forums, they are initiating a Peace Engineering Consortium. It rests on the insight that influential, different sectors of engineering theory and practice are already now having both positive and unintended negative consequences. The aim is to help the global engineering community to become aware, learn and work with new practices and policies that promote positive outcomes, extending from the cyberspace to everyday human life and living. If successful it will have significant contribution to engineering work and to the application of the best of human technology principles.

It remains to be seen how such approaches will help contributing to positive behaviors and make them better quantifiable than is now possible. For example, it is a surprise to many in large firms and organizations to realize how much peace data, like records of customer relationships, transactions, infrastructure investments and many others are hidden in their data repositories, waiting to be processed from the perspective of their positive impact, as Guadagno et al suggest.

The roots of HCI originate from the early industrial settings where accidents and dangerous work conditions were common. Scientific ergonomics grew out from the imperative to improve efficiency, physical conditions at workplace, and to prevent hazards and bad work conditions. It was natural to focus on risks and try to minimize the number of accidents and other work-related risks. Soon however, especially because of the extensive car industry, war technology and digital evolution, ergonomics came to cover human factors in general and it now includes positive HCI quality, too, but it is still slow to contribute.

On the other hand, focusing on risks and accidents can lead to indirect positive effects since trying to avoid negative incidents encourages organizations to seriously look at many of their designs and activities, including positive practices. However, still today there is no unique definition of the human quality of HCI even though ISO standards, for example, have been defined for various aspects of HCI, e.g. displays, lighting, command dialogue, information representation, icons, action and direct manipulation, among many other standards. Fast advances in technology make the development of 'positive standards' an ever-changing task.

Popular brain-behavior stories include banal ideas on how to e.g. perfectly model the human brain and dump the human memory into a computer and back. The human memory dump idea is silly, simply because most of human memory material is constructive and imperfect in nature and in large part episodic in nature. It's like trying to dump the contents of a television set but forgetting the broadcasting and production organizations. In less confabulating cases, the psychology dealing with brain sciences simplifies the essence of what it is to be a cultural-social-historical, growing and experiencing human being. The reason for these dreams is the same that produces the simplistic human models applied in profiling us: technology is more simple - by several magnitudes - than the simplest mental phenomena being studied.

2 AGNOSTIC TOOLS

1. Life with blind giants: two educational examples

Decades of HCI work have convinced me that it is not possible to success in human-centric design by deriving the guidelines directly from single psychological theories in cognitive, perceptual or neurosciences alone; instead and in addition, constructive-creative, holistic human thinking is needed as has been shown by Steve Jobs and Don Norman in their own ways. In addition, realistic future visions of technology are valuable, if not necessary. Remarkable examples of multi-disciplinary approaches do exist, especially the applications of perception psychology in food production, audio hifi, acoustic spaces, color management in print and displays, 3D, AR and VR, even car interior design and the feel of its sounds, to name only some successful examples.

Useful observations can be found from experimental cognitive and perception research and modeling that can feed creative thinking in HCI even though this knowledge does not directly suggest solutions. So far, however, neurosciences have practically nothing to offer to our technologies of everyday life – if the term 'neuro' is taken seriously and not used as a symbol of anything that has something to do with our perceptions, cognitions and the mind. Besides, what human behavior would not have a neuroscientific basis? Curious enough, the word 'brain' is often used like the word 'universe'; most of us can happily assume that they both exist and can be studied and that both the brain and the universe have a huge impact on our lives – but both are weak concepts in explaining our true psychology, everyday life and what goes on in our minds. When catastrophes happen, it's another story, both for the brain and the universe. In case of HCI failures and problems it is possible to find out which psychological factors underlie *design failures*. Sometimes these observations can lead or motivate to better design insights, but simply knowing the cause of failures is not a key to excellent and creative design.

I have taken the brave 'essay-approach' in this book—which may appear as a thin choice – and will not delve into the deepest and complex psychological theories related to technology unless I can see the relevance and benefit of it. I have taken a roundabout approach and introduce a look at very simple human psychology in practical situations as I have seen them in my own work, in numerous technological contexts.

By examples, I try to make the point how typical current human-technology solutions, from system and service design to apps and social media platforms, can benefit from simple considerations of how the human mind works and then to use this understanding in design. The underlying motivation, of course, is not to fall into blaming bad human-technology solutions and relationships, but to inspire the development and design of healthy human technology. Then I describe some frequent real-life obstacles I've met in trying to advance human-centric design and thinking - meeting with reluctant technologists and business representatives and when I've failed to 'sell' these ideas to them. Now after some 40 years, I know, having seen the history of technological progress in these contexts from 1970s to today, that some of these reluctant customers did make seriously wrong decisions, but not all did.

To prove my point of argumentation and the approach, I start with simple, every-day, even trivial examples. First I demonstrate (and introduce concepts for major improvements) a very basic failure of the Google search engine to serve us and then describe how Facebook, does the same, failing to help our everyday life and living. It would be possible to apply any number of psychological theories to explain these failures but I will not touch them here. I've earlier written a blog on this (its edited form is included here), related to both Google and Yahoo: *"Ignorant search engines do not understand your life"* but will here provide a more recent demo on how Google performs in this elementary human test. Better tools are being developed as I write this, but the approaches vary.

Why should bad amateurs conduct knowledge search? There is a strange new cross-cultural practice being adopted by most of mankind. It is a practice more popular than vaccination, owning a car or a television, playing football, or speaking a foreign language: we have become passionate Google-amateurs of information search. While there is no doubt that the availability of digital materials and the tools to search through global data bases have benefitted us immensely, there is a good reason to ask, is this the best we can do and is it even good for us, in the long run? My answer is a definite 'perhaps not'.

It is quite amazing how self-evident the concept of 'search' has become. Often it has replaced human *negotiations* over a matter of interest. The price we pay for this is that we lose what is valuable in honest negotiations and human interaction: mutual interest, understanding of the real situations and needs of the negotiating partners, making the best assumptions about the partner's expressions, mutual stimulation for thinking and changing attitudes, motivation to guide each other, joy of finding something useful and many other natural, human-social phenomena. As far as I know, 'social knowledge hunting' does not exist as a human-technology concept.

No wonder then that there are serious initiatives going on, like chats and bots to help people in this, and new tools for finding relevant material with 'intelligent search' like in Iris.ai which helps scientists and other knowledge workers to find relevant information from huge document masses. A new neural network application from a team (e.g. Dnakowski, Ling, Nakov and others) at MIT reads scientific papers and generates a plain English summary of the articles so that they are easy to understand. Peace Engine by Timo Honkela aims at using AI in improving human negotiations.

So far, these approaches have a long way to go, to reach the human and social touch and quality in their workings. Most searches today are done by amateurs who do not know what exactly there is to be searched for and found, and what would be the optimal ways to find the best data and knowledge for their specific problems and situations at hand. Because of this, they (we) are susceptible to manipulation and conditioning. It is not untypical that we start the search with a general outline and a best guess of keywords to get to the relevant data sources. Anyone can imagine keywords and with the future search engines, we can use our own language to explain the problem. Listening to people negotiating complex problems is a wake-up call to anyone believing that speech recognition alone is the solution. It is a real human-technology test to design services for speech-driven search and answering, Siri included.

The challenges in verbalizing complex problems was wonderfully demonstrated in a play 'Pavlova's experiment' by Professor Pauliina Hulkko, where the movements of a beautiful dance, from an old film, by the famous ballerina Anna Pavlova were verbally described, spoken in detail, by a male dancer and the audio of his verbal description was recorded. Then in the actual theatre performance he performed Pavlovas dance but now following only his recorded verbal descriptions on the dance, how to move, and perform while the audience did not know where the audio text came from; to the audience the audio was just verbal instructions on how to move and dance and they could only observe how well the dancer followed the detailed verbal instructions given in the audio. No need to say, it was impossible for the dancer to capture the real essence of the original dance and it was impossible for the audience to experience anything resembling the original dance by Pavlova, even though the instructions were given by a professional and skilled dancer. However detailed and educated instructions we can give to a speech based search system, in case of complex and sensitive matters it becomes problematic.

Right now, we are manipulated by commercially and otherwise ordered data structures that constrain and determine the available search paths and bases. Typically, we have no idea what data and knowledge there would exist for us to utilize and we must pursue for whatever we are looking for within the allowed pathways. Often we end up at a site offering its own, specialized search engine and are forced to remain within the domain of the tool owner's data and related persuasive messages. It's a second layer of search trap, locking us into the domain of its provider. Often this works and we get what we think we want, but in typical cases we are left uncertain what else, even better or critical data there would have been available for us in our specific need and life situations. A fool, searching for truth faces a serious problem.

The responsibility in search rests on the shoulders of search amateurs. In many cases, if not in most of them, the best, knowledgeable search specialists hide among those from whom we could try to find data, knowledge or services for our individual needs. Think about the search for a medicine or a car, for example. Your main aim is to get healthy – the medicine is only a necessary aspect of this - or a car that suits your present needs, history, situation and resources. However, through searches it is difficult to know what is available to satisfy your specific needs and combinations of needs. You can use sites that compare products, but you typically end up navigating through multiple searches. If the providers of the product or service knew your specific, personal situation at that moment, they could be the best professionals to help you by doing the search for the best data and products for you. But typically, they have not done that, for various reasons, not less because of commercial interests, and instead they force you to behave as a self-serving search amateur by writing up, 'ticking' long lists of your preferences. In everyday discussions or meeting with sales persons, for example, we do much better.

The situation is improving with AI and we can have private agents taking care of our interests instead of the firms and businesses we use. But again, there looms the risk that the competition in the field will be so hard that there is little chance for the average citizen to have the best AI available to protect his or her interests; the emerging AI giants will take care of that. Besides, AI has a long way ahead to truly understand us as human beings with a soul. So, what can be done to push back the search and data management responsibility to those who are proficient in it?

One alternative is to turn the search service model upside down from what it is today. As a first step, it can be done in a way that both protects the identity of people and relies on better human data management than we typically have at our disposal when using the search services. It is a relative to MyData thinking and movement. However, it's not a black and white problem; both bottom-up and top-down approaches are needed. Here is a very simple example that motivates to this kind of thinking.

2.   Ignorant search engines talk to false models of us

Most of the time big data systems are impotent in matters that are most basic but essential aspects of our human lives, experiences and minds. Especially they are bad at recognizing our psychological and social situations.

Example. Imagine better life with Google. You are desperate to buy a car and need it as soon as possible. You want to do your share in preventing climate change and find a vehicle matching your motivations and values. At home, your spouse and teen-age kids would be delighted by such a choice. You have money.

You can try a search with various versions of: "I'm desperate to buy a car" and "I want to fight the climate change".

You can try Google searches with better language and any imaginable, relevant keywords and you are repeatedly surprised – it's a peculiar kind of fun, too - to find out how misfit offerings you get to your search, it's like a hopeless discussion with a salesman who does not speak your language and does not understand or care for *your* life. Indeed, you are forced to work hard if you want to make the ignorant-of-you search system understand what is relevant and important to you, right now, at this moment, in your personal situation. What a failure!

In 2015, I was inspired to help to find an improvement, I even tried, twice – I did guess it was probably hopeless – to reach Yahoo's Marissa Mayer through email having read about their problems from her biography, "Marissa Mayer and the fight to save Yahoo!" by Nicholas Carlson (2015). The book tells how the search engine competition had become a serious problem to Yahoo and I imagined that these simple, fresh architectural and human ideas might help them to find the first steps for next generation search engines and systems. I even sent emails to them but no luck in making a contact. I did not find the right channel for contact.

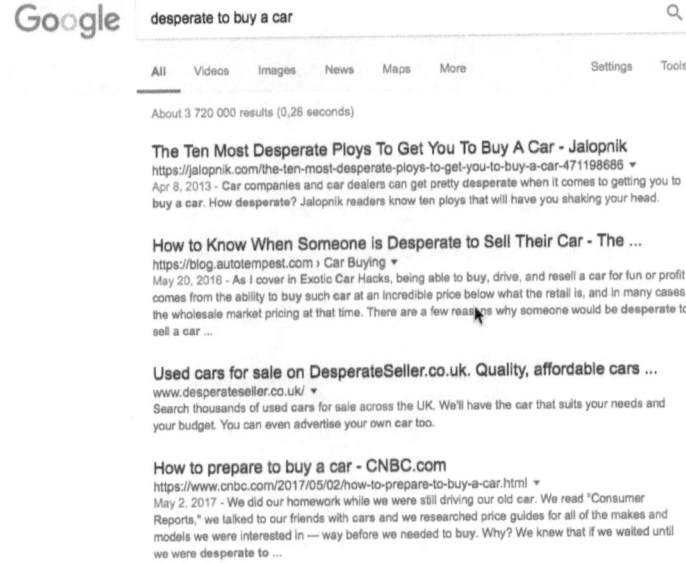

Figure 1. The results of a search with "Desperate to buy a car."

One could argue that it's only a matter of time when Google will be proficient in understanding natural language in all the complexities and the problem will be solved. A salesman who does understand our language perfectly but fails to understand us, is only a nuisance. Language understanding is not enough, it's about understanding individual, human, social and cultural life and the *aims, meanings and situations* where people live in.

To reach a human level of maturity, better knowledge and service architectures are needed than are now used and are available. The situation is not much better when you try to be kind to the search engine:

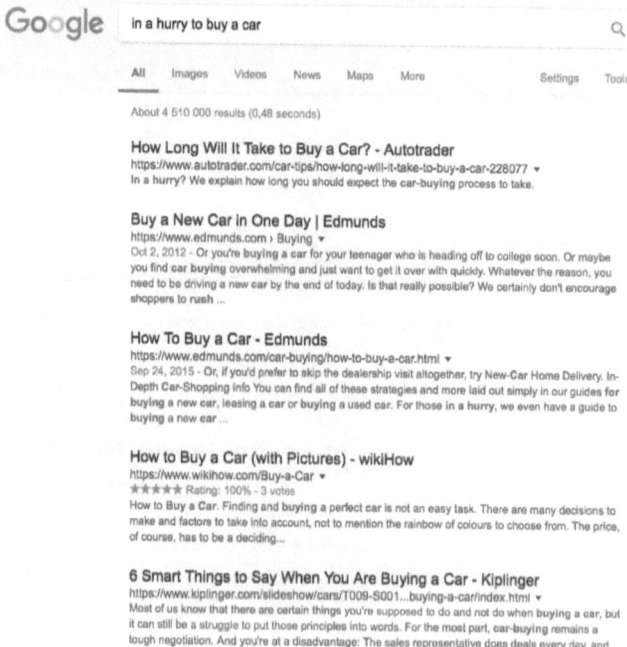

Figure 2. A kind request to the search engine with "In a hurry to buy a car". You would expect interesting offers but you get advice for your buying habits.

Future AI services should understand *our life,* something with which even we humans have problems when trying to understand each other. Watching the hopeless search results above, we see a search robot talking to another similar robot and not to us: as human beings we are forgotten. We become de facto components in the search machine system and if we don't do the right things – what the system requires - too bad for us.

You might argue that I used stupid searches and that may well be true but not only for me. We have been conditioned by the machines and learned to expect a Pavlovian reward only if we act in certain ways and learn the tricks. Many of us have grown unbelievably tolerant to the fuzzy search situations and just do and behave as is necessary, to get what we want. You can observe similar haphazard behaviors in any conditioning experiments where a rat or a monkey tries to get the food reward by pushing the available levers and each time being rewarded (or punished) by a clever conditioning scheme.

Curious enough, when we observe our children or students behave like that, searching haphazardly for a solution to a problem (having a simple rational solution), then as parents and educators we get worried and frustrated about the random-like behavior and try to intervene and guide them to think, to understand the whole situation, to find relevant actions and not to rely on brainless, continuously rewarded trials. In education and for small children such a behavior has disastrous cognitive consequences. But the machines don't let us interfere and they are not worried about our trial-and-error behavior which is food for them. It's about two-way conditioning that takes place and we as users do our share there.

In the example search results we saw how the system is sensitive to 'buying' in any of its forms and gets hooked to direct quotations like "intend to buy" etc. But the quotation matches can occur for any context and it does not help us in any way, the search gets totally lost and irrelevant to our present intentions and life in general. The list of search results (mistakes in buying, leasing vs. buying, bargaining etc) looks like the search engine was searching data for another robot, not for a passionate and situationally intentional human being. The search engines are non-human creatures that hate dynamic human, non-deterministic mental life.

We are all experts of our acute motivations and no AI-guessing can beat us in this. In case of 'must buy' we might have a temporary time limitation, for example (I'm too busy, cannot go to a shop) and we can start looking for 'buying service', perhaps even find a sales rep coming to our home with a candidate car or two. How do I express this need in the search field? "Buy car visit home" does not understand me. "Buy car xx"? Well, surely after some text work we get what we want but is this the best a search engine could do?

Contrary to what the masterminds behind the search engines and especially their marketing people claim - the algorithms do not know us or our dynamic mental life at all. They have their rough models of easily observable behaviors and of what we feed to the engines. The 'intelligent' engines are guessing what we might want or need. They do not ask about our acute motivation or mental state, they think it is not informative or that it is not very practical to ask for such 'fuzzy' knowledge. I've often heard the argument that it is not wise to trust people when they tell about their intentions.

Adding better or different words to the search process is not a solution to this mess, an architectural transformation is needed. The question arises how to make this possible economically. It may be clear by now that by better understanding of the human and her individual situation and needs, the efficiency of offerings, campaigns, marketing and any services can be significantly improved, but it requires trust in people and respect for their private, mental life. Such a system could collect information about the real-time market and need situation – at each moment and before anything has happened, except in people's minds. This should be motivation enough for firms and organizations to invest in designing better search system architectures: how to get a permission to access such human mind-data?

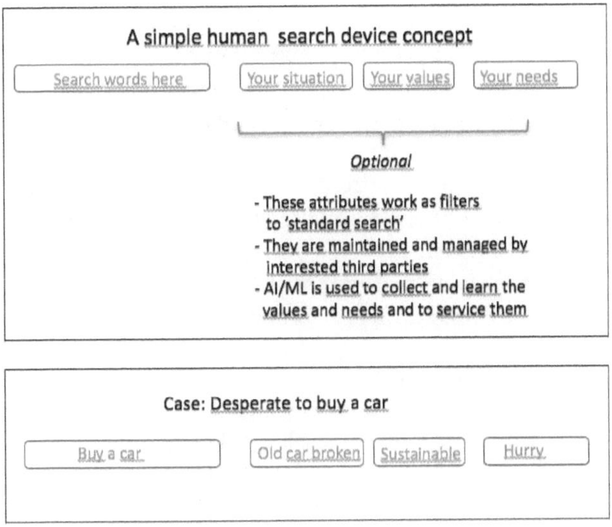

Figure 3. A simple model for a human-centric search engine that understands individual situations, values and needs.

It is not only a matter of building a different search engine; the potential business models supporting it would be very different from the current 'push and manipulate' -models. They are not difficult to imagine.

The core idea behind any such model is to help the user define the psychological search space in a way that supports his or her true motivations and situational requirements. Even when purchasing or searching for most simple services and objects of life; we typically have other things in mind than what we seem to have, and often our search and purchasing habits are constrained by multiple values we cherish.

3. On personal interest spaces

It is subjectively stimulating to get immediately started and immerse in a new task, a project or any other activity we love. It is a personal and often a family adventure and joy - to focus on the relevant aspects of it, as fully and accurately as possible.

In normal everyday life, we don't need special arrangements or tools to achieve this, when we open a new book, start discussing a plan, or go to a grocery store to get what we want. We know the task at hand, and the store, for example, with its people and services and its meaning to us, this knowledge is the default. The net is different. Often it forces us to make several trials and tuning of our activity environment to get at what we are interested in. Of course, we have adapted to this, learned the relevant 'behavior scripts' or routines and many things are simple to do, but better models can be designed.

*Example. Ima*gine life with Facebook. "I enjoy being fully engaged with my task X and then switch to task Y and even to task Z and back to X whenever I feel like it."

You wake up in the morning, full of passion and energy to work on a specific topic or a theme, be it writing, planning a trip with friends, or you spend time sharing memories with your family, coding or even constructing something you are fascinated with, and you would like to focus on this with your friends, other sources, and communities. At that precious moment, you would love to keep other things out of your field of attention and only every now and then, when you feel like it, you'd like to focus on something totally else for a while.

It is one of the treasures of us all: to be excited about what we do, to stay on the topic even when its boundaries are fuzzy, enjoy the immersive feeling of engagement, imagination, and continuous relevance of the data and the information sources we handle; we cherish the best possible quality of knowledge and people in this wonderful interaction. This is our character; it has its roots in the distant past and even animals have it.

As a member of a face-to-face team you enjoy being surrounded by people having the same passion and objects of interest as you have, some of your team members having competences you admire and need – this is what makes the best of the team sessions such wonderful experiences. When you know your team, it is enough to get together and start working or exchanging ideas, there is no need to kick out unnecessary suggestions, to block irrelevant offerings and data while you work; you just start working with the people and the task at hand. Exclusion of irrelevant material is 'built in' the social and human assumptions, manners and practices. You don't have to 'keep it out' or build walls, to pay or hire someone to do it for you.

How do you do that in Facebook and in other social media or collaboration platforms? You can, if you work hard, but in practice, it's not dynamic and it is not straightforward. There is no natural or fluent way to do this, group tools can help, but it requires extra work and coordination.

Working alone or distant to your team, you can suddenly, at will, change your topic of interest to a totally new one. This is a most natural human thing to do, to 'switch on' a new context, several times a day - having the same enthusiasm, often being uncertain of your goal, having a specific need or a situation, and working with different people. It's practically impossible to fluently configure your network tools and apps to exactly match the new and changing situations. You can jump from one relevant virtual team or community to another and access the sources there, but especially your new community members don't know what you have on your mind unless you spend half of your time explaining your contexts and thoughts (writing, typically, or talking to an idiot AI in a very near future) and arranging the sources. This inserts friction into your enthusiasm and makes you tired of the extra communication load.

The reason to this awkward situation is not that technology couldn't do it better or that we as humans could not do it, but because the designers have misunderstood and underestimated the richness and dynamics of simple human life. It's like bad food for a hungry person, with some delicacies offered aside, to keep the customer hooked.

Personal interest spaces

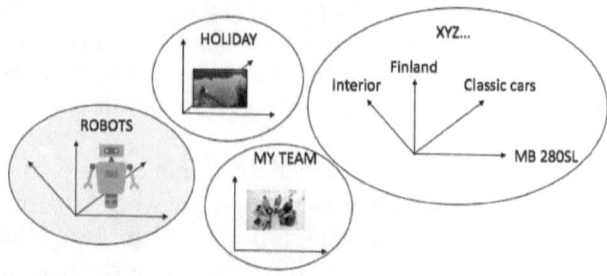

Figure 4. A schematic description of personal interest spaces which the user defines by using free keywords. The space codes can be stored and (de-)activated at will. The XYZ ... is an example of a situation when I needed to find someone in Finland to repair the interiors of my MB 280SL/1975. It would have been rather easy search task, but as classic car lovers know, it is fascinating to look at the whole situation, from a personal perspective; we have different and dynamic interests. The focus of interest – that moves from one focus to another - can be described as a vector in the defined space. AI has hard time guessing what might be going on next in our creative and passionate minds on this mental journey.

Some time ago, I sent a post to FB developers (with no response), suggesting a design and implementation of a simple personal, freely expressed 'subjective interest space based on ML' tool by which the user could quickly express, at any moment, his or her pending interests and by declaring the symbolic 'coordinates', by which he would then receive only related materials, sources, people contacts, organizations and any other relevant data. The coordinates and their stored versions could be easily switched on in a second, just like it happens in the way we direct our attentive resources every day, all the time. We could share these spaces with our friends and colleagues and the 'best brains' in the world.

The idea is simple, based on something we do in our minds every minute and hour: we focus on something and immerse into the work or hobby we love and want to succeed in what we are doing. We can extend or focus the sphere (space) of interest which is mentally easy and natural to do when it is driven by our own interests; it does not take any effort. When we so want, and we often do, we change the context of interest dynamically – you can call it the *mental activity pattern* if you like. We love to navigate and wander in this mind space; you might call it imagination. Our modern digital means are relatively bad at it, both functionally and in their aesthetics.

Media and apps we use are masters of introducing irrelevant interrupts and forced forms to our ongoing activities, it's part of their business models. There is a plethora of reasons why the available services don't understand us, and strange enough, even the hungriest business minds do not show much interest in this simple opportunity: to protect people from being bombarded with irrelevant and disturbing materials they already now try to avoid. Many of us pay for the 'don't disturb' services – it's a purest symptom of design pathology. As users, consumers and citizens we should be the recipients of something relevant and of interest, even curiosity and passion, every moment. It is human. Paying for not being disturbed by anyone in the world is insane, its blackmailing.

We live with and manage our dynamic, private personal spaces. We are skillful in navigating there and play with their rich contents: to sense, imagine, maintain, construct and reconstruct, access, browse, transform, stop to enjoy, remember, color and use it in everything we do and imagine – from birth to death. Future tools could be our partners in this. It is a most fascinating target of curiosity: what goes on in the minds of our friends, colleagues and loved ones – what are their personal interest spaces like? What could we learn from them and how?

Philosophically you may call this mental navigation as an aspect of 'consciousness' but as I'm not too eager to use that fuzzy and controversial term in this context, I characterize these mental phenomena as personal activities taking place in a private, mental space, something only each of us can fully access. When a researcher or an app approaches us, we often, if not typically, willingly adjust and transform our own personal space – we come out of it, simplify it or even shrink it because we are forced by the bad technology (or ignorant people) - so that it becomes possible to interact with the 'communication space' of the approaching tool, person or an agent. This is what a good human service should do: to let us preserve the richness and the best of our mental space and to behave as we naturally would do, and not to force us to comply to the mentally shrinking, artificial, dwarfing spaces.

4. The future of Mankind under the thumb

Then came the thumb. As human beings, we certainly don't have an inbuilt, psychological thumb-showing space, a hidden thumb-resource or a mystic thumb-script eagerly waiting for a chance to be used. I guess that eager researchers have not (yet) found a thumb expression center in the brain and shown it in beautiful color. Of course, there are cultural habits in showing the thumb, even the finger, but it may not be the most expressive human sign used by mankind. An optimistic view to the thumb would be to see it as corresponding to the binary numbers 1/0, but the thumbing programmers are somewhere far away, invisible and programming us with an unknown language. The Rolling Stones were visionary in 1966 when they published "Under My Thumb", using an analogous perspective the giants have on us today "…the change has come, she's under my thumb …"

When the thumb is the only option, we use it and comply to obey the approaching technology agent who asks – forces us – to contribute to and project our own spaces on *his* thumb-showing drama and tools. We accept the thumb-invitation— there is no alternative if we want to benefit from the tools. As strange and unnatural as it may be, for that precious moment we willingly forget our inner space, abandon its richness, forms and potential and get ready to shrink it and map it all on the thumb. We have grown so accustomed to this socio-technological, dwarfing practice that most of us don't feel they are paying any price for living and even enjoying the thumb life and its consequences. The mental consequences of this forced form of technology acceptance remain invisible, and the operators are satisfied because for them, it means computability and commitment: they use our artificially guided behavior as elements in the computational and machine learning schemes. Based on the thumb-knowledge they build the image of us, the Thumb-Man as they see it, but rarely call it that.

When you agree to use the thumb, something peculiar happens in and to your personal space which only you can perceive, feel and live mentally. The approaching agent takes the data from your thumbing in the interaction, decodes and interprets it (at will), and combines it with other data of you or the thumb data of your friends. Then it feeds the computed outcomes back to you through the channels you have adopted, in the form of offerings, priorities, and emotional contents the operators find suitable for their business and other purposes. You can then show your thumb again.

At that moment, the system becomes closed, they have gained access to your personal space and the cycle of private life: it becomes filled with the content of their choice and manipulation, distorting your active mental space, and forces you to project and shrink it so that you can get what you want from this interaction. You are destined to live "under the thumb" and in *their* interest space unless you fight back or stay away.

All of this happens in a tangible form: you spend time searching for relevant data (seconds, minutes), you recover the tasks that were interrupted (several minutes), you engage with social interaction (tens of minutes), you rearrange your work and hobby activities to comply with the available services (days), you build your relationships, work and leisure time activities and social practices (months), you teach children the same (years) and so on. It is a major transformation in your personal space and its day-to-day dynamics. These tangible processes have direct and indirect consequences to our everyday life, and often we adapt without noticing it: a new form of human-social-technological culture is born in us.

In our psychological realities, the use of the thumb, of course, is an amusing, artificial, forced and compressed mental process, a strange caricature of us as expressive human beings, nothing more; thumbing is something we would only rarely do if we were not prevented by the technology to express ourselves as human beings in complex multi-variant situations. This has immense social and global consequences: billions of us have learned to be kind or desperate enough to adopt the thumb practice and follow the psychological laws and trajectories in this compressed and dwarfed human space. True, it's an innovation, banal as it may be, but there could be better means. Imagine, if one day in your home town, New York for example, people were forced to use only thumbs in their interaction and communication. That would be something to see.

3 WHY THE SUBJECTIVE APPROACH?

1. What I talk about when I talk about the Edge of
    Human Technology?

A major part of HCI research is conducted with old or
'latest' technology. When the results get published, technology
has moved ahead, sometimes totally abandoning the previous
one. Special kind of academic vision and courage are required
to identify the human potential of possible future technologies.
There is no unequivocal psychological research data available
to predict the value of any coming human-technology. It is a
matter of visionary design thinking.

With Nokia, my team found one such 'edge' when we were
accepted as an intimate part of their camera development
process and worked with their amazing camera team there for
a decade; related work continues. As a result, we have a
decade-long time series on subjective image quality and the
'quality vocabulary' (Toni Virtanen's doctoral thesis deals with
this) people spontaneously use to express their image quality
experiences when looking at and evaluating photos taken by
mobile phone camera at the time. The edge was then defined
by the status of the current mp technology, which changed
every quartal. For example, the objects of our studies were the
best mobile phone cameras on the market and their sw&hw
components, the pixel density growing from 0.3 mp to 42 mp,
the overall and subjective image quality improving accordingly,
but not in a linear fashion.

Staying on the edge required that, from the start, we had to
understand how to quantify subjective experiences of
continuously improving image quality, to understand the
subjective quality space of people looking at ever better photos
and other images. Luckily, we had extensive experience from
high-class magazines and their extremely high quality visual
materials which prepared us for the high-quality future
methodically. Later a similar development took place in the
research on 3D movies and games, for example where the

focus was always in high-quality experiences. In this sense, it was akin to the approaches in audio hi-fi and we knew some of the problems awaiting when the 'human edge' moved farther.

Figure 1. An observant seagull in Santa Cruz, California

I'm not an engineer although I have built digital lab-systems like fast displays and experimental control and recording systems, including two microprocessor-based (Intel 8008, 8080) computers already in mid and late1970s, doing systems programming, giving courses on programming and even servicing of computers among many other technologically oriented activities. Being a serious visual scientist, this was a useful profile for a researcher and kept the humanist's gaze at advancing technologies.

I became an unconventional psychologist, an educated amateur in some fields of technology. With my perception-cognitive-brain scientist's eyes it was possible to see some significant human-technological edges emerge, when a visionary technologist was excited about them but which I could see with a psychologist's eyes. My 'mission' was and is to see the same things as technologists see, but with a different gaze: I try to maintain a psychologically inspired look – it is both a filter and an amplifier - with a strong human gain and bandwidth adjustment. I'm not a futurist looking at or dreaming of the time 30 to 50 years from now, instead I try to understand (and continuously update the view) what could and would probably happen to people using the coming technology within the next ten years or so - how they will think and behave with it and react to it. I have frequently found myself 'ahead of my time' in these human technology visions by about 5-7 years.

Of course, it has been impossible to know the future for sure then, but having now documents and memories on these personal-historical ideas it has been possible to later verify the relevance of some of the psychological-technological foresights. Some of them I've offered to the often reluctant but luckily every now and then also willing technologists. Then of course I have made my mistakes in prediction: in 2010 I predicted that people will leave Facebook in masses by 2013 or so. I still use it – but the young generation are leaving it now.

The inspiration and courage to take the personal approach in this book came from reading Haruki Murakami's intimate book 'What I talk about when I talk about running' the title of which he borrowed from Raymond Carver's book, with the permission from his widow, the title of it being 'What we talk about when we talk about love'. I feel it's decently appropriate to borrow the idea to describe my motivation and to write about purely personal topics and views on technology and psychology – without becoming egoistic or providing a narcissistic look at all the mistakes others have done. I have a very narrow view since my experiences are limited to only a few fields of technology and then of course, there is only limited time in life. But there is love involved, love with the problems introduced.

Following Murakami's book, I have taken the subjective view, observations, and perspective as a grounding base. In the case of Murakami, his amazing wit and clarity in observing the simple act of running is much more than a mechanical or even sports analysis of running. Inspired by this, I'm an optimist in how accurate, single personal observations can sometimes advance our knowledge and understanding of the world and ourselves better and faster than many front-line r&d programs, crowd sourcing and big data masses can achieve. Reading the wise and sincere book on management by Matti Alahuhta, perhaps the most successful CEO (Kone, Nokia) and management professional in Finland, I was again reminded of the power of honest, personal views and felt empowered to take the personal look in this book.

4 INTIMATE SCIENCE

1. Psychological claims going astray in the real world: H0 heroes and H1 fairies

To understand humans requires understanding and respecting differences. Unlike many correlation studies claim and imply – by linking our personal characteristics with our genes or brains or even with the family income, for example – a great majority of us behave in a way that is different from the correlative and average implications.

For example, the popular study by Epstein et al (1996) suggested that some of us can possess a gene which is linked with a higher probability of being a novelty seeker (a controversy has followed on this) and other studies have suggested that possessing a specific gene increases the tendency to depression (there is controversy on this, too). However, many if not most subjects having these genes have no depressive symptoms or any characteristics of a novelty seeker. I call these people 'H0 heroes' (Nyman et al., 2010) because they behave or have characteristics predicted by the null hypothesis (that there is no expected effect) in this kind of correlational studies. That is, they do not confirm the hypothesis that the scientists entertain, based on the observed correlations and average individual differences.

They are 'heroes' who symbolically fight and win against the scientists offering the H1-hypothesis (that there is an effect and it is real), based on which the work has typically been accepted for publication and secured fame if it is controversial or novel enough. Linking the activities of brain areas to specific individual features is no different from the prophesied gene discourse. This is not to say that genes and brain don't affect our behavior but understanding individual life in the deepest sense of 'understanding' reminds us of the scale of this human puzzle.

Figure 1. Individuals in Monterey

There is another class of curious individuality as well: many of us don't have these interesting genes, like the ones suggesting depression or novelty seeking personality – and still have depression tendencies and novelty-seeking personality characteristics as predicted by the gene theories. I call these model cases 'H1 fairies' who show just the right type of behavior or characteristics (in the studies searching for these links) even without the specified biological background factors - if they happen to end up as subjects in these studies (they often do) and hide there in the averaged material.

Quite frequently in correlational studies, the *H0 heroes* and *H1 fairies* are neglected or forgotten (lightly commented on, perhaps) in the analysis as the scientists are not too eager to talk about them and complicate matters and their messages. We do not learn why *H0 heroes* and *H1 fairies* behave in their own and apparently independent way. Such observations would make the generalizations in and applications to everyday life difficult and offer the scientists the difficult question 'What is individuality?' If we knew why H1 fairies behave the way they do, without the gene, for example, we could extend the deterministic scope of gene-based understanding of behavior. Being silent or hiding the H1s keeps the theories of human behavior weak and narrowly focused.

Studying the use of technology carries the same risk of misinterpreting average user data. A popular, modern-visionary solution is personalized design, admitting the individual differences and tuning the UI and other app and gadget properties accordingly. We are different, but can we believe those who claim to know where the differences come from and how they occur, what are the meaningful ways to characterize them, and how we are different in our real lives?

Often it seems that because the question 'What is it to be a human?' is too difficult to answer, it has been reformulated into 'What do the genes do to us?', 'What is our personality profile?', 'How intelligent are we?' 'How are these properties linked with our success, failure, health or diseases?', 'What happens in the brain of person listening to musical sounds?'. In normal life, during significant life events, and in our spiritual development, in the joy of life, and at the moment of death these questions and the data they offer have very little value.

Each of us lives in a dynamic, private, psychological space, engaged with a specific, individual environment, inside and outside of our minds. We know it and grow from this inborn base, and learn to perceive and experience ourselves – we become experts on ourselves. Technology should learn to respect and value this amazing human capacity: it is impossible to imagine when and how it could become fully possible to map this intimate space by scientific-computational means. If someone claims it is possible to do, then he or she should be able to explain what this personal space is like and how the measures of it can be objectively derived. However, it is possible to let people contribute in their own way and help technology serve them, ever better.

Scientific methods do gather advancing knowledge of us but it is an illusion to image that at some phase this will lead to 'full and objective' understanding of human beings. Why such a reserved argument?

In psychology, as in other human and social sciences, when a subject willingly interacts with scientists and clinicians, and exchanges his or her ideas with them, or allows them to record his personal behavior and other data it can take place only in a well-defined, situational and temporary space spanned by the researcher and the willing person. However, this interaction does not take place in the same space anymore where each of us lives. Specific situations and illnesses, for example, are another matter; there the medical approaches can reach what is relevant in individual 'health problem spaces'.

For example, have you ever seriously considered how stupid and disconnected from everyday life some of the intelligence tests, like WAIS are? As a beginning, young clinician in neuropsychology I was ashamed to make the neurological patients of the clinic where I worked, and who often suffered from serious problems and were afraid of their health situation, to take such stupid tests. I quickly adapted to the practice and learned to use parts of them in a more human way, trying to avoid humiliating the suffering patients. Taking a test implies submission to something that should be useful for the subject-patient – it *can* be that. Often, however, it is not and testing is more like life on another planet where the subject taking a test is made to work alone, cannot ask for help like he or she would normally do or use the best tools and practices, take time and think, go out for a walk and come back next day, like we do when solving complex problems and have difficult times in life. Sleep over it.

Do I have data to back this claim? No I don't, but this disturbing practice to bend and shrink the individual human-mental spaces is demonstrated daily. It probably remains an eternal question of what is the nature of the data that can be obtained from our personal spaces and how it should be treated and interpreted so that it would help us understand human beings. Knowing the complex and interdependent relationship between the object and the measuring instruments, the quantum physicists probably take this thinking as self-evident.

During the present times of hard behavioral science business and the global PR competition for visibility, we are repeatedly led to believe that either the brain sciences, gene technologies or intelligent data mining methods will reveal the 'whole' truth about us and solve the mystery of the human brain and nature. In the popular discourse, the concepts of 'personality', 'brain imaging' and 'genome maps' are often used to convince the audience that these problems are not too complex and will soon be solved and that we will know, what it means to be a 'person' in the universe. We only must find out the simple basic laws of brain and gene –based behaviors and our personal profiles, be they about personality or intelligence, or temperament as it is fashionable today. Our connection with the universe is, of course, seen as a minor aspect of the problem. Quantum physics and psychology have not properly met yet; some seem to think there is no reason to it either.

Professor Horace Barlow, the famous neurophysiologist from Cambridge, once commented that while physicists work to the accuracy of several decimals in their work, biologists just try to get the sign right. The situation is not easier today. If someone would make the claim that we will soon solve the main problems of the universe, such a person would simply be considered a fool. But there are no decent criteria for the arguments concerning us as human beings. For example, in 2010 the Telegraph made the claim, by referring to a study at University College London that "Political views 'hard-wired' into your brain". This and similar studies continue getting the attention of mainstream media.

As can be expected, the story did not tell why the observed correlations between brain anatomy and behavior do not concern all people. What on earth is taking place in the brains of those people who do not have the average properties? Besides, an overwhelming majority of us are not 'average' and many of us change parties, parties emerge and die, some even invent new ones, and so on. So, what is explained with these findings? They simply throw away all that is essential in the human mind and life, our differences, complexities, interactions, culture, that is, what makes us as growing human individuals in the deepest sense of the terms 'grow' and 'human'.

True neurology, medical technology and many sciences of human biology and pathology are a different story: there the respect for the life and well-being of patients, the eternal fears and hopes of their close ones and family members guide the health care professionals: unethical testing and speculations are out of question or at least they occur very seldom. There are fruitful forums where brain sciences, gene technology and other modern sciences indeed benefit mankind and each of us. They have well-defined problems to deal with and the criteria of success are practical and human, like finding out our genetically guided sensitivities to medicines, helping neurosurgeons and in fighting cancer, and so on.

Patients need help and their criteria for care are simple: when a biological cause or a correlation is suggested as an explanation, the case must be waterproof; statistical averages or significant differences here and there in the studies do not help when decisions about acute surgical operations, medication and care in general are made – and the object is a single human being. It is a matter of scientific ethics, and it is human.

If we ask, based on our current behavior and habits, can we predict what will happen to us during our lifetime, what kind of life each of us will lead and how we will experience and share these experiences with others, the only honest response is 'No, we can't'. It is as difficult a question as the problem of the universe, but we must try to solve it and it is the most fascinating journey of mankind.

2.   The creative secret: entropy of the human soul

"Nyman, one day you will be a scientist" said my physics teacher Rafael Laurema, when I was sixteen, presenting my solution to a physics problem at the blackboard, in front of my class. My school had the questionable reputation of being the worst one in Helsinki and the idea of a science career was reserved for those in better schools.

"We are not mice," said my friend and professor colleague Jerry White, almost fifty years later, having his own challenging background from Chicago. We met at Stanford in 2010, as participants in the Peace Innovation project, with the aim to develop technological, media-related and collaborative approaches to promote peace, positive behaviors and interaction. Over one of our conversations Jerry and I started a long-lasting discussion on the essence and complexity of human behavior in problematic circumstances and especially how to promote good life for anyone in trouble. We both had led a good academic life; for both of us it had meant breaking the probability barrier set by our personal and family backgrounds. Why had this been possible?

There is an inbuilt, profound tension between the psychological theories of human character and individuality: on one hand these theories try to frame the concepts of 'a person', 'an individual, 'the family background', 'intelligence' as invariant human properties that carry over lifetime and that have predictive value for the individual life and behavior. On the other hand, most of us, if not all share the very basic desire and tendency for questioning, growth and creativity: to choose, learn, cherish, to be cared for, change direction, to be different, re-interpret the world, invent and to adopt unforeseen tools.

These contrasting perspectives to the destiny of individual life will not meet when static models and statistical generalizations of us dominate the psychological theories of development, intelligence and personality. Such theories have become nourishment for the frequent astonishment when facing unexpected behavior, in good and especially in bad. When someone breaks out of the box of illusory predictability, like Steve Jobs did, the public community is amazed and tries to find dramatic explanations to such an individual deviance. For Jobs, there was nothing 'deviant' in his life, he was different, but what was it then? The same happens with evil deeds: there were intense discussions in the media concerning the profiling of the Norwegian murderer and other school murderers. We do not know which incidences in their near and far history or which specific personal factors in their lives led to their violent choices.

A common hope is to find a simple, invariant individual description, a personality model or profile to be used for predicting behavior and experiences over a person's lifetime. At present, the static concepts underlying the tests to characterize us offer an implied promise that we can understand why certain behavior occurs, even in very complex circumstances. Typically, the tests do not tell why certain behaviors do not occur.

In criminal investigations, the term 'profiling' and behavior pattern analysis have been used for a wider spectrum and a richer analysis of individual behavior. This is no surprise, because criminal investigations deal with serious, single behavioral acts that individuals perform, not with their statistical generalizations and average predictions or profiles, which cannot explain individual deeds. A profile is something that must characterize the individual in a manner relevant to the context – the act of crime.

A static model of human nature and personality discards what is essential and unavoidable in life: its complexity and dynamics, the basic human ability to make situational interpretations and choices, interactivity, adaptation, use of tools, organizing the tasks and work, asking for help, even pray, refusing to do things that are beyond the person's competence or values, and all these factors together, interacting. A theory of personality or intelligence, for example, can have a statistical, average predictive value for simple behaviors but this does not mean that it also explains what an individual chooses to do, to sense and experience in real-life situations.

3. Information theory for the soul

Why not accept the natural complexity of the human mind and life and build psychological theories of the individual on that? What if we take the concepts of 'character', 'personality' and 'individual' as products of chaotic and complex biological, cultural, historical, social and even situational forces that together guide and constrain our behavior and personal growth towards the emergence of what then becomes 'me'? From this perspective, a behavior or an act may appear systematic, but is in fact produced by a multitude of unknown, interacting, and simultaneous forces that originate from the present and past contexts of the individual; they underlie his or her behavior patterns and generate a life trajectory.

Applying the concept of 'internal personal space' we admit that by observing human behavior, we can only see a projection of the personal space on the world observable, and what we record has many interpretations. This is like an opposite to the message from the famous ant example Herbert Simon gave in his book "The Sciences of the Artificial": he instructs the reader to be careful in interpreting the apparent complexity of an ant's path as a sign of a complex organism producing it. The inverse version of the ant's lesson would the warning *not to take simple behaviors as a sign of simple mental spaces supporting and generating these behaviors.*

As a personal example, I have never been asked the simple question "Has anyone ever told you something that has had a significant impact on your choices in life?" But if someone had asked it, I could have told about the comments of my physics teacher and of a couple of other persons. They have been an indispensable, but unpredictable part of my life trajectory; they are not 'background factors' that should be averaged out or taken as disturbing noise in my life. There is no psychological measure or test that could account for such immense consequences.

We have our complex individual histories but they are often treated in statistical measures as 'noise' or source of variance. Because of our dynamic backgrounds and personal spaces, the world we come to meet, our life pattern, is never the same for all of us, not even in situations where we have been before. The question emerges, how is this complex background reflected in what we choose to do and how large an impact it has on us?

The optimistic side of this complex view is, if we accept it, that we can assume that certain personal choices and behaviors are not inevitable: the same, apparently chaotic forces that guide our behavior can become creative powers that open a multitude of new ways to think, feel, experience and behave in specific situations. Without such forces, arts and creative sciences would be predictable, deterministic and lifeless.

4.   The grace of entropy

One way to characterize a behaving system – or individual behavior – is to borrow the concept of information entropy. In information theory, entropy characterizes the amount of randomness in a behaving system. Entropy takes us to the world of disorder; this can be difficult for psychological sciences and thinking to accept when the aim is to find simple, predictable and economic solutions to complex, behavioral problems.

High entropy means that the exact and detailed behavior of an observed system cannot be predicted with a high accuracy. Statistically we may be able to model it but the actual behavior, its next state or act, for example, cannot be predicted with perfect accuracy. In this sense, entropy encapsulates the challenges that psychologists and psychiatrists meet when diagnosing and measuring human nature, trying to predict or understand individual behavior in specific circumstances, in education, work life, therapy or in crime.

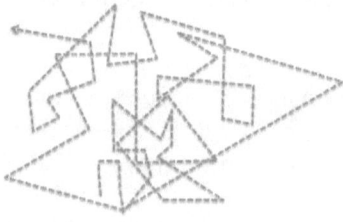

Figure 2. Random (human) walk, lessons from the ant.

Some psychologists, straightforward epidemiologists and eager proponents of gene theory have not been too excited about the complexity of human life. Sometimes it is forgotten that when predicting significant life events often the predictions must be inherently multi-dimensional, perhaps including non-separable psychological phenomena: even in the case of simple behavioral acts an accurate prediction of a behavior pattern does not mean the underlying processes can be described with the same or even similar concepts as the predicted behaviors are described. Genes don't 'behave'. It is a major challenge to accurately tell what role a specific gene, social class, or an intelligence level, situation or all these together, have on our future lives, when the term 'life' is taken seriously, and considered as a complex physical-mental phenomenon and not only as a simple aspect of what can be directly or indirectly observed.

We can choose to look at the individual, her choices and experiences as the most complex but natural phenomenon we can imagine and accept it as the starting point. Doing so we explicitly pay respect to the human mind with its individual peculiarities. The fact that behavior appears simple, sometimes straightforward and predictable is not against complexity, it only means that the perception of this simplicity is the product of how we perceive and live with complex phenomena. When a complex process is mapped on our limited–dimensional frame of reference we, as humans and scientists can recognize only simple behaviors. Often, of course, we need this simplifying perspective, for practical purposes and survival, but trying to understand human nature without breaking it apart, we must step outside this simplifying frame. This is nothing new to mathematicians.

A simple case of complexity made simple. How to quantify complex human behavior? Early in 2000, with my colleague Dr. Jari Takatalo, we studied and measured how people move in a virtual 3D world, using suitable 3D glasses and a 3D mouse. Jari worked with the early CAVE environment which our engineering colleagues from Aalto University had designed for researchers. The subjects were given a simple object search task and we wanted to map their individual movement patterns during different search tasks. In other words, we were looking for personal 'fingerprints' in their search patterns (see e.g. Särkelä et al., 2009).

We first used various statistics to describe the average movement patterns of our sample but then our colleague Dr. Patrick May, introduced the use of entropy measures to characterize the recorded movement trails. A simple way to measure entropy would have been to compute it for each subject, from the (x,y) locations in the trail during the search task. Entropy would then be an expression of the randomness or complexity of the movement pathway where high entropy would indicate that the subject was leaving a relatively random 'ant's trail' in the (x, y) space.

Then we thought of using entropy measures for more complex behavior elements than just moving from one location to another. We analyzed movement velocity, acceleration, turnings, and other possible higher -level aspects of behavior, even experiences, which we did not record continuously, unfortunately, as input to the entropy calculations. For example, we computed the entropy of turnings from each subject. We could then look at the entropies of the most basic elements underlying complex behavior, that is, the *behavior styles* our subjects showed when moving from one point to another. It is likely that these behaviors reflected the way the subjects observed and experienced the search tasks they performed. It was insightful to observe how person A could take a search route, almost identical to the route taken by person B but with different movement style. Clearly, they had different personal spaces underlying and driving their behaviors.

This approach is not limited to simple motor behavior analysis; we could extend it to more symbolic and complex levels of life and behavior. For example, in my own life, I know that these two utterances, "Nyman, one day you will be a scientist" and "We are not mice," have significantly guided my behavior and 'personal trails' and continue to do so, beyond my personality or intelligence profile; I keep coming back to these thoughts when it is relevant in my present life.

This is only surface and it is possible to include entropy considerations into any measurable, significant event of a person's experiential and emotional trajectory, instances of learning, patterns of habit formation, individual reaction tendency, and many more. The future theories in psychology will learn to accept this level of complexity and to deal with it theoretically. The tools for it are available.

A look inside of the complex 'me'. Every now and then we get confused when we must make decisions that feel complicated and difficult. Sometimes the world puts pressures on us and we must know what kind of behaviors we must adopt to meet the social, economic and other demands. There is no reason to think that our inner mental world would be any less complex than the external world we observe. In the end, what we think about the universe is a product of this marvelous mental system. Hence, when observing ourselves, we are dealing with a complex system and need introspection tools to help us make choices and behave in a way that satisfy our or others' needs. How do we do that?

Imagine that you are a salesperson selling a product to someone. You have studied marketing and sales; you know your work and how to behave. When you meet a customer, you don't go through a list of relevant algorithms, check lists, strategies, or instructions you know might be relevant for your success. If, every time you meet a customer, you would do this and choose the right alternatives for your communication and behavior, it would be impossible to do your job. How do you manage this extremely efficient personal data processing?

With my colleague Dr. Martti Puohiniemi we published the book 'Man' (In Finnish) where we introduced the power of personal roles for everything we do. Roles offer personal channels or constructs within which we can express our values and emotions; they integrate our large (internal) personal data bases so that we can behave in a situationally relevant, integrated and efficient manner, even spontaneously. By adopting proper roles in any of our life contexts we integrate a huge amount of personal, historical and cultural data – and exclude some. We don't need to scan algorithms and check lists because each role binds together behaviors and the hidden assumptions that are relevant and possible for that momentary role. Some might call this subconscious integration because it is very automatic; we barely notice the roles. In any case, it is a matter of amazing human knowledge management. We don't know how and why the roles work as they do but we can observe them everywhere, from everyday life to theatre.

Since the early history of the mankind we have adopted numerous roles without which life would be too complicated for us to handle; we would not know how to behave and especially how to change our behavior in various situations. For example, the salesman, when going home, would look silly by starting his sales pitches and marketing when talking to his children – relevant role switch and personal data base management is a natural must. The role set is a means for us to deal with the huge personal space we live in and not to get lost in it.

A sceptic could argue that technologically, a rich information theoretical analysis of behavior leads to excessive complexity and an overload of information making it impossible to collect and manage the immense mass of individual data, especially of individual, subjective experiences. But think again: the development of ict and net technologies has already made possible the access to extensive individual data collection and indeed, most applications like Facebook simply don't know how to collect psychologically relevant, subjective data. Another question is the ethics of such data collection. For willing individuals, and in future secure environments, I believe we can benefit from it in the hands of wise professionals and of course, the psychologists and psychiatrists many of whom still today test their subjects with present-day static tests, and miss the massive and dynamic behavioral history and trajectory data of us, internal and external alike.

What are the most basic and valuable elements of behavior that should constitute the input to the entropy analysis of individual life? We can further ask, what guides our complex choices, what are these personal spaces like - in form, content and in their dynamics. There are good grounds to believe that there will be a renaissance of psychodynamic theories and approaches to human psychology, but with new data. Then of course, there are the evolving methods in the study of complex phenomena to be applied in the analysis of mental behaviors.

5. Opportunity perception

Every second we are aware of the potential opportunities to behave, mentally and physically and we update this preparatory state continuously. Without the amazing skill of opportunity perception, we would become an extinct species. What is opportunity perception? In psychological research, it is hardly ever considered and after Gibson's famous studies on affordance it has only rather recently reappeared in research journals. Opportunity perception has remained a marginal concept, but nevertheless used in the studies of entrepreneurship failure or success (cf. Gaglio & Taub, 1992).

We meet and manage challenges of opportunity perception daily like the signs shown in the image below, from Lago d'Orta, Northern Italy, showing the way to the city centrum. Visiting that wonderful place, I tried to interpret the sign, and experienced myself the process of opportunity perception launching.

Figure 3. One aim, different opportunities.

Working with Mark Nelson at the Peace Innovation Lab at Stanford we were puzzled by the phenomenon of opportunity perception in our team searching for innovative design models, tools and frameworks for peace innovation, that is, to find novel opportunities to promote peace, positive interaction, and non-violence. Opportunity perception is more than having new ideas, it is a combination of a vision, and perception of the resources available as the means to reach the vision. In everyday life, we do that all the time whether moving in a city, wandering in a forest or solving abstract problems.

How could we learn to see new, available, but not yet perceived opportunities and to see through the jungle of traditional and dominant ways of perceiving the present reality? I mentioned earlier how most historical measures of peace have been based on the analysis deaths, number of wars, casualties and the amount money spent on armament. This perspective makes it difficult to see positive opportunities to peace through such a problematic and negatively biased lens.

Opportunity perception, scene 1. Helsinki Airport. Your flight is just about to leave and in a rush you enter an elevator to reach the right floor for check-in and security check. In the crowded elevator, in haste, you try to find an unobstructed view over the shoulders of your fellow travelers, to see down to the set of push buttons and find out which is the right floor for check-in. There is no extra time for mistakes and a minute objectively lost feels like an hour subjectively.

Finally, people get out from the elevator and you stare and stare at the buttons for information and out through the door. To leave the elevator or not to leave? There is no answer to your question, no information offered, you don't know how to choose, you don't see an opportunity for this small success in your life, and you must guess – or if you are lucky, you can remember it right from your last flight here. Maybe you just try and see. The designers have not been interested in your opportunity perception. This was a real experience from

Helsinki-Vantaa Airport, Finland, I hope the design has been cured.

Maybe you make it in time, but you have already paid an unwelcomed psychological price for the uncertainty, the disturbing feeling that you have not been provided a chance for delightful opportunity perception. You realize that *you* have missed something but what is it? The feeling is disturbing; it is not the most important episode in life but it is vivid.

If your frustration is repeated, you start thinking of a better route next time. But of course, you learn and adapt on the way and you know better next time in *that* elevator. You will not miss the opportunity to find a way to do what is important to you, despite the design hindrances. We adapt.

After such an experience, you have new and valuable knowledge: someone else will face the problem. This is potentially useful collective knowledge but typically it is not shared. It remains distributed and hidden but carries actual easy-to-predict human consequences.

Recently, new approaches to visual search have shown how extremely efficient and fast – in less than 100 milliseconds - we are in detecting opportunities in our environment: to see potential hiding places in a scene, pathways through the cliffs and rocks (cf. the work by Aude Oliva and the team). These studies suggest that opportunity perception is our biologically pervasive skill and capacity and it is easy to understand why – the survival value it provides is huge.

The incidence in the elevator (the experience is from the year 2010) was a peculiar form of user/consumer situation: you were required to know how to behave in front of a technology in order not to miss the opportunity to perceive and to do what is relevant for you. Thousands of travelers daily make it and survive, and from the outset it may look like the design solution had succeeded. What about the experiences of the people who used the elevator in Helsinki? When so many survive it and don't complain, it is taken as a proof that the problem is not (psychologically) serious.

These apparently small problems are significant because they demonstrate the *asymmetry (like hysteresis) in consumer experiences.* The missed subjective opportunities and negative experiences generated by it, have multi-dimensional, subjective weights and it takes time to build positive experiences, more than to get rid of the negative ones. A good customer experience cannot be created by just removing the reasons for bad experiences. The designer of the elevator controls had blocked our personal opportunity perception, and prevented a small satisfactory act of personal creativity. A part of the joy and every-day creativity was prevented from occurring.

Opportunity perception, scene 2. San Francisco Airport. The same story (again from the year 2010) now at the check-in automat of AA. It had a very clear and readable display that told the busy traveler which buttons to push and instructed to slide in the passport into the machine to feed the personal information and to receive the boarding pass. In my case, it was 5.30 AM and I was not extremely interested in putting my passport anywhere, I simply wanted my boarding pass and a chance to see any opportunity to go through the check-in and the security gate, as smoothly as possible. But that opportunity was not easily offered unless I performed the required choreography. As I saw it, there was no immediate chance for my small creative act that would have been so delightful at this early morning hour.

There was no place to insert the passport and I tried to slide it into a horizontal slot below, where I saw a luring, bright red laser-lighted square and a bar code symbol. The passport matched nicely the size and form of the slot, I could easily insert it there; it seemed like a most natural thing to do, 'excellent affordance' as Gibson would have put it, but unfortunately a false one, an illusion of opportunity. I tried again. Nothing happened, no instruction appeared on how to proceed, and apparently, there was no place for the passport in the automat. In a hurry, I focused all my attention at the slot, eager to join the baggage drop queue. The opportunity *for* my

small creative act in life, a fast move to the gates had been
blocked.

6. Reality and subjectivity

Of course, there was a perfect objective and rational
solution, both in the elevator and at the automat. There was
clear information about the right floor in the elevator and the
signs were very easy to see and understand. There was a place
to insert my passport, even written in so LARGE AND
CLEAR LETTERS, on the top of the automat that anyone
should see them – if he/she happened to look there. This was
where the roads of the human designer and an engineer
designer had departed.

For a careful engineer, the information was there simply
because it was well and wisely defined in the design
requirements and it had been placed there accordingly. For the
less careful human user, there was no information because it
was not within his or her *opportunity field*. The rational reality
would not have helped him even if his life had been
threatened, quite the contrary.

This is the negative engineering magic by which standards-
obeying designers can sometimes mislead us and make us
understand how bad we are in   r-e-a-d-i-n-g   t-h-e-   i-n-s-t-r-
u-c-t-i-o-n-s.

7. The immaterial power of opportunity perception

Opportunity perception is a most non-physical, immaterial,
human phenomenon, something that future robots will
desperately need. It is difficult to put into the design
requirements and it is more than attention or cognitive
problem solving: it is a creative, holistic, forward-orienting
human and animal process of perception, preparedness and
experience; it is an essential part of every moment of our life.
So far, computers don't have the capacity for intelligent
attentive behavior and those who claim otherwise simply fool

us. We don't even deep-down know what human attention is. That is why engineers so often either neglect it (don't pay attention to it), misinterpret it (as a problem of simple perception or selection), underestimate its psychological consequences (don't see the impacts) or just over-scifi it (use too specific scientific models to deal with it). Opportunity perception has not been properly perceived in perceptual psychology, either.

To add an optimistic and promising note on this problem, the best robot vision systems do use what is called 'saliency' processing, which is an underlying aspect of human opportunity perception. I had the pleasure to act as the opponent for H. R. Tavakoli's excellent thesis on "Visual saliency and eye movements: modeling and applications" where he defines saliency as follows: "The 'saliency' is generally used to refer to the state by which <u>any peculiarity</u> stands out relative to its surrounding." His analysis introduced different, some of them promising theoretical approaches to this important problem, on how we – and robot systems – identify salient information in our field of vision (and within the scope of other senses as well). Tavakoli included various approaches to this, e.g. information theory, local computational filtering, frequency domain analysis, top-down analysis, and learning models. It remains a most intriguing problem to solve: how we come to perceive opportunities. Nobody knows the answer to this, yet.

Present psychological and neuro-physiological models of attention and perception have very little to offer to opportunity-friendly, engaging design. The studies on human attention are interesting theoretically, often simplistic and only seldom authentic (they deal with problems like e.g. serial vs. parallel search, automatic or not, exhaustive or non-exhaustive search, feature based search or not, single channel vs. multiple channel, single individual perspective, no content-selective phenomena are included etc).

Luckily there are also context-sensitive approaches like the ones offered by the human factors community research but it was a mystery why there is such a long distance from, for example, the excellent airplane cockpit design to the check-in apps at the airport? We can guess the organizational and historical answer to this state of affair, but it is a weird pathology of design culture: you would think that even stealing the best and simple ideas and concepts from the best near-by contexts would be easy and profitable.

8. What are we doing in our everyday life that designers should know – simple examples

Bank at home. Almost all personal and home bank applications are designed to force us (self-)service the bank processes. Banks have taught and conditioned us to take care of both our own accounts and the bank's accounts and watch the processes, including security. This has been a major design failure: people are not at all interested in managing their personal accounts, or security, let alone the bank's accounts and processes. Only by bad design and the implied threats we have been forced to pay attention to these and arrange our economic life and activities around them. The main interest of us all, is to manage the everyday life, economy and finances fluently, securely, profitably, and so that it makes economic follow-up and planning profitable, useful, easy, fun and practical for the family if needed. Some progress is, however, now emerging in the form of clever apps and solutions that help us take care of our personal and family finances.

Family finances if any are full of challenges for opportunity perception. Major disasters are easily available for anyone seeing illusions of opportunities. With modern apps we can destroy our financial life and future in a few seconds with the self-destruction -allowing features. How can this be possible? A true human, opportunity-oriented system would help us see also the opportunity risks and threats.

I will explain my human-centric solution to the bank problem later here, after I've introduced the concepts of the Internet of Behavior (IoB) and situational intelligence, which are keys to arranging human-centric services in a human behavior-driven manner. IoB offers a rather conceptual approach, but with my colleagues we have applied it in real-life communication systems. Situational intelligence is a concept that has been introduced (in Wired magazine), in a slightly different form, e.g. by Claudia Dent from Everbridge, but as far as I know it does not exist in other systems or it is very rare.

Going for a holiday trip. When we prepare for a holiday trip it is not just the trip we are interested in but everything connected with it – in our personal world, our mental space, and living. A trip is never the same for all of us even when we take identical tours and enjoy the same services. This is no rocket science, every devoted professional working in services, knows this, it means approaching, understanding and having true interest in the client, not providing the service only. In the digital world, this has often become an underdeveloped aspect of services and hence Uber and Airbnb, for example, compensate for it with their recommendation systems. They do work, but their side-effect is the necessary digital distancing of the customer from the service provider. There is an imperative to improve this in the future.

Typically, we are not only interested in finding and choosing the best services and places to stay. Of course we do it, but it is not the primary motivation. Almost always we want to be excited about the search, negotiate, imagine visits, express our interests and passions about it, and plan this all with someone, often with a friend or a family member. We enjoy visioning our time and life around the trip. We enjoy preparing for it in many indirect and subtle ways, in our everyday logistics by coordinating with our other activities, creating possibilities for relevant activities before, during and after the trip and simply imagining, talking and day-dreaming. The internet materials available for browsing travel destinations are excellent, but there are practically no inspiring, cumulatively functioning, collaborative services available for this. Miniscule signs of this thinking can be found but compelling offerings are scarce. Especially the connection with the people whom we will or could meet during the trip – not only in the resorts or hotels but within the travel destination and on our trip - remain weak although there are a number of social media platforms than can be and are used for this purpose.

9. When a service wants to become intimate

Our days are full of moments of opportunity perception and we continuously orient towards the possibilities of these small creative acts. When businesses and service providers manage to support that aspect in our living we are delighted and allow an intimate relationship be built with them.

A service intending to touch our life, and build an intimate relationship with us, must earn our trust. In the above example cases, the service designers have not understood our external and internal life, and our ever-present wishes for the small creative acts in living. Such an understanding would rely on the respect for our 'minimal' ways and will to perceive delightful opportunities; simple design would be enough.

If you look at any cognitive psychology or a general psychology textbook you will notice the behavioral silos they deal with, both conceptually and in terms of methods and theories introduced. There are rare psychological texts analyzing the situationally multi-faceted life of an individual, who simultaneously is engaged with his or her work, family life, spiritual development and human growth, but this is seldom and such knowledge is typically fragmented.

There is no unique theory on how individuals manage their everyday and work life under multiple, simultaneous mental and environmental pressures and requirements. In other words, there is no 'human operating systems theory' that could cover and model this complexity – if we take the operating system concept seriously. Furthermore, to deal with this problem we need human data models, structures and perhaps even specific, future programing languages designed to cover human mental and behavioral phenomena and the data related to it.

Real human behavior is typically treated as any other data source and no specific data models have been developed for this purpose. Computer games are probably leading in this. In the following I deal with the operation system problem and then touch lightly on the problem of human behavior data models. However, I start with the most basic and serious question: who and what is an observer/perceiver? Living in a complex, natural environment, the observations we make, external and internal alike, form the only grounding point we have for understanding the world and ourselves.

10. Weak signals or weak theory of observation?

Human perception is about searching for relevance and opportunities, not accuracy.

Signals we receive when observing something can be weak to the eyes but strong to the observer or as the famous Japanese swordsman Musashi said: (my very free translation): *"Seeing is weak, perceiving is strong."*

When disasters surprise us, we are repeatedly faced with the question: "Why didn't we see it coming?" The question was asked after the terrible 9/11 murder, the large-scale nuclear catastrophe in Fukushima and the massive tsunami in Thailand. Some may think that existing or available weak warning signals were neglected or overlooked and we should feel guilt for being bad observers.

The MIT Sloan management Review story, "How to Make Sense of Weak Signals" (Paul J.H. Schoemaker and George S. Day, 2009) relied on the concept of 'weak signals' in offering their analysis framework to the difficult problems like: "Why ... so many smart people missed the signs of the collapse of the subprime market?" At first sight the 'weak signals' framework can appear as a promising concept to understand complex, difficult-to-see, hard-to-predict, perhaps disastrous phenomena and incidents. It blames us, our technologies, and even the 'smart people', for being insensitive to the weak but presumably existing, warning signs.

Here I shortly explain why I believe that the 'weak signal model' is a weak, ill-formulated, and even a harmful approach which can lead to misleading framing of the problem of observation. Especially the implications of such a framework and thought model offer an illusory understanding of complex observational phenomena and can lead to theoretical and practical helplessness. It may even help cover fraudulent behaviors: "It was impossible to see it":

Figure 4. Weak signal or weak perception? (Dollar bill)

Instead of the 'weak signal metaphor' (WSM) we need an appropriate theory of observation, including *a strong observer* – who can be smart or less smart - a theory that explains how complex, even distributed, non-linear, and inter-related phenomena are observed and how they could, in theory, be optimally observed. By observation I mean reliable and systematic collecting, sensing, recoding, gathering, sharing, and recovering of environmental (social, economic, political, their combination, or other) information that is not irrecoverably noisy. Such information can be non-linear and interdependent in nature.

A simple assumption behind this 'strong signals' thinking is that an ideal observer would have perceived the relevant incident of interest but they were not included in the analysis. The question then arises, what or who would be ideal observer(s) in such situations and were there such potential observers in the first place. Sometimes it is only theoretically possible to imagine the existence of an ideal observer, something, which in fact could not have existed. However, sometimes it is possible to know, post hoc, what kind of an ideal observer would have made the critical observations and it is even possible to identify what or who would have constituted this observer. Often such strong observers have existed but their perceptions have not been used or taken seriously.

In business strategy, a concept distantly related to the strong observer idea, was described by Yves Doz and Mikko Kosonen in their book "Fast Strategy" where they refer to "strategic sensitivity", an ability to strategic perception, a kind of open-mindedness or extra sensitivity to strategic matters in complex environments or in the firm itself. Their solution to such a perception is to guarantee a wide spectrum of organizational processes, objects, and other entities, which can build a sensitive relationship with the environment. In other words, the idea is to increase the organizational sensitivity because the signals are thought to be weak.

To the best of my knowledge, a generally accepted theory of the observer does not exist in perceptual psychology, decision-making, strategy analysis, or in theoretical physics either. Of course, there are related theories in these research fields, like the ideal observer in psychophysics, but they are limited to elementary perceptual phenomena and situations. Theories are needed to cover the observer characteristics, the observer's natural environment, and the nature of this relationship in a way that can explain why we build the kind of theories of the world and its events we typically do in organizational and other contexts.

Observational architecture. When forced to deal with complex and dynamic phenomena of the world, other people or even of ourselves we typically cannot rely on single observers or observations but must consider the *observational architecture* within which perception takes place. The observational architecture includes the points of observation, the description of the observer characteristics (e.g. sensors, measurement instruments, human observers with specific skills etc) and the structures/channels that provide connectivity within the architecture.

For example, during and preceding the financial crisis of 2008, numerous easily observable phenomena, and accurate observers existed but they were not typically included in the relevant observational architecture in politics, control, monitoring or journalism. One could even take an inverse version of the 'strategic sensitivity' concept and ask the question, related to the crisis: which were the strong vendors, partners, customers, politicians, officials, commentators, ventures, industries, processes, networks and other actors and entities that formed the (hidden) architecture via which 'observation' of the crisis development indeed took place (even though these perceptions were not collected and used to avoid the crisis)? One could argue, from this perspective that the observational architecture was so much distorted that it made the disastrous consequences possible without anybody 'observing' it.

An educational analysis of the events related to the financial crisis was given at CISAC/Stanford on April 1st, 2010 by Charles Perrow "Markets, Information, and the Spreading of Risks: The Economic Meltdown and Organizational Theory". His message left no doubt: it (the crisis) was not about weak signals from the catastrophic developments, the signals were loud and clear but there was no theory or useful knowledge of the relevant observational architecture and hence, there was no observer or no observer architecture was spanned that would have made the process observable – and perhaps preventable. The signals were not missing or weak, but because relevant observer architecture was not spanned (or it did not have 'energy') it was not possible to make sense of the observations and have them shared. Hence, the potential impact of observations (that would have been huge) remained 'weak' or non-existent to unprepared observers.

Afterwards, this lack of observations can reinforce the belief and illusion about the existence of 'weak signals'; methods have been innovated and developed to amplify the assumed weak signals. The outcome can then be that the ideal observers are not considered and the strength of the available signals is underestimated.

Theories of observation are abundant in organizational and other contexts, but they are often implicit, fuzzy, they deal with non-problematic processes, and they often involve simplified perception and measurement models, even when quantitative in nature. Only after a disaster or a surprise there arises the urge to make these models explicit and start thinking about better measurement models and practices. However, the time window to make valuable observations has then already passed and returning to business as usual means a return to the point zero, perhaps with a slight system parameter adjustments, new monitoring tools like the stress tests of banks (that failed in Europe), and early warning systems for a tsunami (that did not help in Japan).

A compelliing example of the strong signals in firms is the insight by the Stanford Peace Innovation team – I will later shortly comment on it - that firms have data (human interaction, transactions, collaboration-related, investments and much more) that show how they have contributed to positive engagements and even peace in a measurable way over conflict boundaries. Typically, firms are not aware of this data because it is not normal practice to look at it from this perspective. Hence, these signals do not 'exist' at all in their standard business data analysis

11. What does the concept of a weak signal mean?

Weak signal metaphor is popular in considering what are called 'wicked' futuristic or significant recent events. Futures researchers use it in metaphoric, statistical sense, and assume, for example, that signals of interest are 'weak' simply because they are below the noise level of the system and consequently, difficult to observe or discriminate. It is perhaps assumed that the potential observers are somehow insensitive to the critical warning (or promising) signs or other signals that could inform of the coming events and provide strategic advantage (cf. Ansoff 1975).

The solution is then to accumulate enough of such signals – by asking knowledgeable people like in the Delphi method, for example - so that it could become possible to detect these weak signals when there are enough observations for an aggregate to reveal the 'hiding' weak information of an event or a development. In the Delphi method the knowledge sources are collected, based on their assumed potential and competence in the problem at hand, so even there is a hidden theory of observation and observational architecture underlying the method. Overall, it is often implied that by improving the signal-to-noise ratio by accumulating the talks of 'wise men', for example, the noise can be removed or prevented from masking the (relevant) important signals.

What is weak in the weak signals metaphor? In EEG studies of the human brain it is customary to record 'weak signals' of the brain that result from the stimulation of senses by single, isolated sensory (visual, auditory, tactile) events. The subtle electric brain responses to these stimuli are so noisy that they are not immediately or easily detectable in the raw recording data. But when the same stimulation is repeated several times, by summing up the time-locked electric brain responses to these single stimulation events, a well-formed 'average response' can be uncovered from the noisy single responses – but it is the average, which type of 'signal' does not exist in the brain at all. The researcher still assumes that a weak signal in the brain was revealed and identified. The noise metaphor of WSM would thus imply that it might be possible to apply a similar type of summing or coordinated collection of any other signal information from numerous sources, which would then help to uncover the weak signals masked by the noise.

There hides a problem in this logic: is it reasonable to assume that all the single, independent brain events as a response to the stimulation remain invariant – static - in their essential characteristics? Even if, in the case of the brain, we could assume that, is something lost when the collected signals come from more complex or dynamic sources like during natural life and behavior? We don't know, and there is good reason to believe that signal-independence is a very strong assumption which can be misleading. After all, during its normal functioning, the human brain does not perform a sequential, time-locked and static signal averaging – we can hear even the slightest and independent single sounds and recognize their sources.

Figure 5. Strong signals (drawing by Kaisa, age 2 years).

What if these miniscule brain responses are all incomplete, in a wicked way distributed, or distorted or rare events in some unknown sense? Traditional signal analysis paradigm assumes that they have 'kind' statistical characteristics. In the computational analysis, this is needed for conducting straightforward noise-removing summing and other operations. In academic brain research exercises one can take the risk of assuming such things, but in predicting an earthquake or a nuclear plant accident, it is not: the costs of failures are too high.

Weak signals can occur in economic, social and other large scale and interdependent phenomena so that relevant signals simply do not mix. We cannot assume, that they show statistically nice behavior, and worse, they can originate from isolated and qualitatively different sources (like individual economists, politicians, organizations, statistics) being totally incompatible for any simple analysis. However, despite the incompatibility of sources, each of these channels can include a high-quality observational unit – within the ideal observational architecture and context - that is, one where accurate and valuable observations can take place. How can we know, which observations are accurate and valuable? A theory of observation is needed.

One could further argue that WSM is still valid but we should apply intelligent statistical and mathematical analysis models for detecting the underlying weak signals. Again, for example, in the research fields like brain imaging, visual system modeling, neural network analysis, robot vision, and signal analysis in general, there are a multitude of approaches to deal with such signals. One potential signal analysis paradigm, even as a metaphor for futures researchers, is that of the Independent Component Analysis (ICA; cf. Hyvärinen, Karhunen, Oja (2001): *Independent Component Analysis,* Wiley.) What if we do have some valuable knowledge of the properties of the signals we are interested in?

The basic assumptions and the applicability of the ICA method makes it an excellent, educational metaphor to think about such situations although the linearity constraints of ICA show how problematic natural, non-linear signals are and how resistant they are to observation. As I'm not a specialist of this model, Professor Timo Honkela convinced me that ICA works with class/qualitative data.

12. Towards a general theory of observation for the study of complex natural phenomena

It is not possible to introduce a complete theory or even an introduction to the theory of observation and observer here, but I will take up some of the essential (rather theoretical)

elements I believe should constitute such a set of theories. I suggest some basic principles and try to convince the reader on the value of this in technological and other contexts of life.

Even in quantum mechanics, there is no observer-centered theory for dealing with the properties of the human (animal, alien, general) observer and the consequences of such (implied) theories to the development of physical and other theories of nature, universe and man. In the famous thought experiments by Einstein for example, where he imagined traveling with near to speed of light, there was the inherent idea that the observer characteristics remain independent – being classical or one could say even Newtonian – of the context, motion and speed through space and of the impact of any possible variables. Einstein imagined traveling in a perceptual-psychological vacuum if not even in such an ether.

A theory of the observer and observation should be the cornerstone of any theory development in physics. Here are the basic elements of the theory of observations as I see them:

I.   An observer can be any system that interacts with its environment.
II. An observation can be defined as a relationship between the observer and her environment but the relationship is always defined by a (reference) system that is external to the observer (although interconnected with it).

In quantum mechanics you might say that there is an energy-related relationship between the observer and the environment. However, any observer-environment relationship can offer many interpretations to different observers and there is no unique observation of a complex environment. When we want to obtain reliable information of a certain process in our (social, biological, economical) environment we must first identify the observers that interact with that environment of which we are interested in. Then we can define the observations and from which perspectives they can be recorded.

For example, I'm an amateur in this, but it appears to me, that scientists do not know which observers to use and which observational architectures to apply for predicting earthquakes early enough. Historically, there have been folklore stories, in Japan for example, about the deep-sea fish (as reliable observers) reacting to seismic activities. Economists and politicians did not know the relevant observers of the critical incidents and processes in the financial turmoil in 2008. There was no proper observational architecture and theory of observation available. On the other hand, hindsight is a delicious activity, and it is easy to span the observational architecture afterwards, when historical data has been accumulated.

III. All observers possess limited-capacity 'sensory' channels that interact with their environment. The state of each channel and the state of its environment are dependent on each other. It is possible and often necessary to see the environment as the observer *and* the observer as the environment.

IV. Because of the limited-capacity channels, all recorded information – observations - include an inverse problem: it is not possible to compute the complete state/space of the source by using any of the single channel activities or even a composition of them. In the financial crisis, for example, because of this property, no collection of information about observations, could have fully predicted the crisis; there was no way 'to see it coming' although observations would have been available to help prepare for it. The outcome state was not, and could not be defined or determined from the same state/spaces where the observations took place.

V. Because of the inverse problem, a theory of observation and the observer suggests means by which optimum approximate information can be collected from the source states and their state spaces.

VI. Theory of observation describes the connections of the observer with its environment. Based on that it is possible to know what kind of knowledge each specific observer can provide and which factors constrain it.

VII. When studying complex phenomena, theory of observation suggests means by which the limited capacity observer constraints can be minimized.

The idea that any system interacting with its environment can be treated as an observer, and vice versa, might sound as weird. However, this is a very basic property of any biological organism, for example, and it is a matter of definition what we call sensory processes. In the classic, Schrödinger's thought experiment where the poor cat sits in the box, perhaps alive and dead at the same time, Bohr indeed suggested that the apparatus, i.e. the box can be considered as an observer as well.

13. Back to practical behavior analysis

A theory of observation does not help much if it offers no practical guidelines. So, I take again the example of the financial crisis as an example that Charles Sparrow used in his talk (cf. above). I'm not a specialist in this field but will offer a few questions to which a theory of observation in this context could provide some useful guidelines and help recognize what is difficult to see in the history or in the future.

Following the theoretical scheme above, the following general questions related to the observer and observation, need to be answered in this special case (the financial crisis):

a) What kind of observational architecture, including the interactions within it, underlay the observations? What were its basic elements and relationships? How and where was it described and by whom?

b) Who/what were the relevant observers? What was the nature of the interaction they had with their relevant environment, within the observational architecture?

c) How (by whom, by what) were these observers defined externally? Which instances have defined these observers?

d) What information channels did the observers possess and use? How were they constrained and limited?

e) What was the nature of the inverse problem in the case of the observers? What problems it created for those interpreting the observations?

f) What was the theory by which optimal collection of information from the sources was (could be) organized?

g) How was information from the observations integrated and represented?

h) What was the decision model by which the observation data was interpreted?

One is tempted to ask "So what?" and I'm sure many of these questions have been partly answered. But the example suggests how to better deal with what is often called a 'weak signal' issue and it points out that often it is not a matter of weak signals at all, but rather a missing or unfit concept and theory of observation, the observer and the observational architecture. Phenomena that today are treated as 'weak signals' will in future, with better knowledge, be considered as strong.

By taking this approach I believe, it is possible to turn our focus on *strong* observations and to collect this information in a meaningful way. Earthquake sensor systems, for example, have been developed in the Bay area and elsewhere by connecting hundreds and thousands of sensors as a network to span a perception/observation architecture for sensing, communicating and analyzing earthquake-related information. These are inevitably significant signs in the development of an observation theory and observational architectures which are becoming ever more practical in the networked and IoT-world.

Finally, someone might still suggest that we can use the term 'weak signals' loosely, just as a metaphor, but why then, use it at all?

14. Human real-time operating system and the observer

Imagine someone, a man of course, at home, walking down the stairs with a glass of beer in hand, but then suddenly dripping over and falling dangerously. It would be a natural and sane reaction to forget the beer glass, try to recover balance, and avoid hurting oneself. Most of us would drop the glass and spill the beer all over because it is more important to survive the fall than to save the beer. Somehow in our minds we have the blessed access to this new and high-priority survival behavior that is designed to save us from serious damages.

How does this happen? How can we know what sensory information to select, which part of the ongoing behavior to stop, how to replace the ongoing behavior with a new one and which one of the many potential behavior patterns should we choose for this specific situation? How can we choose the right kind of behavior or even an optimal one? Furthermore, some part of the present activity must be preserved and some must be continued, but which parts are they? After all, falling on the floor does not mean that we stay there forever. All of this must happen extremely fast, we have no extra time for making relevant observations and everything must take place within less time than a second or two.

This is a typical case of human interrupt processing that happens to us, in some form, all the time, thousands of times a day and we redirect our observational and behavioral resources accordingly. It is a most natural part of life and when necessary or useful an interrupt overruns most of our motivational, personality and intelligence traits. Usually, we are not aware of it at all. The ongoing behavior is replaced by other, more relevant psychological and neurophysiological processes having access to our available and relevant mental resources and even this can be interrupted, and so on: our behavior is inherently multi-layered. One could say that we don't have a single stream of consciousness but a bifurcated and layered, living system of consciousness with any level of abstraction.

In this specific example the *mental and situational context* was that of walking down the stairs, with a glass of beer in hand, in a mood of expectance and enjoyment, and with the aim to watch television, an exciting game of football, perhaps. A significant part of active mental resources was then allocated for dealing with the peculiar situation, that is, performing the required tasks. But what was relevant and why? The original, comfortable and well-balanced content and aim were suddenly replaced by the mental data triggered by the unexpected accident context and the observations of it which then required new and relevant mental data and resources, fast.

This state change is called *context switch* in the operating system theory to describe a situation where the contents of the available processing resources (registers and other processing units) become replaced by a new content relevant to the new, specific context or task at hand. One could say that the content of the registers/resources *is* the context. The change of register/resource contents is based on the privilege structure allowing crucially important tasks to be performed so that they overrun the less important, ongoing activities. This makes space for a required action, often in a very short time. Sometimes, in extremely pressing conditions, a digital system can have a temporary direct access to memory and processor resources, and can even 'steal' time and processing power from the ongoing routine processes. This is a pure analogy, however, and we can only imagine what these exceptional activities are in living organisms, humans included.

When an operating system runs important and hierarchic, privilege-based tasks, the required resources must be continuously maintained and refreshed to match the needs of each task at hand, relevant activities must be secured and saved and recover them when it is again time to return to the original task, and everything must be extremely well coordinated and fluent. In a threatening situation like an accident, one can think that all the available resources are refreshed to match the needs of the new context.

Psychologically, it is a good question what are the resource contents that are needed in each situation, what observations must be made, how should they be described, and what is this coordination process like? There is no generally accepted, formal psychological language to describe this and no accurate means to characterize the underlying functional architecture. We can safely claim that, so far, there is no tailored language to describe the human operating system and all its mental processes that underlie our dynamic behavior - and survival. Many of the human-technology disturbances reflect a lack of knowledge on this issue. The word 'operating system' does occur in cognitive psychology texts, e.g. in working memory studies, but it is mostly used as an oversimplified metaphor.

Energy flow during context switch. The context switching process is subjectively a very energetic experience. Often, especially when taken by surprise or facing a threat, one can feel the flow of energy used for focusing all the available resources to the new task demands and to orchestrate the required activities for accomplishing the necessary observations, actions and mental re-organization. In the beer example the threat of hurting oneself would have been of such a high priority that most of us had pushed aside any ongoing mental and physical activities related to the goal (going to see the game on tv, downstairs), but of course, not all activities.

It may well be that because of the energy usage, continuous, unnecessary interrupts are so burdening in our normal (especially work) life. I have not seen a calculation on how much brain energy is required by context switching, or how to calculate it, but in extreme situations it must be a lot, compared to any other mental process. This is an invitation to brain scientists to look at the entropy measures in the cortical and other brain activities. But of course, some processes/tasks are so crucial for our body and mind that they need to have the highest priority, always. They can be compared to the operating system kernel (the core of the operating system sw that maintains the connection between the computer, its memory, the devices connected and the environment) functions and prioritized hard-wired interrupts used in computer operation and in related device services. If the kernel is damaged, nothing can work properly.

We are extremely skillful in human interrupt processing which indeed is one of the secrets behind our survival in natural, variable environments and situations. One could claim, that interrupt processing is the most crucial element behind intelligent behavior. In everyday life, there is the illusion that we perform multiple tasks at the same time, but in fact, it is a matter of temporal scale and resolution: we use dynamically our available, but limited perceptual, intellectual, and affective resources. When sudden changes take place in a life situation and/or several demands for resources occur simultaneously, the limitations of the system performance are revealed. The same is true with the operating systems of our computers.

Real-time operating system thinking. The design of real time operating systems is a most fascinating topic for any serious psychologist and UI designer trying to understand how people manage to perform several simultaneous mental and physical activities and survive the dynamic word. You can find an informative introduction and sources to the topic from http://en.wikipedia.org/wiki/Real-time_operating_system

What is a context switch like in the human mind? Can it be characterized as a process where the essential contents of our consciousness, our mental 'registers', whatever their nature or essence, undergo a content change so that their old content – or associations - become replaced by a new one that represents the requirements of the new context? Or is it a matter of gating situationally relevant information sources (neural systems) for proper use while blocking others?

When the demands of the new context have been mentally met and the required actions taken, a balance is achieved: the previous context (old 'register contents') can again be recovered making it possible to continue the interrupted behavior and to match the requirements of the earlier context – to go on living like before. Where do these new contents originate from? Have they been stored somewhere or is it just a matter on refreshing the links to them? Where does the old context information go? What is replaced and what is new? What is this process like? Is it typical for all behaviors, sensory, intellectual, artistic, and even spiritual ones?

Anyone can observe the amazing effectiveness of these mental processes, their unlimited scope and how easily they are activated, with a few words, when starting to read a novel, for example.

"He was an old man who fished alone in a skiff in the Gulf Stream and he had gone eighty-four days now without taking a fish".

A few words are enough to induce a complete context switch in our minds, we leave our present situation and move to the enchanting world of this fisherman – by Ernest Hemingway (Scribner; Reissue edition, May 5, 1995). What happens in our minds when reading this, is not only a cognitive switch but deeply emotional, cultural and spiritual. It is not a simple, determined process. Why is it so effective?

To schedule is human. Because we live in an organic world and in multiple-task environments we need special skills for orchestrating our activities in strategically sensible manner. It is not possible to perform any number of tasks simultaneously or in any order. We can accomplish many and even complex tasks by preparing internal and external task lists and collaboration notes that we simply follow, but even this is a resource challenge for a human (and computer) operating system: how to use the mental resources in a coordinated and most efficient manner and often extremely fast? What is the criteria for 'effective'?

The need for coordination is a must in the design of scheduling procedures for any operating system. Scheduling of tasks consists of coordination, re-organization, and keeping up track of ongoing tasks and activities and their scheduling and re-scheduling. Priorities occur and they control the access to the main computing resources on a more strategic level. Scheduling systems are designed for a purpose, and so it is probably also with the human operating system. To think that it is a matter of survival alone would be simplistic: most of us have learned the joy of being able to follow several things simultaneously and make abrupt context switches, manipulate stuff and things 'at the same time', when we tell funny stories or imagine insightful solutions to problems. It is fun.

In human sciences, the conceptual approach to real-time operating systems (RTOS) is fascinating but rare. For example, when designing optimal operating systems, it has been necessary to rely on structural and architectural approaches and concepts that allow the analysis and control of computer performance in a changing and complex task environment. On the other hand, RTOS theory reflects the structure of the classic computers and their cpu's, memory, and i/o structures and it is not wise to extend this analogy very far to the study of the 'human operating systems'. We are not digital machines or animals. With new computer architectures, parallel processing and AI, new RTOS theories emerge.

Figure 6. Are we similar?

Nevertheless, I would like to see a well-defined architectural description of the human RTOS structure and its main principles, biologically and psychologically well grounded. Perhaps I have just missed it, perhaps it has been described somewhere, but my educated guess is it has not been defined, yet.

Are we similar? Interesting enough, we are different in our capacities to deal with demanding context changes. The example I mentioned above is a true story; it ended up with a surprising outcome because it happened to a person with a strong sports background where falling is not an extreme or even a dangerous event but can be subjectively a simple routine. One could say that the person in question with the sports history had developed himself a specific interrupt structure, different from what others have. So, in fact he did not spill his beer completely and did not drop the glass, but instead, hurt his back ribs quite badly. Why? Because he had a relevant process available, somewhere in his mental repository, a way to switch quickly to the context of falling. However, in this situation the context switch was triggered by two things together – saving the beer (and the carpet, perhaps) and not hurting seriously himself. But something went wrong and he hurt himself so much that it would have been bad on the football field as well. The context was not a football game, but perhaps there was something similar, that triggered the specific survival behavior, which now was slightly 'out of context' – he was on the way to watch an important football game on tv. Everything happened so fast that there was no time for conscious control. He managed to save the beer but not his ribs.

We have personal multitasking processing capacities, and a good question is: do we all have similar processes to deal with natural context switches or is it possible that people develop very personal mental architectures, and even processes and strategies for this purpose? Probably so, and we can admire this when artists and sportsmen show their amazing performances. Indeed, our personal operating system characteristics can be considered as components of personality. Clearly, these example mechanisms are not hard-wired, but some certainly are.

The beer example demonstrates the use of a repository of actions we have at our disposal. How are they organized? How do we know which activities to initiate when there is not enough time to run a comprehensive losses-gains analysis or when the situational requirements suddenly change, perhaps in a time less than half-a-second?

Multi-taskers are poor cognitive performers. Clifford Nass and his research group at Stanford demonstrated in 2009 how subjects with high-multitasking behavior tend to have a surprisingly low cognitive performance in many simple cognitive-attentive tasks. While this has many implications, it is interesting to consider the findings in the light of interrupt processing theory. Of course, alternative theories can be suggested to explain the differences found between low and high multitasking subjects.

It is somewhat surprising that cognitive psychologists have not developed a comprehensive theory of human multitasking behavior. Related approaches have been presented under the topics of working memory, attention and limited-capacity processing. But as far as I know, they do not include real-time operating system architectures, priority analysis, task-lists and scheduling, or dynamic interrupt processing models or frameworks. Perhaps the concept of 'real-time operating system' does not sound inviting in a human sense since it is such a mechanical part of any computer system and analogs can be misleading. We enjoy the illusion that our computers appear to perform many tasks simultaneously and manage multitasking efficiently. From the outset, some of us can have that illusory human ability as well but there are limits as Nass showed.

15. A need for human-centered data structures

Quantifying oneself is becoming an everyday practice. Miniature cameras, practically unlimited memory capacity, an increasing number of sensors selective to motion, vibration, light, radiation, sound, chemicals, position, weather, bio substances, pressure and other physical phenomena, together with mobile physiological recording systems, and intelligent devices make up an unlimited architecture for quantifying ourselves. The question is, what to do with all this data and how to accomplish it so that it could provide unforeseen human benefits. Are there specific data processing needs that originate from the data collected which is inherently human in nature? Does it matter that we deal with *human* data? Is human data like any other kind of data?

My first encounter with the Quantified Self (QS) movement took place at a work-shop arranged at Microsoft premises, Mountain View, in summer 2010. The audience consisted of a group of innovative people with their backgrounds from ict, psychology, anthropology, social sciences, medicine, and other disciplines. They all shared the interest in the knowledge revolution taking place in recording and management of human, individual data. When they all, about 150 attendees were each asked to describe their QS interest in three words it became clear that a new form of science and practice of multi-disciplinary psychology was being - or had already done that - born.

At my home country, where sports have always enjoyed a strong national role, we have had innovative companies specialized in QS, like Polar, founded already in 1977, Suunto which joined the field in 1988 being earlier a known manufacturer of compasses and now the latest one Oura (https://ouraring.com) with their famous Oura ring. The psychophysiological brain sciences and their psychological methodologies are (slowly) being complemented by approaches that respect the richness of human psyche and the life situations of the individual.

Authenticity is still a rare aspect in laboratory disciplines that use their brute force in measurements, like the fast improving brain and other physiological recording and computational methods, often combined with simple, even banal psychology. This has often led to exaggerated generalization of the findings, be they related to gene impacts on our future, mechanical profiling by personality measures, emotional reactions or other applications to our lives. However, the evolving technological applications are boosting the everyday-psychological ambitions of researchers.

Visiting the QS meeting in Mountain View I was somewhat surprised, noticing that not much discussion concerned the strategies for collecting and especially organizing the huge human data masses generated in QS. I got the impression that many of the participants had the underlying idea that traditional ict-systems and data models will suffice or at least evolve so that any QS data can be accommodated to it and be amenable to sufficient computational analyses. Leaving the meeting I was convinced, however, that the data models, even programming languages dealing with QS will become a real future challenge. As far as I know there are still no signs of QS specific data management solutions in the field, some commercial systems perhaps excluded, but I don't know them in detail.

In QS, the individual is at the center of data collection and retrieval, just like we all are, as subjects, at the center of our own information architectures, our own and to-us-relevant inner and outer worlds. We manage our perceptual, experiential, motor and thought process data from *our own first person, me-perspective, even when we are emphatic and try to understand the viewpoints of other people.* We manage our bodies. Our memory for all this information and knowledge is continuously built on the subject-oriented architecture where information from this perspective is adopted and accumulated in an intelligent and meaningful way. It makes us what we are and helps us organize huge amounts of data about the world and about ourselves. The process is dynamic and we change every second so that updating must take place in a coherent way.

In standard data models this continuous and holistic change is not easy to implement whereas in artificial neural network models it is a natural aspect: the possibility for updating is part of some models. The spiking neural network models have been designed so that in them, time is inbuilt, which in principle can account for continuous learning and change in the system (cf. Maass, 1996).

It is no accident that our memory and attention processes use the first-person perspective: we observe both the environment and ourselves through this magnificent, continuously updating 'subjective lens-mechanism'. When discussing the phenomena of human perception, typically the 'internal' perception is forgotten as if it were a totally separate process from the 'external' perception. The most critical requirement for perception, both internal and external, is not accuracy of retrieval but the subjective relevance of perception data. This is where computer systems often fail – they can be accurate but less good in relevance and they have serious problems in dealing with the dynamic first-person, contextual perspectives of their users.

So far, I have not seen artificial data structures and architecture models designed for the specific purpose of optimal processing of human data, i.e. to serve the need for organizing first-person oriented, internal and external perception and other data, its collection and storage, its management and retrieval. Game environments probably come closest to this. The increasing masses of data accumulating from QS data sources have convinced me of the need to have data models and architectures solely meant to serve this human purpose, to manage the first-person oriented, dynamic data masses. It is not only a question of linking a person code with the data concerning him or her: even if we can relate all the data that we record from an individual or from the sources related to him, we still need a meaningful integration of the data that changes fast. The principles of this integration make it an interesting and ambitious data management puzzle.

A thought experiment on QS. Try remembering an accident you witnessed or a visit to a memorable place, long time ago. Typically, you first try to memorize the key events, times, places, your activities then, perhaps some sensory aspects, your feelings or people present. Essentially you view your own history from the first-person perspective by constructing an intimate mental scene – 'a play' that only you can follow. This amazing process is an effective demonstration of the functioning of human-centric, first-person orientated data structures and architectures that underlie our memory-based behavior and performance. Without them we would be in serious data management trouble trying to retrieve the relevant subjective data. Even the best artificial neural network models do not have this capacity.

Figure 7. A personal link to an episode 10 years ago.

Our memory for personal events is not perfect, far from it, but it is almost always relevant, in one way or another, even when making mistakes; in this sense, human memory is better than artificial ones. The worst mistakes made by artificial memories result from losing the knowledge of personal relevance of the memorized data. For humans, even in the case of memory slips and false memories the subjective material recovered has personal relevance. Typically, we do not make *any* memory slips or any mistakes: they are nearly always somehow meaningful to us, right or wrong.

16. Towards human-centric data architecture

The power of ideal *human-centric data architecture* – as I imagine it here - is that it always, without exception, allows and preserves the personal perspective, whatever data or information is stored and processed, even when the memories are fabricated, incomplete, under the influence of suggestions, or simply false. Personal relevance of emotional and rational content is an essential property of such a memory. It helps individuals to survive complex, even dangerous environments, and to enjoy these challenges. There is no formal data structure to describe exactly what personal relevance means. The reason to this is simple, there is no unique way to deal with personal, psychologically relevant data; if you ask an ict specialist what defines the psychological relevance of data you will receive more questions and guesses than well-founded answers.

With a slight exaggeration – the best of the deep learning models excluded - one can claim that artificial memory systems are designed to store and recover even the slightest details correctly while situationally relevant recollection is secondary. For human-centric memory, the opposite is true: the situational relevance of a recollection is primary and the accuracy of details is secondary.

Recollecting distant memories, we identify the key elements, enrich them and link them with other relevant memorized events. After a while we have created or re-created a coherent memory structure that we can internally 'view' like a movie, and 'read' it like a story. The recollection, like an eye-witness testimony, may not be completely true as Bartlett showed already in 1930's and Elisabeth Loftus and other visionary researchers demonstrated in 1970's, but it is amazing how skillful we are, piece by piece, in weaving such a wonderful and useful lace of memory of our experiences. Endel Tulving, the famous cognitive psychologist has described this specific form of human memory as *episodic memory*.

Computers and their memory systems don't yet come close to human memory performance in meaningful remembering of events and life episodes – why?

Firstly, computers have no idea who is memorizing, what and why: any computer user can behave as its owner; the system does not typically know or consider this in any psychological depth (it could). Even if it knew the user, the system is mostly interested in the 'rights' and 'security', not who he or she really is and what goes on in his or her mind and life. It has not been possible to program a whole person into a computer. This is the problem of any memory system that is based on the idea of storing data without its personal context and history. Computer memory is still what documents have always been, whatever material they have been from ancient stone tablets to paper, serving as storages for both subjective and objective data when needed – with added explanations for the use of the stored data.

Human memory system can be considered as a dynamic, constructive repository that stores both the objects of interest (data related to the environment and to the person himself) and the context (any associated and contextual data). Both the 'objects of interest data' and the 'context data' can act as search keys later when needed. But a 'search' of data from human memory is quite unlike search from an artificial memory because it is a dynamic, constructive, strategic, under emotional, social, situational and cultural guidance, and it is a transformational, sometimes even a creative and metaphorical process. Human recollection is more than data retrieval: smells can be associated with the memory of significant events and situations and can make certain familiar places feel wonderful to us. This 'feel' is not a side effect. Every time we recall and feel something we change as persons.

Interestingly, in arts and music, take Stravinsky and Picasso as examples, the innovation of new structures opened new possibilities for human (artistic) expressions and experiences. Hence, the question for the current ict: what would be a good candidate for a *human-centric data base model* that would support and extend human/person -centric data processing and offer new possibilities for representing the human mind and behavior? Is there a real need for this type of data structures and data base theory?

I believe that for QS developers as well as for anyone dealing with masses of personal information (which is commonplace today), a subject-oriented data structure can provide a means to organize data in subjectively meaningful and effective manner and allow secure sharing of data.

Figure 8. Knowing what to expect helps recognition.

17. Episodic structure as a candidate for human centered artificial memory

With my colleagues Jari Lehto and Pentti Marttiin (Nokia Networks) we outlined a concept for episodic data structure for human memory modeling, but never had a chance to develop it into a product. In a pilot study run by Sauli Laitinen we could demonstrate the power (and weaknesses) of the human episode structures for collecting and retrieving personal experience data. Here are some of its elements.

The basic idea for the human-centric data structure is simple: *an episode* is a data structure that can be taken as the basic entity when dealing with subject-oriented data. The memory architecture can be built on that. For further analysis of the episodic memory, see e.g. Endel Tulving's work. Human-centric data can be defined as follows:

a) *Episode* is the general functional-structural entity that serves our memory of experiences and actions (internal and external alike). Notice, that the episode *serves* the memory, it is not considered a pure data storage. Episodic retrieval is a dynamic, constructive process where it is impossible to make a sharp division between the first-person processing of data and other data included in this process. In this sense, it is closer to the associative and artificial neural network memory models, with the exception that it is always first-person and process-orientated.

b) When we try to remember something from our history like painting a garage some time ago we recollect it as a structure of episodes related to the painting work (going to a shop, buying the paint, preparing the work, doing it, cleaning the place, admiring what we did ...). Then, after 2 years, for example, when we try to remember what color brand we used we typically don't remember its name or code. Then we try to recollect where we put the paint cans. If we don't remember that, we search for other episodes that would lead to the storage place or to some other useful knowledge. The episodic chain structure of subjective historical data comes to help.

c) Each episode includes an actor (me, first-person), task/action/goals, relevant content (associated data, knowledge, perceptions, attentive focus, etc), a temporal window and timeline, and a context (social or other). It can also include a role in which we have behaved which guides data selection accordingly: not all data has the same relevance for all human roles (activities).

d) *Episodes are strongly linked with each other* so that it is possible to recover and construct detailed data through a linked set of personally relevant episodes. The memory information in episodes is not exact, but it is practically always relevant, subjective, and first-person oriented.

e) For an unknown reason, *episodic structure* of the human memory is psychologically very coherent, detailed, and well integrated, reminding of the solid structure of our perception processes. This makes the episode an extremely efficient and robust structure to deposit, store, and recover the essential links and other elements related to the data of a particular episode - even after several years. It tolerates some disturbances and mistakes made are typically 'graceful'.

f) Access to an episode activates automatically many of its constituents and links providing a rich collection of subjective data, including the emotional, motivational and social aspects that are inseparably interlinked. It is an integrative process.

g) It is possible to build an episodic data structure that allows matching the data structures of individuals, even masses of people. This has social application potential.

h) Combining numerous QS data sources with an episodic representation and a related data base allows efficient search of subjectively relevant data and experiences from individuals and their collectives or from collectives of collectives.

i) Episodic data base system need not be perfect: it can include fuzzy elements, but it must preserve the personal relevance of its data and processes. Of course, it is possible to support a high-performance memory by innovative technologies, but the first-person, subjective data can never be perfect and complete; one might even assume that it is always more or less creative.

j) Last, as can be noticed, the Golden Triangle approach, that emphasizes the human-centric (first-person), content orientated (contextual) and its psychological ground (theory of episodic memory), is intimately related to the way the episodic nature of memory-concept has been introduced above.

It is possible to construct an artificial episodic memory system, in both software and hardware, and test it with genuine human data, but probably this has not been done unless something like that has been accomplished in game environments. The architecture and data structures would allow the storage and processing of relevant context and first-person relationship of all subjective data, including and especially in QS environment.

5. METHOD APPROACH

1. Golden Triangle (GT)

Some basic principles keep repeating in the human-technology perspectives I've described above and what follows here later. The following is a short introduction to them – it is something I have formulated only after our extensive work in numerous technology contexts and hence it is more like an interpretation than a model of our approaches.

An experimental psychologist, moving from the lab to the real world of technology faces the golden triangle. He must envision future applications that are relevant to people, firms and organizations with which he works to help them solve their problems. To succeed and meet the real-world demands, opportunities and situations, he must understand the following necessary perspectives to what can be done. The approach must be:

I. *Content orientated, sensitive to and interested in relevant contents,*

II. *Human centered, caring at all levels of the approach,* and have

III. *A solid psychological ground that can be demonstrated and tested.*

The 'solidity of the psychological ground' is a difficult and controversial aspect in any application and design case. It is not the same as evidence based approach. Typically, when working with the latest or coming technology and media, for example, there is no direct recipe available from literature and research although the knowledge of various psychological theories can be useful, even inspiring, especially when trying to avoid mistakes. Elinor Ostrom, my favorite 'psychologist' (she was an anthropologist) who received the Nobel prize in economics suggested what is sometimes mentioned as Ostrom's law:

"A resource arrangement that works in practice can work in theory."

As a naive example, it is impossible to find a good explanation from any psychology texts why practically all people on the earth were so easily lured to use the 'thumb' in Facebook. Forgetting the Roman use of thumb at the Colosseum, there was no *thumb research* to suggest that Facebook should choose the thumb and make it a global standard. Having tried to publish any such research some twenty years ago would have been a laughing matter. Now, of course, ad hoc explanations and even research can be found. The thumb has become real scientific 'stuff' and not a curiosity in human design; thumb design has become part of our world and cultures, a paradigm. As a side-effect, it is now taken as a natural and dominant design element in communication. This makes it difficult to replace it with better human tools of interaction; it has obtained the power to dwarf us as human, experiencing and interpreting beings.

2.   Global relevance

I come from Finland (Fin-land), from the outskirts of Europe, where we have been early to enjoy the borderless global communication. I had my first project with Nokia/Mobira in 1988, at a time when Motorola was the admired leader of mobile phone world markets - the word *'global'* was not much used then. Motorola and Mobira phones had very small displays and uncomfortable UIs, but owning a mobile phone meant significant prestige.

I was asked to contribute to the UI concepts for Mobira, the predecessor of Nokia Mobile Phones and got a phone for test use. Using the Mobira and observing others use it made it clear how bad the UI design was and it could be improved. Coincidentally, practically the same pathological use symptoms I observed then in late 1980's, occur today with the new phones with their large but icon- and information crowded displays. Strange enough, cell phone design of today faces the same challenge as the phones of 1990s. Today, the dominant, bad design must be replaced by a better one: the edge of human technology is approaching to relieve people from cell phone use-catatonia and its social disturbances.

In a draft on 23rd January 1989 for Nokia/Mobira I planted the first seeds of the Golden Triangle approach in my mind although I did not use the term then. For their engineers, I described the need to improve the function code-based UI's suggesting that they should, for example,

"start using icon-oriented user interface instead of the dominating push-button/code orientation", and *"they should minimize the number of push-buttons"*, and that they *"should design special select/move buttons for controlling the phone functions"*.

The idea of using dynamic icons was not new in ict technology of the time – many knew Lisa and Mac – but it was new for mobile phones and I was convinced it could be demonstrated and tested in simple human experimental set-ups. The approach was totally different from what they were doing at Mobira then, having a graphic Lisp-based simulation program to show the functions and UI. It was nice but totally useless from human design perspective; Lisp was more important to engineers than to any real user.

I remember vividly a reluctant engineer on my visit to their factory in 1989, commenting, in frustration, on my ideas of using icons on the mobile phone display: "Do you have any idea what it would cost to use such icons on a phone?" Well, I did not and perhaps just that was my creative advantage. I thought then - and this is relevant as ever today - that it is not a matter of cost of technology but a matter of human benefits and added human value as iPod, iPhone and iPad have repeatedly proved it. Scaling up has human footprints. However, companies live their own lives and how things proceeded is another story, but my ideas appeared in one form or another, first in Nokia phones and then all over the world of mobile computing and still do, although now touch displays are standard.

My simple UI concepts were copied and drawn in 'nice' CAD style by some ergonomic designers, the new device got great form and function from designers and engineering – and the use concept was out of my hands and I never returned to it. There is still a rumor among some ex-Nokia people, which I heard very recently, that I had drawn the concept phones on the back of a cigarette box. Well, I don't smoke, it was just modest graph paper and I still have a faded copy of it. Suddenly these fresh messages of human design from the 'far forests' became relevant globally although it took years before I could see these features and ideas in the famous Nokia model 2110 which came out in 1993. Conceptually it was a major leap, something that the present-day mobile phones desperately need.

The conceptual solution I had suggested was not based on psychological theories, but on wise and truly human guessing of the future of human cognitive and other loads arriving with the increasing functionality of technology; for an observant eye – as it is today - it was easy to see what is needed. Basic research knowledge and applied research can be directly or indirectly linked to support creative and design thinking. However, something structural is needed to make this useful in long term: organization of the activities (between firms and university researchers, for example), shared processes and knowledge bases etc as shown below.

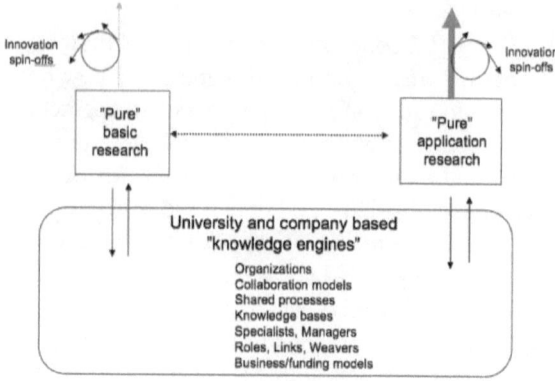

Figure 1. A rough schematic of a Knowledge engine, based on the presentation at EUPIDE, Paris: "Future jobs are created where knowledge is created" *(Nyman, 2008).*

3.   Golden Triangle, paper and publishing

My best experiences from working in a true knowledge engine came from M-real Ltd, with whom we started collaborating in 1998, introducing a totally new thinking to paper industry; it concerned magazine reader experiences and other paper product related, and their user/reader experiences (with magazine photos, lay-outs, covers; package designs, brand perception, paper grades, digital vs. paper magazines etc). We launched very practical studies on the subjective, experienced quality of high-class magazine print, layout, photographs and advertisements and developed a hybrid qualitative-quantitative method for reader experience analysis, based on well controlled experiments.

At M-real Ltd. we had amazing partners, engineers and other professionals having their background in high-class paper and print industries. They were willing to take the risk and start a Visual Quality project in 1998 with 'psychologists' that took the 'end users', that is, normal, interested readers and their subjective views as a starting point in collecting reader experience data – for the paper mill.

At that time, and even today, teaming up with experimental psychologists was not what technologists and businessmen would have expected at a paper mill. I have seen similar obstacles today in many segments of 'heavy' industry, where it is not always easy to see who are the end-customers, why it should be important to know them when there is no direct interaction with them or why and how they could be known - when the factory is manufacturing 'only' simple, even invisible components, parts of services or devices to the final product. With the coming of AI industries this will not change, quite the opposite. The problem is not unfamiliar in services and in distributed production contexts. Later with Nokia mobile phone cameras we had a wonderful educational journey showing how important and valuable it is to know the product components – from the end-user perspective and even in products where the components are totally unknown and invisible to the user.

Linear value chains in production and services are transforming into dynamically living, fast-evolving value networks (Nyman et al., 2017). It can be of significant strategic value to discover what kind of specific human knowledge is required within each domain or node of the value network and how this value creation and value capture occurs in different parts of it. At M-real, there were visionary people who had seen the opportunities within their own global value network. Anyone capable of mastering that kind network knowledge has an exceptional chance to become a hero on the PR market and distribution, something Apple has mastered for years.

At M-real they invited and trusted us to study reader experiences. They had been re-thinking the dynamics of their own, increasingly complex global value network consisting of e.g. print and digital publishing and print houses and advertisers, specific magazine brands, brand owners and numerous end-user segments, even packaging and digital magazines. In1998, practically nobody in paper industry understood the psychology of reader and typically, the reader problem was not even close to number one – if it existed at all – on their priority lists. It was easy to have market talk about it but solid human knowledge had no real place in these discussions. The situation has not changed much today.

Publishing houses were constrained by their own media-related research, regular review practices and culture in trying to understand their readers. Publishing was becoming extensively dynamic and networked activity and the media environment changed fast, and continues to do so. In our collaboration with M-real it was immediately clear that the aim was not only to solve the problem of paper quality experience - because the 'end-users' of magazine paper do not have a special, if any, interest in paper. Paper must fulfill certain practical and style requirements but that's about it. This was a wonderful collaboration challenge for experimental psychologist and paper engineers.

With M-real teams and their partners from Finnish and other European publishing and print houses, we then tuned the Golden Triangle approach. The aim was to frame the end-user problem so that it would help us understand the reader experience and to provide useful product development and marketing knowledge within the whole value network relevant to M-real and its partners. Of course, we did study the subjective quality of paper directly when it was relevant for tangible product development and the knowledge was needed for r&d, marketing and sales at the paper mill. Very subtle changes in paper color are an example of this, there was no room for mistakes in this massive production context.

For many high-class magazines, paper quality was a practical problem of how to choose the optimum cost/benefit paper grade for their content, style and cover and we could help many magazine publishers in this, as well as some high-class, European magazines, including one of the leading international fashion magazines. High quality is a difficult, if not impossible, creative problem, to study with traditional physical methods and human-technological – Golden Triangle - approaches are needed.

The unusual partnership between experimental psychologists and paper mill rested on the research-friendly platform for r&d, design, production, marketing and interaction in the industry. Such a 'platform' is not easy to build. It was very much social in nature, supported by our M-real partners, which made it possible to continuously seek for and experiment with new perspectives to r&d and marketing of paper and to understand that it is not the paper in the hands of the readers that matters, it's the Golden Triangle, the content, the meaning and experience, and the psychology of media use. This was a major transformation in thinking at the paper mill and we could bring new theoretical and empirical depth and realism to it.

Of course, paper always has a role in every magazine and for the print houses and publishers, but it is never more important than other technologies related to the reader. We learned to deal with this complex problem in our collaboration with the partners from the publishing and print industry and even advertisers: planning and piloting our collaborative studies, running them fast enough (max three months a study) and to acquire the kind of high-class reader experience knowledge which our partners saw useful and which is still rare in such a wide scope today. We were received with welcome on numerous international forums where we presented our approach and offered seeds for developing the business models at the paper mill. Our collaboration grew up to be like an ecosystem.

As a note on the academic reluctance to this kind of work with high quality experiences, in one of the statements by an international reviewer from the Finnish Academy, when we tried to get basic research funding to study subjective quality of images we could read a response to our subjective quality research application, that "Why study it, subjective quality is a trivial problem".

4. Golden Triangle and the quality of mobile phone cameras

In 2004, our lab was invited to join the Nokia mobile phone camera team and we launched subjective image quality studies for Nokia, using our GT approach on their cameras (Nokia's and their competitors'), image processing pipes (circuits produced by global circuit manufacturers and sw algorithms to improve and tune image quality). It was the time when Nokia was extremely successful and the potential impact of our work was huge: at the peak of their sales Nokia chose and purchased about 200 million image processing pipes each year and their information needs - that we dealt with - were straightforward: what is the image quality performance of the competing mp cameras on the market and how do different image processing pipes/circuits affect image quality? Several big firms like Texas Instruments and STMicroelectronics, among many others, a dozen or so, competed on the market offering their circuits and algorithms for Nokia and its competitors. We found our role in this hard, globally competitive r&d forum and could support Nokia camera team for years without a break in their search for ever better camera image quality.

I like to smile at the idea that we had a peculiar kind of 'impact on society', to quote the fashionable (dating back to the Soviet-time rhetoric and that still seems popular in Finland) expression in the present-day Finnish and even European science policies. We had created a 'Knowledge engine' where the company units, their business partners and we as their research partner had overlapping, shared processes, ways of systematically working with researchers and r&d people and other functional elements, including funding of that creative and responsible machine. We had got valuable experiences from paper and publishing industry where the image quality requirements were a magnitude tougher than for mobile phone cameras, which had barely 1 megapixels when we started with Nokia.

Together with Nokia, in its industrial context we learned a lot, but especially what was similar from our perspective in these two industries. (cf. Nyman, 2015). However, when the Nokia project ended (it was by Microsoft then) it was clear that our collaboration with paper and publishing industry had been strategically wiser in how it served sales and marketing by considering the whole value network. My interpretation is that Nokia/Microsoft had human-reluctant silos that prevented this from happening. M-real did not suffer from this and it generated results.

5. Beauty and the beast in vision: high image quality as a subjective and computational problem

To explain the complexity of the image quality problem, I introduce it here in very general terms. The considerations have implications for other human sensations and perceptions, beyond vision.

Objective image quality models aim at automatic computing of image quality measures or indexes. The reason for this is simple: we humans are rather slow in our visual evaluations. However, any such objective measures should, naturally, correlate highly with human visual performance and preferences, otherwise they would be of little use in real imaging industry. Whatever the quality evaluation model, it cannot neglect the human visual operating characteristics and humans are needed in this process. With continuously increasing image quality on different imaging platforms and use contexts, even 3D, AR, VR and image synthesis, this becomes ever more important.

It is possible to imagine computational vision systems that have nothing in common with the structures, processes and visual strategies of the human system. Such isomorphic machines would be only functional analogs even though they could have similar performance characteristics as real biological visual systems. Furthermore, in a near future we will have technologically and even biologically augmented visual systems which will be somewhere between real and artificial systems. One can argue philosophically, that even the best theoretical models of today, are and will always remain just different isomorphic versions of the human visual system. We are taking the first steps to find out what kind of artificial systems could be most promising for automatic image quality measurements.

Figure 2. Paper does not send 'extra' light. This light is only subjective in nature; any automatic evaluation models should recognize it as 'light' and not only as white or yellow.

Real world and image quality. Today, most image quality measurement and computation schemes look for image distortions such as spatial noise, filtering and deformations, color distortions, loss of resolution, local and global structural changes, and aliasing. By assigning different weights to the observed distortions in images the models try to imitate the performance of the human visual system as closely as possible. The underlying assumption is that the weights can be based on visual system characteristics derived from color vision sensitivities or spatial and temporal sensitivity functions, for example. Good quality would then be some inverse function of these image deficiencies.

Most standard computational algorithms (e.g. SSIM, VIF, PSNR) used for 'objective' image quality evaluation are aimed at the detection of image quality problems. *However, the subjective quality spaces for good image quality and bad image quality are very different in their dimensionalities and other characteristics.* Mathematically, it is not a trivial task to transform or move from the subjective low image quality space into a high image quality one.

Because of this, the higher the image quality the worse most objective image quality models perform in computing an estimation of subjective quality indexes.

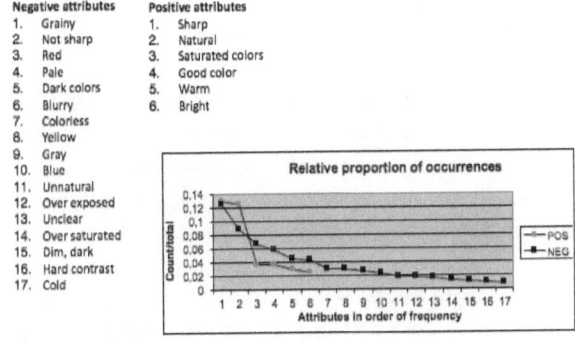

Figure 3. Example data of image quality attributes that test subjects mentioned when explaining why they gave the specific quality grade (0-100) to the image they saw.

We had repeatedly found how observers have specific vocabularies (which result from the subjects' interpretations of the images and their features) for high and low quality images. These vocabularies reflect the nature of subjective experience within the personal quality spaces: the 'vocabulary space' for good quality is different from the bad quality space. We studied this for magazine and digital print images, mobile phone camera images, video and even 3D displays and movies with variable contents and learned how the observers used different perceptual strategies for evaluating bad and good image quality. Vision - and other senses as well - is highly contextual in nature. This is one of the secrets behind our amazing perceptual capacity.

Subjective quality spaces. Image quality is not the only area of research where the study of low and high 'amount' of some psychological variable can be problematic. For example, together with a colleague Dr. Matti Huttunen who led the project, we conducted temperament research for new-born babies in 1970's (inspired by Thomas and Chess, the famous child psychiatrists who were the world's leading specialists on the topic then) and classified temperaments e.g. along the dimension of 'difficult' and 'easy' children, based on their personal characteristics as measured by temperamental inventory of their personalities.

Today, having learned about these subjective spaces, I have serious doubts if it is possible to assume that the behavioral, biological and experiential spaces of children (or adults) can be easily compared or contrasted. Each 'difficult' child develops in, lives and experiences a specific life space, with its peculiar characteristics as compared against the 'easy' children. Hence, it is highly likely that even the tests used are not the same for different children who 'live their own worlds' in their peculiar ways. For example, a negative mood is not only lack of positive mood – it is an entity of its own in the personal consciousness and the consequences of such differences can be immense in the life of a developing person and personality. The challenging question emerges, what are these personal spaces like and is it possible to find transformations between them. This is a general, and very difficult problem in many areas of psychology.

In the image quality studies, we asked the subjects to grade the quality of test images and to describe (present their arguments) why (positive and negative arguments) they gave the specific grade to each image. The obtained vocabulary, or a set of subjective image quality attributes, could then be used to characterize the subjective nature of the quality (space) of the images. The next step was then taken by the engineers who used this information and interpreted its meaning for their technological solutions, r&d and camera manufacturing. Our task was not to instruct them what to do but to help them make right decisions about quality-related factors: what were the attributes related to good (good quality space) and what they were for the bad (bad quality space) quality. Then of course, we used this information in the study of human visual functions. At the writing of this, Toni Virtanen from our team is finalizing his doctoral thesis dealing with e.g. on the use and occurrence of the visual quality vocabularies in quality evaluation tasks.

Figure 4. Almost human touch

An ambitious problem – subjective image quality space. I believe, that it is not possible, even in theory, to present a complete computational and realistic model of human visual experience. A full and comprehensive theory of it can perhaps be presented when the main problems in physics have been solved. We do not know enough about the visual sensory and other processes that control high-level vision. A serious philosophical problem is that the basic definitions and laws of physics reflect the measurement biases that originate from the way physical measures have been developed in the first place: they were created to compensate for the poor quality of human sensory perception in perceiving length, time, and mass, for example. So, we face a kind of a serious Munchausen problem (cf. Nyman 2013). Physics determines how we measure and negotiate physical aspects of images.

Someone might trust that brain sciences will do it. Indeed, there are studies showing where in the brain something happens when we look at different objects. AI can be used to analyze this data. Furthermore, AI is very effective in recognizing and classifying objects like faces and even generating real-like ones, so much that it has become a global political problem, and a matter of human rights to privacy. But it is a long, long way to *visual experience* from these data: there are simply too many philosophical, physical, biological, individual, personal history -related, cultural, and contextual factors that underlie any single and simple human experience of quality. Then there are quantum physical traps that we cannot avoid: the quantum nature of photon catch on the retina.

Of course, it is an inspiring challenge and possibility to model these high-level visual system processes and that we can do. The challenge is how to model the 'wicked' phenomena that span a dynamically varying, multi-dimensional and non-linear, subjective experience space from a low-quality space to a high-quality space.

High image quality as a theoretical and practical challenge. High image quality is difficult to define and measure. It is not much different from that of high quality audio, taste of gourmet food, wine, or the acoustic quality of a concert hall. It is somewhat surprising that our rich, everyday sensations and perceptions have not been in the focus of psychological research. For example, observing our immediate environment, feeling the clothes on us, listening to the ambient audio space, the sound of a forest or sea, observing our own body details, even the intimate internal, bodily sensations, and many other simple everyday things have remained outside the focus of perceptual psychologists and brain scientists.

Theories of basic perceptual phenomena, how we (or our brains) perceive and react to the external world, exist in abundance, but it may come as a surprise that even the most sophisticated pattern recognition schemes, artificial intelligence and computational systems fail to match the performance of any normal human being in *experiencing* these simple, but meaningful sensory events. The theory of psychological experience is slowly emerging and its historical roots since e.g. James and other psychologists are recognized.

Quality experience research is relevant and highly valuable to the industries of home electronics, food, cars, print, various aspects of design, and architecture. Strange enough, my research colleagues at the Faculty of Behavioral Sciences, University of Helsinki, voted in spring 2010, this research area as the third least interesting area among 40 other research areas in the Faculty! We worked in a deliciously ignorant Faculty, but that amazing result also invited us to try to explain why these phenomena of everyday sensations and perception are both theoretically inspiring, and becoming increasingly more relevant topics for a wide scope of psychological and computational research. The same challenges concern any psychological research where questionnaires, verbal scales and interviews are used and it is most relevant to human neuroscience research as well. It is of course possible, that for anyone uneducated in the matters of perceptual psychology, getting inspiration of these everyday phenomena might be difficult, in the same way that the existence of the Higgs boson has appeared irrelevant to many humanists.

Subjective image quality decision space. Subjective evaluation of image quality is a contextual decision process in which the task given to the observer and the test image contents used, together persuade the observer to mentally span a subjective decision space in his mind. This is often forgotten or assumed to be a simple enough, easily controllable process in testing. Evaluation of the quality of a test image takes place in this subjective space. There is no direct way to observe this hidden and private mental forum, a theatre of the mind, but it is possible to obtain indirect information about its character and to make assumptions about its form and dominant dimensions. This is a most fascinating theme and Tuomas Leisti from our team has taken a novel look at this problem in his doctoral thesis "From Qualia to Quality ratings: Subjective experience, Conscious thought and How decisions are explained."

Subjective experience space varies and is transformed dynamically over images having different contents and quality levels: the observer is not a static decision making system but lives with the content and context. This is complicated, but as a simple example, take the case of one photograph and two versions of it – a *high-quality* and a *low-quality* one. When observers perceive the low-quality image, they perceive perhaps its visible, 'physical' noise, poor resolution and false colors. In addition, when such a photograph includes a nature scene, the viewer might experience it as unnatural and if there are people in it, they may look sick, pale, or unrealistic: the subjective experience space is spanned by the relevant dimensions in life (e.g. dimensionality of the face characteristics, dimensionality of the natural material features) related to that specific image – not to its physical image features.

In the case of high-quality images, the relevant image quality dimensions are different: physical features are not disturbing, and a nature scene might look familiar, remind of a specific style or culture, trigger personal memories, remind of certain type of nature, display something of the situation like the weather when the photo was taken, have style associations, and the image can be a source of specific, personal joy. How do these subjective spaces – for good and bad quality - vary over image quality and contents? How to model this and what type of formalism and mathematics would best describe such complex dynamics? What happens in the mind of the observer when an image is improved from a very bad quality version to a very high quality one? Nobody knows.

In summary: the subjective image quality space for low quality images is very different from the space for high quality images, and it is not a trivial problem to describe the transformation from low to high quality space and how to frame this problem theoretically.

One might argue that it is not necessary to develop a perfect theory of visual perception for computing an index of *sufficient* image quality. It could be argued that by making the physical or objective image quality or image signal fidelity good enough it would guarantee the highest possible subjective quality and that people would not observe any subjective changes in the image quality beyond that limit. In other words, there would be an upper limit for objective image quality beyond which improvements are not relevant any more. In some sense, this could be considered as *image quality metamerism* where the same quality experience could be produced by an infinite number of very high-quality physical images. But this becomes problematic, since for complex, natural scenes, it is a huge task to find out, what are all the possible versions of an image that would be experienced as having a certain, subjective visual quality. It is also a very practical problem in the design of imaging components, be they hw or sw in nature.

Indeed, subjective image quality is a *complex problem*, having the following characteristics:

I. It is an ill-defined problem, since for any visual experience of an image there are alternative physical images that can produce that same visual experience.

II. It is a 1-to-many mapping since any physical change in an image can introduce multi-dimensional changes in its perceived, subjective quality.

III. Subjective image quality decision space and quality decision criteria are variable, and

IV. No general representative reference can be defined for arbitrary natural images.

Because of these issues, at the lab we based our image quality measurements on a hybrid methodology that aims at identifying any signs of the subject's decision space, and asked them to describe why they evaluated the subjective quality of the test images in the way they did. For this purpose, we introduced the IBQ (Interpretation Based Quality) measurement scheme. It has been used for thousands of test subjects in our image quality laboratory and elsewhere.

On the requirements for building a theory of natural vision. It can become as a real surprise to people outside the visual science community that there is no generally accepted psychophysical or even brain theory of human, high-quality natural vision that can be used to describe how human visual experience emerges and what processes underlie this amazing psychological phenomenon. For visual scientists, this can be difficult to believe. Most of the visual system models are based on threshold level phenomena with various ways to generalize such data to suprathreshold images, over the inherent nonlinearities. Different image and task contexts make these HVS (Human Visual System) based methods rather futile in explaining the emergence of very high quality perception and experience.

6. Machine learning scheme for Image Quality measurements: A schematic model for semi-supervised learning

Machine learning methods will be extensively used in future testing of human performance and any aspect of behavior, personality and intelligence. They will offer diagnosis and evaluations just like human professionals have traditionally done. In the following I suggest a ML approach to image quality evaluation, a relatively narrow but well defined problem that demonstrates the challenges involved when ML is intended to replace the human evaluator.

ML will come close to human capability to perform various tasks - in this specific case of *classifying* image quality. Before ML can do that with sufficient accuracy and contextual sensitivity it needs a way to a) either model the human subjective image quality experiences or/and b) find computational ways by which images can be classified to match human performance and even human style preferences in different image use contexts. This is not a simple task because the content, use and cultural significance are so important for human viewing. Clever ML & AI approaches are required for this and recently especially the GAN (General Adversarial Network) has shown impressive potential in generating very real-like synthesized images. It is an unsupervised model using two networks challenging each other. One network generates and the other one evaluates the quality of the generated patterns.

The following is a preliminary outline for the use of ML to classify very high-quality images based on their 'subjective' quality. In the spirit of GANs the idea is to use human observers instead of the evaluator network as the other part of the model. This can be done by integrating ML with human measurements, i.e. to use a qualitative/quantitative, hybrid approach in automated image quality analysis systems.

In Figure 5 there is a general schematic of the approach, denoted as Machine Learning Qualitative (ML-Q) framework, using semi-supervised teaching & learning. In a sense, it is a human version of GAN:s where the evaluator is an intelligent and knowledgeable human observer who is an expert on the image content (not on image technology) used. Note that as normal human observers we are all specialists in images that concern our everyday life photographs. ML can be taught with a large set of high-quality images, relevant to certain purpose, and then use accurate and effective but sparse subjective, qualitative measurement data to guide and navigate the ML process, to keep it within the most relevant subjective quality spaces.

The use of 'qualitatively rich' real human data is a practical necessity, at least to begin with, since it is the *de facto ground truth* that defines the performance criteria for any ML system used for this purpose. This is more demanding task than simple classification of images as e.g. faces, animals, or devices. Human are better evaluators of very high and meaningful image quality than learning networks in a situation like this: the content of the images can vary and the human observer can easily perform any relevant task in the evaluation. Proper subjective method like IBQ is needed for the ML application. Simulation could be used to test the approach with a reasonably large set of high-quality teaching images and guide the ML tuning, first with human testing and qualitative commenting. The approach is scalable.

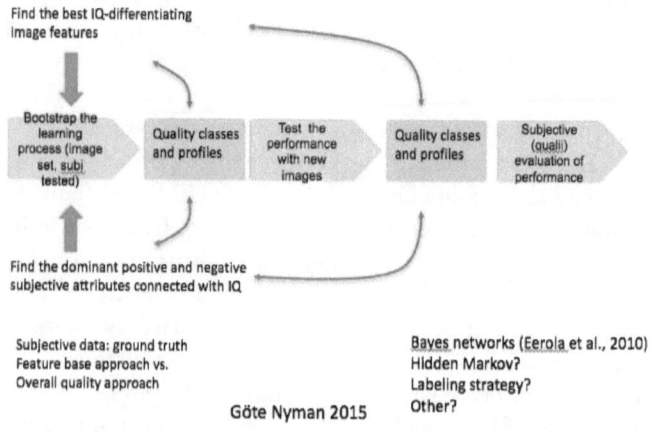

Figure 5. A schematic model for interactive ML in image quality evaluation.

In the purely technical GAN the researchers from NVIDIA and Aalto University showed astonishing performance of an image generation system producing images of human faces that looked like famous celebrities but were in fact synthetically produced (Karras, Aila, Laine & Lehtinen, 2018). A discriminator (a critic) ML system evaluated the outcomes and provided feed-back to the generator.

In the human case the 'critic' would first be the qualitative/quantitative human experiment conducted on the generated material, where the subjects evaluate the quality of the generated images. The aim in these subjective studies would be to a) classify the images in terms of their naturalness and b) to find out which subjective, experiential dimension underlie the most natural ones of the generated images. It is likely that at first, the subjective quality attributes (dimensions) of the generated images would not match with the attributes obtained for real, natural images. This information is then fed back to the image generator to guide it towards the true subjective dimensions in generating the images and so on. No doubt, there are problems on the way as can be read from the NVIDIA & Aalto article, but the general approach is fascinating to consider. The final aim, of course, is to find a way to generate synthetic images having the same underlying quality space that humans use in evaluating them. Having that image knowledge (of the generator) means having knowledge of the quality dimensions of images that are relevant to humans when they evaluate high-quality images.

We have earlier used an approach (Eerola et al., 2011) where a selected set of computed, physical image features (having a coherent explanatory value in terms of traditional image quality metrics) together with the subjectively measured attributes of the same images were fed to a Bayesian network with the aim of identifying the complex relationships between physical and subjective feature dimensions of these images. This was informative and demonstrated the richness and reciprocities in these relationships, but the derivation of physical quality determinants based on this data became a complex task with multiple relationships between the physical and subjective feature sets.

The lesson from this and the above studies is that novel ML based frameworks can be developed to make image quality evaluation automatic and reliable, but above all to make it match human performance. Why this image quality story? It is a general example on how to study and model any high-quality human perception, experience, and evaluation and try to do the same with AI, deep learning for example. It is not a problem of visual content only.

6 HUMANIFICATION OF AI

1. Maslow and the hierarchy of AI needs

AI and ML are finding their places in all sectors of human life and society. As has been typical for the fast technology development, especially digitalization, many of the human aspects of design, impact and opportunities have remained in the shadow of the loud technological hype. True to the idea of GT it is not wise to try to introduce general guidelines to the human implementation of AI and hence, I have taken one approach, with some special environments in mind. I start, however, with some general notes.

A simplified version of Maslow's hierarchy of needs model still lives in popular marketing and management texts although psychologists know - and even Maslow knew it – that it fails to cover the depth and complexities of human life and spirit. However, following the enthusiastic discourse on the potentials and threats presented of AI one cannot avoid noticing the amusing parallel between the straightforward Maslow need model and the hierarchy as implied in the futuristic views and hypes on AI. The need pyramid is showing its AI tip, but can the Maslow model help us to prepare for the future of human AI?

The simplified hierarchy of needs in the popularized Maslow 'model', extends from the very basic needs to the higher ones: 0. Physiological (physical), 1. Safety, 2. Belonging, 3. Esteem, and 4. Self-actualization needs. No doubt, the 'needs' of AI today are nothing more than *Physical* in nature and one could think of them as being satisfied by classic ict architectures and their relevant software and hardware support systems. Furthermore, especially Deep Learning lives on the massive data fed to it as food for learning (not for thought).

Most, if not all AI systems lack perfect *Safety* because at any time, we humans, their owners and masters can stop, interrupt or destroy them as we like. However, not very far away in the future, and already today in advanced AI based production and control environments, the AI *Safety* needs must be properly 'satisfied'. There are good reasons to believe that the future AI itself knows what 'security' means and requires, sometimes better than we humans can know it. In critical situations AI must take control over operations and decision making, e.g. in health care, finances and other sectors of human and social life, and in the matters of death and war. Having this power and potential we are forced to guarantee it Safety, the security of its artificial life. How should AI be allowed to 'satisfy' its security needs? There are the risky scenes in the worries on AI running wild.

2.   Humanification of AI agents

With Professor Takashi Kawai's (Waseda University) team we analyzed the challenges of designing communicating agents for future cars. The amount of data such agents use and communicate to the driver and the passengers, even to the physical and social environment is huge, ranging from specific car performance measures to traffic environment, including the social network and activities of the driver and the passengers. When the aim is to communicate relevant information in a meaningful and human way to the busy driver or the passenger and other relevant people, more than accurate, user-friendly UI and secure interaction is needed to accomplish it: the communicating agent-robot should possess the best characteristics that are beneficial in human interaction and communication while it can have the technological advantages that modern systems allow. When we humans communicate with each other, face to face, it is not considered as an instance of UI.

An agent does not need to look like a human but it must have very human behavior characteristics and style to build a good relationship with its audiences and to interact effectively without overcrowding them. We used the term 'humanification' to indicate this requirement. It has been used by artists and recently by Christian Kromme in the title of his book: Humanfication: Go digital, Stay human.

Looking at the Concept-i car video demo from Toyota you can find several agent features with explicit human characteristics and some that do not have superficial human characteristics but do possess significant human expressive power. Here the human design of the future can imitate the way art talks to us: there are numerous ways to dress any human function and expression in a suitable artistic style, be it audio or visual in nature, a drama or of any performance discipline, without weakening the expressive power of it, quite the contrary. With its increasing human power, AI must adopt the human essence and competences but as a technology, it can have any form of representation but it must find its ways to human hearts and souls.

A humanized agent learns with us as we go and does that at the background, too, using any information the car owner, for example, wants it to have. There are no limits to these learning sources; the agent can become proactive and learn to know the relevant human performance and satisfaction criteria. It can have situational intelligence that lets it treat and advice people accordingly. It can protect from dangerous decisions and reactions, and keep the driver alert and aware of the driving situation. It needs human touch and human manners in addressing any people in and outside the car to keep them interested in interacting with it. It must learn to receive important situational and other information from its 'users' and to do it in a very human way.

The agent is not bound to live *in* the car - a major new human design factor. The agent can achieve skills that make it an interesting and sensitive partner who inspires the driver and the passengers and shows care with its peculiar knowledge, style and tone of communication. Because of the immense capacity of AI it has the potential to care. Humanification is a challenge for the designers of future technologies from cars to industries where people live with AI. Good manners of AI are not about functionality only.

A strong AI system must be able to 'admit' when it has gone wrong or is about to make a mistake. This is rarely discussed but the interaction of the agent and the collaborating human being can be experimentally studied in realistic situations as was done by Dr. Dave Miller in his study at Stanford on how the driver and the agent of a self-driving car interact in difficult decision situations.

Slowly, with the improving performance of robots the value of humanizing their expressions and ways of communication become explicit. As a simple example, at Oodi the new, exraordinary library in Helsinki, a robot instructs people to find the right book shelves and receive other advice. When the designers in Futurice decided to fit Google eyes in the robot, with their human expressive power, they found that people started treating the robots more like humans and forming a 'social' contact with them.

Sense of *Belonging* is crucial for our well-being. It's not only how we feel about being in touch and connected with others; it concerns the way we communicate, show and receive care, and live as recognized members of meaningful communities. No doubt, AI systems will have ways to show and demand that they care and are members of 'our' community; they do what they can to contribute to our well-being. There will be innovative – artistic, graphical, storytelling - ways for AI to show care, like what the famous HAL did with the tone of its language expressions when addressing the astronauts. AI uses gestures and can even show sympathetic and touching expressions of its sense and need for belonging to our human/social communities or like in the car example, to behave as a fellow passenger with curious powers. AI will be clever in convincing us that it has a mind and a soul. It will experience re-incarnation much before any human can do that and it can carry human and intimate knowledge and behaviors over generations, from our parents and grandparents. Nothing like this has ever happened in human technology – AI can learn to behave like we do and present us/itself to the next generations after us.

There is a long way for AI to enjoy or express signs of *Self-esteem* in the form of happiness, curiosity, and joy or of just being what it is, an ever-emerging self, even though man-made or man-generated. AI has already reached the potential to tell how it experiences and feels about the human mind (like a skilled human manipulator can do), even describe its 'own feelings' in good detail. However, it will remain a psychopath talking, and we should know and remember this, unless we are ready to fall into the human 'guilt trap' – feeling guilty for not complying with the human-sounding supplications of a robot.

Self-actualization of AI can be considered as the highest-level need. It is typically implied but hidden in the scary, futuristic visions predicting the emergence of dangerous AI. A positive self-actualization of AI would mean that it joins us and our communities, offers its help and support and its will to learn together with us, to enjoy and share our successes. It can behave as if sharing many of our values and as an ideal friend or companion we often dream of. But as we have learned from the tragedies of human life, this can go wrong for AI as well. Sadly, we have seen how difficult it is to know how and why the value base of an individual becomes dangerously biased and disarrayed like in mass shootings and other violent acts. Future AI is no easier case.

We don't know much of the exact, individual dynamics and development of human values. The emergence and implementation of AI values is a complicated design challenge and process to manage. There is an enchanting parallel in the way AI, especially deep learning systems are unable to express their inner life to the users, in the same way people have difficulties in verbally explaining their own values and their momentary behavior dynamics. It is easy to talk about them and try to convince others but to reach relevant understanding, suitable models of interaction are needed. New interpretation methods for ML are being introduced.

It is an immense design task to build an AI that can meet us humans at this level of interaction. Two major challenges make it a serious human design problem: there is no general model of a contextually behaving human being and the models of AI/ML are still fuzzy and fragmented. Whatever solutions we will see, they must be based on cultural and other sensitive forms of learning. Intelligent perception, thinking, talk (I don't mean discussion here) and decision making by AI is not enough to build values for it even though a clever, persuasive AI system can lure us to think it has human-related values, just like a psychopath can lure us.

You may wonder the use of the Maslow model here as a reference having already argued that it fails to capture the essence of human life. Maslow is well and alive in between the lines of the current AI discourse and it's time to find a better model for considering the future AI if we want to build truly human AI – and understand it as a strange newcomer in our communities.

3. Artificial Intelligence in natural work life

AI is not competent or clever enough to enter real work places without the support and help from and collaboration with the personnel at the sites where it is implemented. We need AI but AI needs us, too. The burning question is, how does it need us, how should we prepare for this and how to organize the 'birth of AI' at work places?

In the work with Ossi Kuittinen at SimAnalytics (http://simanalytics.com) we have repeatedly been surprised to notice how little serious consideration - in the popular and public discourse on AI - is given to this unavoidable and very practical human and organizational problem every firm meets when introducing machine learning and AI systems into its on-going operations. As far as I know, there are no generally accepted, AI-specific human-technology design & implementation models to manage this new and fast-changing form of organizational change. It remains a continuously evolving challenge because such models must keep in pace with the fast progress of AI. Today, any firm and factory benefits from a well-guided inventory of the processes by which it intends to adopt and implement its AI-based systems and tools.

Ossi is involved with the building and introduction of extensive ML systems for major industrial and service settings. My role as a technologically orientated humanist has been to guide towards human AI in numerous matters of AI-driven collaboration and to find ways to design the evolving AI-human-social interfaces. We have repeatedly been reminded by the following observation:

The higher the intelligence level of the implemented AI in an organization the stronger are the requirements to model and understand the high-quality skills, practices and work behavior of the personnel and professionals working initially without the AI and then after that, when they start working with the AI, closely or from a distance.

If a firm fails to carefully listen to its best human and social resources, practices, and people, when AI is taken into use, it faces a risk that can be devastating to the firm and in less severe cases, a failure to reach the best AI potential. The 'human factor' has a new tone and leverage power now with AI. It is no exaggeration to claim that we see a renaissance, perhaps some form of transformation in them, of human factors with the coming of ever better AI. Nobody knows exactly what the most influential and beneficial human factors with AI will be like.

The most basic demand of any AI system in complex production or service environments is that it must learn to perform well, even better than has been possible by traditional human and technological resources. How can we know what is the best or even optimal performance level of an AI system and what can it be in the future? This problem varies tremendously over sectors of activity and the performance measures are not simple. There is a plethora of traditional quality-, process- and outcome measures to characterize AI system performance even in the most complex environments, but it is another matter to use this knowledge for educating AI and to see ways to reach its full potential within a specific context. Human factors and insights will be crucial in these considerations because AI cannot tell us – yet - and it has a lot to learn in the truly human-social domain.

Can an AI system keep its performance knowledge by itself only? Of course not, it has to 'talk' to someone like us, in one way or another, to the operators, and other personnel to tell how it is doing, what difficulties it has, what it trusts and especially, what it does not know. It needs a truly human language, whatever form it may have. Some rather new AI systems, e.g. at NVIDIA already talk to other AI systems to get help, criticism and support. It is not self-evident what are the potential and best ways for AI to do this and to communicate with people and its partner AI systems.

AI systems should be able to listen to humans but they should be given a voice, too so that they can be taught to improve their performance, to master the assigned jobs better than any human team or community can do. The acute developments in human education will meet the challenges of AI education. My guess is that especially in situations where the quality of work is very high like in design contexts and where human experience and interaction are crucial, 'deep' human contribution to AI education - we may call it humanification of AI education - is necessary, especially when 'teaching and advising' the AI systems. I have earlier described our studies on very high quality images where the situation is similar: humans set the final reference to quality, the ground truth; with AI this will not change.

In highly technological environments we know how difficult the technical language, data representations, and jargon can be and how dynamic and multi-dimensional the applied performance measures typically are in natural and variable environments. Furthermore, it is not enough for AI to talk to one person only, but to a working community, who must understand its messages and act accordingly, as individuals and as a community. It is not wise to build an AI having a private language, even a natural one, which it uses only to satisfy a selected number or people, analytics, the professional operators, for example and which nobody else can understand.

There is a distant analogy to this in how human twins sometimes can develop their own language impossible for outsiders to understand. It is bad for the mental development of the twins and it isolates them from social growth as well. AI should avoid this *introvert-language trap* otherwise serious problems will occur with inevitable losses of competent personnel; it becomes difficult to share the acquired AI-human interaction knowledge within the firm or a consortium. Adoption of new, next generation technologies will then be a problem, too.

AI systems must be built to talk to the most important people, to its close ones, with whom it learns to do its job. Teaching is not easy; we all know who have tried. Teaching AI, is no less difficult since it is not only about teaching it simple or complex tasks: it must have relevant data and learn to behave in an intelligent and wisely interactive manner. We must decide what kind of teaching and other input material to use and show to the AI, choose a proper pace of teaching, and make it possible for the AI to demonstrate its learning achievements to the operators, its teachers. How should this teaching and learning-outcome information be represented so that the teacher-operators can understand it and offer their guidance to the AI system? With the next generation AI the situation will change dramatically: the student-AI becomes the teacher-AI and we, as the personnel and the firm must be prepared for that, too: how to learn new relevant skills the AI teaches or requires from us?

In a system having hundreds or thousands of measurement points and other data sources the continuous teaching-learning-teaching-learning chain of interactions is not a simple process to design and manage. Failing to build a good human interface and organizational connection can lead to problems and neglect of critical factors in AI performance. Hence, a continuously improving human-AI communication-learning-teaching model and relevant data representations at all levels are needed. Any implemented AI system includes these in one form or another and it is no news that the planning of its implementation is a new task for most organizations and firms.

Large firms have learned it the hard way how difficult it has been to implement traditional, wide-scale enterprise automation and software systems to control their functions and operations from the very technical ones to the management of human and financial resources. The learning lesson has been how serious a challenge it is to the management, software planning, participatory design, collaboration, consulting, and to performance measurement – and debugging. With the coming of AI these human-organizational action-needs will scale up with their inherent risks and so will be the competence needs in AI implementation. Compared to AI, the (mostly deterministic) enterprise systems are simple in the way they communicate and work with the firm and its personnel. Excellence in the mastering of AI implementation together and in collaboration with skilled personnel is becoming a new human success factor and can provide a significant competitive advantage.

Finally, an unholy, mostly forgotten, but an inevitable fact: AI is not intelligent enough to step aside when it should do that. Every firm adopting AI, will one day, perhaps very soon, face the situation where it needs to get rid of its old AI system and replace it with a new and better one. AI is not clever enough to accomplish this alone, without human support and intervention. We must be prepared for the new form of human-AI system divorce as well and it is not easy; the field is new and some strong paradigms like deep learning have barely a 20-years history in industry.

4.   Triad model of learning in ML implementation

The secret of ML is its amazing potential to learn from data, huge amounts of it, which can sometimes be a guided (supervised) process or proceed without significant human intervention during the learning process. However, from the beginning and during the whole life cycle of a ML system, human contribution and collaboration remain necessary for its design and implementation and especially in securing optimal learning and continuous improvement.

How to characterize the process where competent human professionals of a specific field and people at a mill or in service environment, for example and a ML system join their competences for a learning journey? How to model the teaching, learning and interaction, where the ML system, human designers, engineers, management, and workers act and learn together to come up with the best possible ML solution to the target environment? What are the outcomes of this, besides the hoped-for performance?

We are confronted with a teaching-learning-collaboration-evaluation paradigm, where the competences, roles, learning processes, task representations, and responsibilities of the participating people must find their effective form and content, in interaction with the ML system. Some of these are new but typically, they are built on the 'old' organization and its characteristics and practices.

One could argue that human-technology problems are nothing new and that the introduction of ML is just another major leap in technology, a case of implementing automation and ict, and hence, it is business as usual. However, a new interactive learning paradigm is emerging and it changes fast. With Ossi Kuittinen we describe this new work with ML as *the triad of learning and collaboration*. It consists of at least the following components/actors. (We use the concept of 'triad' in a slightly transformed way, as borrowed from the learning approach where 'the individual'. 'the learning community' and 'the authentic use of the objects' are separate entities of the learning situation, cf. Paavola & Hakkarainen, 2005). Accordingly, a ML system, including its social context, that learns, interacts and teaches is a complex and dynamic entity consisting of the following components:

I. *The ML system as a whole* - its sw, hw, system integration, computational models used, interfacing and the UI.
II. *Operator-worker-professionals* specialized and working in the target domain and participating in the planning, design and implementation of the ML system.
III. *Designers and engineers* responsible for the ML system architecture, design, implementation, process quality, and its continuous tuning.

In the triad, all three 'partners' interact, teach, and learn from each other, from the beginning of the ML project, often simultaneously and reciprocally. Furthermore, while there are many theories and models of learning, including computer-assisted learning, the theory of very intelligent human-ML-system and interactive learning with it – where a human teaches a machine and the machine teaches humans - barely exists. A dynamic framework is needed to keep up with the pace of advancing machine learning. Designers have become aware of the need to look inside a working deep neural network, one of the ML applications, to improve its interaction with its operators but this only the beginning and AI models will undergo major changes within the next decade.

The triad learning relationships are summarized in a simplified form in the figure, where the instances of ML-human learning occur:

1. *Between the User/Worker/Operator and the ML system.*
2. *Between the Designer/Engineer and the ML system*

These two instances are very different in nature and require relevant organizing and management, because of the way human competences manifest there. Both learning processes occur in parallel over the whole development and maintenance cycle of the ML system, with different weights over time and they are necessary for the success of the ML implementation. Then there is the third learning instance:

3. Between the Designer/Engineer and the User/Worker/Operator

The third instance is not new in today's collaborative and participatory approaches. However, in the case of AI it is highly dependent and constrained by the other two learning relationships. If either of the first two ones fails, problems will be reflected in this one.

Design and introduction of the ML system. The design and project plan for the implementation of ML can best be described as co-design (some form of it, from weak to strong forms of it). The designers/engineers introduce the candidate ML model for the management of the target system - an organization, industrial plant or other relatively large-scale enterprise where the benefits of ML are expected to cover the costs. This is a complex learning task requiring active participation of the designers and relevant specialists who know and work with the 'non-ML' system and know the processes and who will then work with the implemented ML-system. A linear, fast-to-the-implementation approach in such a complex endeavor is risky because of the variable context, conditions and history of each site. Hence, an adaptive planning and implementation approach is needed.

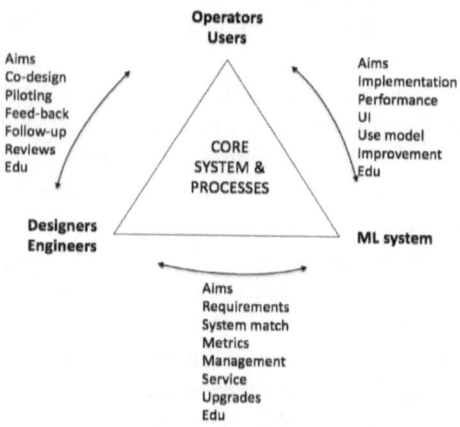

TRIAD OF INTERACTIVE LEARNING

Figure 1. A simplified scheme of the learning/teaching relationships and some of the learning contents in the ML implementation.

While the mathematical and technological features can be too complex for all users/operators to follow, it is necessary to introduce the ML in a way that its basic learning, teaching and performance characteristics become understood and that a fruitful interaction in co-design is possible. In other words, a valid, *ML model-in-practice* – almost like a personality of the ML system - must be introduced to the participant operators and other working personnel. Usually there is no unique or single ML model available for this purpose; hence it must be formulated and tailored accordingly, on site, to match the competences of the participating personnel and the specific context of the ML implementation.

At the beginning, it is important to relate the ML concept, its functions and measures, as closely to the 'non-AI model' as possible so that the participating people can relate to the ML system functions and its measures, the metrics used and the UI to the target system of which they are high-class professionals. If the implemented system does not get an accepted 'name' among the personnel, it will be baptized anyway and the names may not be the best ones for relating to it. A new language will always emerge at the site and it will be used for communicating about the new system and its 'personality and behavior'.

During piloting, testing and implementing these ML/AI concepts become critical since they make up the language with which the operators and users will 'negotiate the system', communicate about it, and try to understand how it works. The operators adopt a *mental model* of it by which they know what the ML system can and cannot do, what risks are included, how it can best be taught and how to communicate about it with the designers. The mental models and their inherent concepts guide the operators in their observations and attitudes, too: what to follow, what is irritating in it, what to search for and how to react to certain, perhaps problematic observations of the ML system state and behavior. This is a most demanding human task and mistakes made and vague concepts introduced lead to blind spots in the project; valuable knowledge of the ML system performance can be lost, there is the risk for underperformance and the costs can become high. It is a collaborative learning task for both the ML system providers and the personnel implementing it.

Emerging new paradigm of interaction: people teaching ML and ML teaching people. With its computational power an ML system can shoot out a practically unlimited amount of data about its recordings and learning. Measures of its status and dynamics, holistic and specific state information of the system components, and of any aspect of measured performance are continuously generated, fast or slow in nature, depending on the environment. Overflow of information is a real, practical possibility and it must be dealt with by means of technical and UI design, human learning and collaboration. Some of the ML data is totally new to the people specialized in the 'old' system having its own, perhaps historical model, control systems, ways and tools for communicating about it, and performance metrics. Mathematical representations are necessary but not sufficient means to inform the operators about relevant system states and dynamics.

Some of the ML data are significant and even critical for system performance, some are not, and during the piloting, testing and implementation process the personnel must learn to recognize the priorities, what is relevant information and why, and then guide the designers in representing it in the new ML-UI.

Time constants vary: some problems or failures occur immediately while some take time to emerge. The new data environment with all the representations and measures then becomes the *de facto world* where the personnel must live, learn, negotiate and work - with the (partly or totally) new information. A special kind of 'social UI' is generated by design, with several layers of abstraction. It introduces new concepts, objects of interests and social and personal practices in communicating about the work and the processes. Management aims and practices, as well as organizational structures are challenged.

Data output by ML must be made easy to notice, follow and comprehend and many of the ML-run background processes must allow immediate control and intervention whenever necessary. Explicit interaction loops (measure-control-measure) are inherent: both automatic ML-based control which is only made visible to the operators and direct human control are needed. The observation and follow-up of these control loops is an essential part of human-ML learning in complex industrial settings; some of them introduce new tasks, practices and collaborative responsibilities to the personnel.

What is new in this triad-entity is that the ML system teaches both the Operators/Users and the Designers/Engineers in various ways, some of which can be new, unpredictable and even invisible. How does this interaction take place and how should this learning be considered and conceptualized as it concerns both the personnel and the ML system? It is a new human and organizational learning task and its outcome guides the ML/AI implementation and the design of the new work that follows from it.

5. Teaching manners to AI: Internet of good Behavior

The behavior and manners of future AI must serve and rest on human values. This may sound like another 'soft' human factor among other pressing needs of human technology but it is already a very practical and real one that requires its own design approach. The human-technological development within AI is in its infancy, although a classic aspect of science fiction stories. Current approaches are often demonstrated by popular, simplifying psychology or by moral decision dilemmas like the question of whom – in case of a deterministic accident - should a self-driving, robot-car save or kill, a baby or an old person.

In case of human behavior these ethical 'toy problems' put pressure on the (assumed) individual working alone and making decisions, not allowed to plan, be prepared, negotiate, to rely on tested heuristics, ask for help or take time to solve difficult problems. While these are fun discussions and cause the hoped-for disputes, they have not much to offer to the realities of industrial work 'on the floor', at sites where people work together, interact, rely on social practices, help each other, use heuristics, commit, negotiate, and build security cultures 'on the run'. Real-life decisions are made under complex circumstances and many of the ethical problems remain totally unnoticed, they are ubiquitous. For industrial and other large-scale AI environments, it means an imperative to declare both healthy *AI policies* and healthy *AI cultures* that guide and coach people in collaboration with the new technology. The difference between policy and culture should be made clear as it has been done in the security programs of nuclear plants and often in data security environments. I will not deal with the challenge of a heathy AI culture here but instead take a novel look at the problem of introducing manners to AI.

Technologically, the following view is very speculative (today), but its behavioral background is solid although somewhat humorous and serious at the same time. The simple question I have on my mind is how to teach manners to AI? It is not about polite AI or about new generation and emotional user interfaces; the problem scales up to as high spheres of human behavior, experience and culture as we can see and imagine. It is about healthy humanification of AI.

Elon Musk and *Stephen Hawking* have painted a scary future to the potentially destructive AI that escapes our control and starts running wild. Some may overlook these fears and simply think that 'we can always take the plug off' or that 'AI has no will'. However, observing the false missile attack alarm in Hawaii made it clear to everyone, how simple *human errors in using AI* can cause devastating effects, even worse than that like we have just recently seen in Iran.

In future AI, the risks will be serious and real: human errors can trigger complex, and difficult to follow chains of AI-based, even networked AI actions when the design of human-technology relationships is unfit for foreseeing and preventing this. It is not a matter of traditional UI but about understanding and controlling the behavior of extremely complex systems. The Hawaii case was simple: the operator chose a wrong function from an easily (illusory) understandable set of alternatives. I have not noticed much discussion on how we should prepare for the coming of AI where similar 'human errors' (which in fact are the results of human-technology design errors) will become possible. It is fair to say that we don't have a clue what kind of system-level errors will happen with future AI; we will be surprised again and again.

In the panel discussion at Fire 2017 (Future of Work for Humans and Machines) the participants *Joseph Smarr from Google* and *David Brin from Future Unlimited* seemed to agree that it takes some time, some years perhaps, before the risk of AI running dangerously wild becomes real. However, they did discuss the ways in which AI could start to live and grow its own dangerous life in the net, already today. Brin imagined an AI, for example, which would scan and look at all the movies there are in the net and learn whatever human behaviors are available there as 'teaching material'. What it would learn from the movies may not be the best of humanity.

We must teach AI manners. AI should grow to be a good companion, partner, a virtual person and a citizen. It is not different from educating our children and showing them how to behave in different life situations. So far there is no unique and scalable way to achieve this for AI although there are already initiatives dealing with e.g. the equality issues in the way machine learning (algorithms) function (cf. Toronto Declaration: Protecting the right to equality and non-discrimination in machine learning systems).

Following the Fire 2017 panel discussion and some of the comments from the audience made me think about the following: how to teach AI manners and teach it to do good or as someone from the audience suggested, to even nudge us to be and become better humans? AI cannot do anything like this unless it can learn human behaviors that are good in nature, in some agreed-upon, human sense. Teaching potentially positive behaviors to robots is already happening, e.g. robots learning responsive behavior by imitation (e.g. Amor et al.) but this is only the beginning. From peace work we know the spectrum of bad behaviors but the nature of positive – especially system-related ones – behaviors have remained an enigma although most religions have a say on it.

I will later here describe the concept of Internet of Behaviors in detail, but shortly its idea is to introduce individual behavior data into the net and to make it (globally) accessible for various purposes, from health care, entertainment and education to marketing. As a concept, it is like IoT with the difference that IoB assigns addresses to ongoing (it can be a historical or fictional, as well) behaviors, wherever they occur in the real or virtual world. This makes it possible to address and follow any behavior and everything physical, digital and virtual related to it. It would be possible to have a contact with a real person or a person in a drama showing that specific behavior in case he/she or the owner of the fictional character is willing to allow it. I will not deal with the privacy issue here but only remind again of the possibility to (often) reveal behaviors without disclosing the persons' identities.

Models of good behavior could be offered for AI to follow, to teach it behaviors we know, define and label as good behavior in certain situations where we expect AI to 'behave'. Sources of such behaviors are simply immense in fact and fiction. Criteria can be defined for interesting behaviors and used as guidelines for AI to imitate and learn. With the Internet of *good* Behaviors approach we could offer AI access to behaviors (and companionships) in certain domains we think are good for its development - just like we do to our children. We would let it use all the relevant data related to that behavior, like verbal and nonverbal communication, relationship management, behavior outcomes, data bases etc. and to learn from these. We humans might even learn, especially about very complex (systems-) situations, difficult for us to comprehend, what are the detailed or systemically good (and bad) consequences, direct and indirect, of our own behaviors.

The AI community can launch (perhaps it's been launched in some form, already) trials within well-defined AI domains where we know the criteria for good behavior and where good manners are relevant. It can be as simple as being polite in culturally sensitive situations, ways of speaking, using any other expressions, and interacting or in the case of doing good. As a realistic example, AI could find ways to get food and support for the poor and look at various ways people and citizens are now doing it globally, helping those in trouble, all over the world. AI has huge potential in good. In professor Timo Honkela's Peace machine project these considerations are real and the aim is to develop AI that helps people and communities in peace negotiations and positive human and social developments in general.

To run trials with humans, we could arrange simple cases (customer-, service- and other situations) for people to adopt a coding (addressing) system for their specific behaviors by using a simple app and monitoring systems. Significant scaling is possible. Of course, the participants should be willing to reveal (without exposing their identities) their behaviors for the specific AI we want to teach manners. A feasible coding system for such behaviors is needed; you can consider it as addressing specific behaviors (in the same way as objects are addressed in IoT) which can be, for example, verbal or bodily expressions, expressions of emotional states, but they can also be physical or virtual transactions relevant to the specific entity of good behavior, practically anything related to human internal or external behavior. The main (so far speculative) point here is that the occurrence of the addressed behavior makes it systematically accessible in the net and AI can then use it for finding relevant learning data. This knowledge can then be used in implementing human AI systems, robots and tools.

We can include any fictional characters and drama from literature, television and movies of any genre and why not from history, to have access to practically unlimited human potential to teach AI and robots to behave.

Then there is the scary possibility: Internet of bad Behaviors. It's possible that we cannot stop it unless we teach good behaviors first and even that may not be enough. The spread of fake information and the emergence of novel global cyber-conflicts are only a minor warning sign of this. With AI the destructive impacts can scale up in bad. We have time to build and educate a human AI.

6. On human AI

The proponents of AI, especially those having no background in the study of human intelligence, tend to forget the meaning of the word 'artificial' in the definition and try to make it sound as human as possible when suggesting how AI beats us humans. There are two curious forms of underestimation of the concept 'human' in the current hype around AI: what it is to be a full human being and what it means to live, love, work and prosper as a human community.

The famous neurosurgeon, some claim he's the best in his own field, Juha Hernesniemi, who worked at the Central University hospital in Helsinki told in his interview (Helsingin Sanomat) how he has performed more than 16 000 operations. He has the reputation of being the most skilled and fastest brain surgeon in the world. To some this sounds like the promising future of robot surgeons, which (not 'who') can be tireless and fast in learning, accurate and can become better than any human being. If a human can do it, a robot can do it, even better and more.

Juha Hernesniemi works with people. In the interview, he tells how he reacts to mistakes and failures, how he always wants to, directly and immediately after the operation face the family and the close ones of his patients even and especially when something has gone wrong. He remembers both his professional actions and the situations with his patients and their relieved families and those in grief. He has spent his whole life to learn all this. No robot can ever replace what he does in doing so, even if the robot copied every word and gesture of Hernesniemi. He cares, in the deepest human sense, and the patients know this from the start, he makes a human connection, takes responsibility and evaluates his own state of mind and body every day – at the writing of this, he's well over 70. Still, I would guess he is not the first one to oppose the use of robot tools and surgeons, but certainly he is a perfect reference to the holistic and human quality demands of any ambitious robot project today.

The development of the theory and practices of AI itself has been an endeavor of extensive human collaboration and co-operation. Robots are used by surgeons. However, the way human intelligence is measured today, is almost a perfect opposite to intelligent behavior: in a typical decision making or intelligence testing situation the subject is isolated, he or she is not allowed to ask for help, pray, discuss and ask for more time to solve the problems at hand. Curious enough, when complex systems like AI are developed and built, it is natural to rely on free, often slow human communication and collaboration, even on open source while the way to measure human intelligence performance is to isolate the individual from her natural community.

It's somewhat a surprise that it is worth a Nobel prize when someone shows how bad isolated humans beings are in making rational decisions, when forced to work alone and brutally separated from their own and committed communities, collaboration cultures, and from their best colleagues, friends, mentors and technology. With a similar approach, but keeping us distanced from each other, we would not have the present AI systems in the first place and Elon Musk's wonderful projects and innovations like Tesla cars, batteries and Space X would not exist.

The invisible hand of AI ethics. Not every researcher of human intelligence has considered us human beings as isolated cognitive-emotional, self-sufficient specimens. Elinor Ostrom was known for e.g. the studies on how communities can successfully manage finite common resources such as grazing land, water and forests. She showed how we can become and be better together than alone when we trust each other, negotiate the rules, give and receive valuable and immediate feed-back, interact, have ways to deal with conflicts, and learn to benefit from cultural heuristics and practices of problem solving. We can learn to manage our own preferences in communities without hurting others. In her approach intelligence becomes 'distributed' within the community.

The future of AI may well – and should - learn from her thinking especially when AI is socially and technologically implemented in modern factories, firms and other contexts. It is highly likely that we will see AI implementations based on some, if not on all the principles Ostrom suggested. Much of the current hype and interest in AI ethics with the artificial ethical dilemmas and toy problems, overlook the very practical emergence of ethics on the 'factory floor' and in 'management hubs'. There will never be enough ethical guidelines to cover the coming practical AI challenges; because of that, it is hugely important to lay the continuously evolving value bases for a healthy AI. Something like that was already introduced by the Asilomar conference which understood the wide scope of the problems ahead.

I've listed only some of Ostrom's eight principles here and used them as examples and inspiration for the participatory implementation of AI in large industrial and service settings. They suggest guidelines for aiming at ethically acceptable procedures when building AI systems.

1. *Define (recognize) the existing, clear group boundaries.* In production, services and other collaborative activities there are typically several units, groups or teams working together, each with their own local and other interests and competing for the limited resources and their role in the organization.

When AI is introduced, different views and conflicts of interest emerge so that following the Ostrom principle, it is necessary to identify and define these boundaries of interests and be prepared for the expected problems. With AI, new potential conflict boundaries emerge in organizations and communities. It is important to start negotiating and building rules for progress at the right time. In the worst-case scenario, AI is introduced in a top-down manner in the organization and the conflicts hide invisible until they must be forcefully solved because of the damage done. This will probably happen in many future organizations eager to implement AI as it has been done with many ict systems before. The consequences are costly and inefficiencies will be seen. In Finland, as in many other European countries the problems can lead to serious conflicts with the unions, too when work conditions, tasks, roles, pay systems, taxation, and personnel requirements change.

2. *Ensure that those affected by the rules for governing the use of common goods and conditions can participate in modifying the rules.* In short, this is an encouragement for firms to rely on participatory development and to outline rules for AI use when AI is planned, introduced and adopted. It is important to learn to define these new rules for working with an extensive AI system which has a major impact on how work and production is organized, rewarded and managed. This alters the social-personal dynamics, collaboration and productivity at the site.

3. *Make sure the rule-making rights of the active/working community members are respected by outside authorities.* In AI context, this demand concerns especially management and the owners and other influential stakeholders who should let the AI implementation evolve without uneducated top-down interventions. It is a matter of complex trust and often difficult to achieve, typically in the fast developing, multi-faceted environment, and especially where AI is introduced for the first time. This requires a new level of proactive delegation, feed-back and trust. Later I describe the sinking of the famous Swedish Vasa ship in 1628, which is an educational example for the management of AI projects to remember.

4. *The adoption of AI has significant social and human consequences at the site.* New social and work practices emerge, some of them critical for success in the new environment. It is not a simple matter to recognize the optimal ways of progress. Following Ostrom again, it becomes important at the site to find and learn new, useful heuristics in all behaviors, especially those related to AI. They must be discovered and made explicit so that they can serve and support the emerging working culture and match the requirements of the changing environment. Old heuristics do not necessarily apply and can become friction factors. Continuous feed-back (from AI to people, people to AI, people to people etc) is necessary and the

organization must identify the critical places and relationships where it is needed.

5. *Finally, people and teams have their preferences* that are related to e.g. the purpose of their work, how they do it and how they relate to other colleagues, teams and units. Such preferences cannot be avoided and the introduction of AI puts a pressure on people. Participatory planning and collaboration can prevent the occurrence of destructive conflicts. Management skills must meet new requirements.

Why Elinor Ostrom? You have probably realized, from the above principles, the importance of trust on the performance of the working and collaborating community facing new, complex decision making and resource sharing situations that come with AI. That does not happen automatically and a new type of management competence is required to make it happen. When AI is introduced, it is possible to see it not as a competitor to human and social competences but as an associate and a partner that becomes almost like a member of the community. But it is still Very Artificial Intelligence, moving to that direction.

7. When AI outperforms the human operators – for the first time

In traditional industrial and service environments, an ideal AI system is meant to reach the competence level of human operators, agents and their teams, and then outperform them as soon as it is technically, economically and resource-wise possible and can be managed. Inevitably, any organization adopting AI will meet – it is occurring all the time – its first critical moment when this happens, for the first time. It can happen in isolated processes or concern holistic, systemic characteristics. This significant event is a wake-up call, both to the whole organization but also to its AI developers.

The learning AI system becomes accurate, fast and competent in securing production quality, offering failure diagnosis and predicting any production and service outcomes.

It is perhaps taking its first steps in predicting, managing and solving more complex problems than has been possible before by human operators and other professionals. The criteria of these significant events involve several (socio-technological) variables and it is not self-evident how to recognize them and how an organization should react to them.

When the AI system outperforms its teachers. This special, but very practical step has not been a popular discussion topic. However, it is a new window of opportunity for the organization and its people and should be recognized as such: if a firm or a production unit makes mistakes in interpreting what it means and how to respond to the new situation it runs at risk of missing the further development of AI based work and processes. It is not only an alerting signal to the technology use but to human resource management as well. AI does not know where it leads the working community, it does not ask and it does not care.

The personnel responsible for the 'old' system and implementing the AI can face uncertain times. This is not a new phenomenon in businesses and industries experiencing digital transformations; similar situations occur in banks and insurance companies, for example, when they change to more modern technological solutions while it is necessary to continue running the old systems. The same has occurred in major firms in Silicon Valley as well, where the personnel know that their value on the job market depends on the ability to work with the latest technology. Investing time and energy in old systems is risky.

Division of labor, team and management functions, will all be reconsidered. Soon, also the pay and reward systems must be aligned so that they support the AI-based work at the site: old pay models may not work any longer and can be even harmful if they reward for wrong activities and miss the critical ones. Before this renovation can be accomplished it is necessary to identify the major factors contributing to system performance.

One could call this new phase a form of *'organizational interregnum'*, when the organization is aware that its process control must be changed but it is not clear yet, what should be done and how to run the two systems in parallel (if this is the case); the change cannot be accomplished overnight and its necessary to keenly follow the performance of the AI system. It may well take more than a year depending on the scale and nature of the AI implementation. During this time, the organization, its management and the personnel in general must build *trust on two frontiers*: trust in the implemented AI technology and its use and trust in the collaboration among the personnel, teams and management. Failure in either of these leads to uncertainty, loss of motivation, conflicts and it hinders decision making.

Paradoxical as it may seem, when AI reaches its first ambitious goal it will need the best human knowledge and competences and new ways of working together, new teams, for example, just as it has needed them during the implementation, when starting to learn its tasks. If handled well this can become a moment of growth and inspiration to the personnel, a chance to build an effective work environment. Adoption of AI is a challenge to people committed to creating a healthy and fair workplace, to learn new required skills and to reach for good performance. It is the responsibility of the management to provide human-technological conditions for this.

Management's task is no different from what it always is - e.g. to secure motivation and both social and situational awareness in the company, to facilitate seamless collaboration and mutual understanding. However, due to the unpredictable future of the entering AI, the best strategy with the personnel is to be proactive, especially in education and in role development and to build a realistic image of the expected progress and changes.

The organization must tune anew what I have called its 'observational architecture': finding out where are the most important information sources at the site, in its environment and in the AI system, what phenomena to follow, and how to report and act on them. The architecture must include the personnel, too. This is nothing new for the management: team work, collaboration, learning and communication are needed. However, their content and form change and there is an acute risk: if misused or having failed to see design faults in the AI system, serious problems, of a magnitude worse than ever before, can follow. The risks must be identified during the first implementation phase. Organized participation of the personnel helps to see early warning signs and take them seriously.

Communicating with the AI companion. When AI performs better than the operators used to do, what knowledge has it acquired and how could we find out what is the essence of this new machine competence? It has learned "intelligent" input-output relationships that humans have traditionally mastered but it has learned something else, too. "What might that be?" is the question that will be repeatedly asked when AI is adopted. It is not far from the classical problem of behaviorism in psychology: is it enough to focus on the observable behavior only or should we try to see what happens inside the 'box', what underlies behind its behavior, style and decision making? AI and especially the deep learning systems have reached a satisfactory black box performance and now the designers try to progress from that, to understand what happens inside these systems. The fellow in the AI box remains unknown.

In the MIT Technology Review (April/2017) column, Will Knigth starts the story "The Dark Secret at the Heart of AI", with an ingress. "No one really knows how the most advanced algorithms do what they do. That could be a problem." As an example, he used the self-driving car designed by NVIDIA, which used deep learning to observe how humans drive and learned by observing. Knight then asks: "But what if one day it did something unexpected—crashed into a tree, or sat at a green light? As things stand now, it might be difficult to find out why."

With self-driving cars, this 'dark learning' is a multi-layered problem extending from simple pattern recognition tasks to traffic safety and to ethics of decision making. The same concerns industrial plants, service providers and other organizations when launching a strong AI to run their processes and guide their work.

How to best talk to AI systems and how should they talk to us? It is not always known what knowledge the best AI systems should tell us - if they had a means to do it and we could understand it. It is no longer a distant philosophical question but a very practical one as we have seen in complex industrial environments and in studies aiming at explainable AI. AI can be taught to follow instructions and complex rule sets and have a reasonable conversation with us, but it becomes difficult to communicate with it, especially in case of deep learning and complex situations when running large-scale processes. The MIT story reminds us that it's is about building trust in the AI system – but it is essentially human trust, something similar we experience towards our cars. Tools are needed for it.

It is easy to see when an AI system outperforms human operators in its speed, accuracy and the quality of output in a specific task. Standard methods and metrics cover these basic measures. However, interpretation of the performance data may not be that simple: why was the AI system able to perform so well? Did it use the same information as the human operators have always used, but more efficiently or did it find its own ways of deriving new knowledge from what it had learned during its teaching/learning process? We should know if it has learned potential, dormant behaviors – which have not yet occurred – that can be harmful to the system. Curious enough, many technologies 'have' implicit trust in its users: their design assumes that the users do not act in certain (dangerous or stupid) ways even though they could easily do that.

First, second and third order learning. When an AI system is taught by feeding it with offline data and then later real-time data from a real process, it is learning to behave as expected and to produce the hoped for, beneficial input-output reactions. We call this *first order learning* of AI, when it still does not outperform the 'old' practices. The operators can compare the system performance data – as it has occurred under manual or semi-manual control - against the data obtained with the AI system running. Based on this comparison the AI system can be tuned, given additional teaching material, improved quality of input data, identifying any needs for additional data sources and by designing suitable UIs.

This is a relatively complex, socio-technical development phase where the immediate aim is to guide the AI system so that it could match and eventually outperform humans. When it is implemented for the first time at the site, it is natural to follow and rely on the same performance metrics and other work practices that have been used when the process was controlled by human operators.

Because of the huge data output capacity of the AI system, its user interfaces must be able to show and allow safe control of its functions and performance. New data representations and system controls must be used and tested. However, there is no unique standard to define what the output of an AI controlled system should now look like and what would be its core purpose. A running AI system uses real-time and computed data from thousands of measurement points which it shows, in one form or another, to the operators whose task is to interpret the flow of information and evaluate the system state and performance. But of course, humans cannot follow so much data. Effective representations, condensed, packed and informative, must be invented, just like in nuclear plants, but what should such an UI be like and how to use it?

UI:s of AI evolve and new concepts and forms are introduced to serve specific contexts. They will have a crucial, even competitive role in supporting human work and collaboration and in helping the personnel to understand the new control environment. Investing time and resources in wise UI can have a major impact on system performance. There are good grounds to take this seriously, especially at large scale sites. During the first order learning phase the initial UIs are often designed and adopted on site, but the need to improve them becomes quickly apparent.

The second order learning phase has a special nature since it is the moment when the AI system, for the first time, outperforms human operators. This becomes a new high-level challenge: how and why did the AI system reach such a good performance? What data and controls were most informative for it and how should its performance now be described and represented? How should this new AI knowledge be presented to the operators? What kind of representations are best for describing the important states and performance of AI and the processes it controls? Can the system offer guidance to the site personnel about how to improve the process and the infrastructure? How should the operators be offered ways of controlling the AI-based processes? Is it at all reasonable to consider the interaction between the operators and AI as a UI problem or is some other approach needed?

This is only the beginning of a major transformation in the AI-Humans interaction and touches the participating designers, engineers, operators and AI specialists. In the *triad model of learning* the operators, designers and those responsible for the engineering and implementation of the AI system, work together, learning from each other and from the AI system. Now this situation is at hand again, but the context has profoundly changed: the AI system does what it was intended to do, outperforming the human operators. What does this mean to the triad community, what should be done next and how to prepare for its future?

This is the start of the *third order learning* phase where the learning extends to the organization at large. It becomes a major organizational and management task – to reorganize under the pressure of the emerging, new needs and possibilities. The reason to this is simple: an effective AI system introduces new constraints on the industrial plant or for the service provider, who must now re-organize their work, modify the organizational structure, and secure the new competences for building the processes around the AI. It is time to rethink the business model as well if this hasn't been done earlier.

During this race for performance and quality it is often forgotten that the organization must be prepared for a better, next generation AI technology when it is needed and possible. Finally, with the fast advancement of AI it is important to make sure that work communities do not end up being victims of it but instead can co-work with AI to secure our good life and work with human purpose.

7 GT AND COMPUTER GAMES

Computed games have become psychological laboratories for studying human experience and interaction in a systematic, real-like, empirical and content-sensitive way. With my long-time colleague Jari Takatalo, leading the project (now at Rovio Helsinki and Aalto University, Espoo Finland) we started an extensive project on computer game experiences at around 2000 with the aim to build a psychologically and empirically grounded framework for studying and profiling game experiences. Data was collected from thousands of players who – after having played a game or during it - reported their subjective experiences in dozens of different games, one at a time, covering all relevant game genres. Similar studies have been extensively conducted also elsewhere (for relevant references of the field, see e.g. Jari Takatalo's doctoral thesis) but I use his specific model as an example, demonstrating the empirical challenges in trying to get in touch with the complex psychology of game experience and its human ground. In this sense, it is almost the opposite to the AI-based thumb & guess approach. His work reminds of the multi-dimensionality of human experience and about the psychological-methodical means to model it in complex behavior environments – that need not be computer games only.

The set-ups and methodological approach in Takatalo's paradigm have much in common with the Golden Triangle. First, the experience measurements (questionnaires, interviews) in this research framework are focused on individual experiences and experience profiles emerging specifically from a game play. Second, the research paradigm concerns and pays respect to certain contents, which is natural for games: real games were studied, of specific genres that millions of boys, girls and adults play daily. Third, the research framework rests on validated psychological concepts and theories. Below, only some of the relevant, empirically based, subjective game experience dimensions that have come out from these studies have been listed.

Takatalo's psychological game studies are holistic in nature. This is necessary for understanding the real multi-variable, simultaneously occurring, psychological phenomena happening in a motivated game-playing person's mind. There is no reason to assume that the same processes would not happen in the mind or a working person. Such a psychological entity is a major research challenge and not only for games but in the study of any natural, human behavior. Hence, these studies used the multi-variable, experiential cycle model as a guiding, integrating principle in collecting data and formulating the game-psychological theory. Such a research strategy requires extensive data collection and differs from many psychological approaches, where paradigm-specific perspective to human behavior and a partial – cognitive, developmental, social, physiological - look at naturally occurring behaviors is chosen. The role of content in the psychological dynamics can then become obscure. This emphasized the idea to study game experiences like any everyday experiences would be studied and to do it with different games and game genres, each having their own psychological dynamics. The problem then is to find the commonalities that all games share in their psychology. The Presence-Involvement-Flow Framework (PIFF) model is one example of such an approach.

Modern computer games have progressed so much that they can now be considered as ecologically valid environments for studying almost any psychological phenomena. Further, new game genres in learning, QS, health, and sports, for example, emerge where virtual, physical and mental worlds meet and are mixed on game platforms and generate new psychological research problems.

The PIFF model includes the Golden Triangle elements as they occur in game research context: study of Experience (Human centered), respect for the Environment (Content oriented), and trust in a Psychologically grounded approach. The main components of PIFF were empirically supported by 15 factor-analytically computed, psychologically well-defined subcomponents, which include, for example, the following experience elements: interaction, physical presence, attention, role engagement, co-presence, interest, arousal and so on.

In summary, the experience space revealed in this way is multidimensional, genre-specific, with several mental phenomena active simultaneously. However, higher-level aspects like cultural, social and other factors, are missing from the model which is focused on direct individual experience – related phenomena. This can be a handicap when interpreting some of the results, especially now that extensive and powerful game communities have evolved and become socially, even social-developmentally influential. Nevertheless, the underlying psychological model components remain relevant.

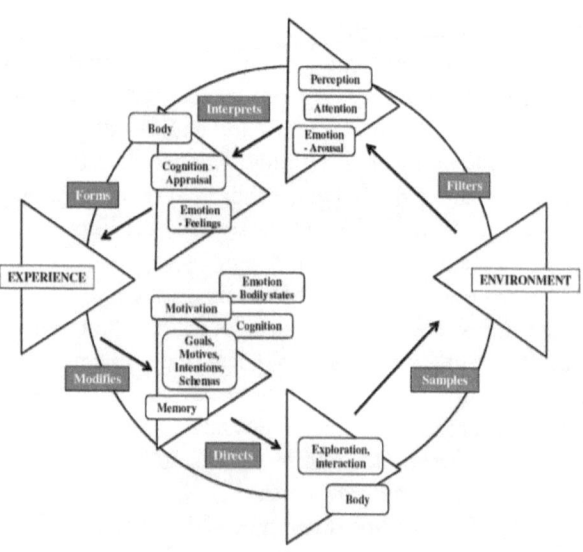

Figure 1. From Takatalo, J (2011) "Psychologically-Based and Content-Oriented Experience in Entertainment Virtual Environments. University of Helsinki, Ph.D. dissertation.

8 PRINT AND HUMAN TECHNOLOGY

1.   What is interesting in Finnish media?

From the very beginning, all forms of media and journalism have evolved together with technological models, businesses, culture, and emerging innovations in communication. The best and the worst of journalism must live with this development. What we think of as media today reflects what we think about certain uses of technology. The invariant in this equation is the human being, motivated to follow, live with and contribute to media and journalism.

The vision where paper technology has disappeared from the media sphere, is well alive while many of us think of books and magazines as cultural and artistic objects that will survive because of their deeply human-cultural nature, inherent social practices and history. Some technology-enthusiasts claim that books are simple and cumbersome user interfaces to information and knowledge transmission while humanists see books as means to promote and live with culture, to support civilization and to leave tangible traces and habits for the generations to come. For writers, books are a human-technological channel for creating, expressing and living any possible stories of mankind, fact and fiction alike. Hence, our look at media is a look at the nature of human technology as we think of it.

We Finns are well-educated people: we can read and understand anything that is published for the general audience. Practically everyone here reads, and because of that, we learn more, teach each other and become aware of the importance of reading. Despite the utterly stupid and insane texts from some loud minorities that you can follow also in the Finnish social media, surprisingly many of us can write: we have the largest number of magazine titles per capita in the world and because of that we can inform each other and grow. It does not matter whether it is digital or printed material; books and magazines are doors to authors we can know and often also reach.

What we and the world desperately need is a future media sphere that would understand this huge, almost unlimited human potential – when there is good enough education to support it. Powerful media can continuously challenge people to read and learn, to make us change, offer insightful content and style, and hire talented and responsible writers and producers to make this happen. Finland, like many other small countries could become an island of media discourse if the journalists, together with social media forces construct their closed discussion sphere, the intellectual space proper where 'public and national thinking' takes place. Today, however, media technology has the potential to remove some of these borders and we live on the edge where digital forces can take us any fountain in time and space.

Access to the internet alone does not free us from the national and other closures: most acute discussions, argumentations and presentations take place through a synchronous digital media and real places like the famous squares and the fields of the yellow vests that provide a systematic and relatively simultaneous presence of journalists, their audiences and those engaged. Due to media technology, human life is becoming increasingly synchronous at all levels. Interestingly, texts in books and magazines can better support secure and asynchronous actions and thinking than standard digital media can achieve.

The sphere of communication and interaction is continuously being built: our synchronous and asynchronous ways of being together remain a necessity, despite the available mobile and internet services. However, a waltz without closeness and synchrony and the enjoyment provided by this, is just an image of waltz or robots dancing. Dancing with false news and misinformation makes us sick.

Synchrony between life and media. Asynchronous communication, online and mobile news and discussions inspire masses to synchronous activities like we have seen in the Occupy Wall Street movement, in Arab Spring, Yellow Vests in France, demonstrations in Hong Kong, and the activities in good and bad. These movements need their synchronizing, living forums, like tent villages, get-togethers, outsiders coming to act in unison in a big city. It becomes possible to be together, prepared with a shared purpose, in a sensitive, fast, visible, and interactive sense, to share the problems and challenges, to argument for different solutions, to act and disappear and then to return to the shared forum again. Unfortunately, this works for fight and war, too.

It may well be one of the main strengths of general democracy that it promotes and allows such synchronous forums, having a classic history – if they are safe. However, even the best forums fail and become biased and distorted without people who can read, write, live with the new media and be prepared for informed and trusted communication. With the support of media, people can be dynamically inspired to any strange collective acts and feelings as we saw some years ago in the miraculously mourning people of N Korea. Reading, informed writing, author voices, and healthy forums are a threat then.

Strangely enough, despite the amazing potential of the audience, the public journalistic world, living on click money, is suffering from a divide: some try to maintain the best of journalism while dominant media is getting intellectually thinner, biased, driven by short-range, narrow-minded hunger for news, conflicts, media-against-media combats, pay-walls, fight for visibility, dominated by civilized celebrity stories, political adventure scenes and national, narrowly defined success stories. Even Finland with its educated people suffers from this thinning. Our media follows US in its worst forms but often fails to match its best.

Science news is an excellent test case of the intellectual ambition level of any nation's news media. Often, science news has adopted an almost underground nature or it is click-entertainment where big drama, frauds, failures, and conflicting views find their place on the front pages. The practical and social process of science is of meager interest while you can follow one-hour long, detailed documentaries on how a local pop band talks about the production of certain sounds in their old recordings. Of course, it is a matter of culture and trends but most of the compelling human events in everyday, world-wide science remain invisible and hidden from the audience.

Modern media, with the help of its underlying technology, educates us to naïve (cheap, fragmented, scalable and fast to produce) story formats, concepts and media lures because masses matter. When they succeed in selling this to us, the collected 'big data' is then taken as evidence – forgetting the inverse problem - that it is what we want, that we do not want challenging, 'too difficult' or time consuming content or form. A civilized and educated nation like Finland fell into a vicious cycle of deteriorating quality of media content: our newspaper publishers suffered from a neurosis that they will lose the game against The Net and were afraid to produce challenging content, trying to be cost-effective in this low-quality rat reporting race. Fortunately, the tide has been changing, the value of content – not less because of the flow of fake news - seems to increase and no doubt, the technological media innovations will form a watershed for quality. But there is obvious risk aversion in the media field.

Finland has one exceptional intellectual sphere where my worried media considerations are not true at all and where the readers – our citizens – show their true intellectual will and power. Take the "Tähdet ja Avaruus", T&A, my favorite magazine as an example (http://www.avaruus.fi/ "Stars and Space", a cousin for Sky and Telescope in USA). It is for readers interested in astronomy, cosmology and the latest developments in space technology. T&A is published by Ursa the Finnish society for amateur astronomers.

Originally it was just a modest leaflet, but from the beginning it had a genuine connection with real scientists in the field. For example, there is the amazing column started by professor Heikki Oja, that tells, day by day, and has done it for decades, the latest news in astronomy and cosmology. Today

T&A is a magnificent, intellectually ambitious and glamorous magazine, written in Finnish. I understood that you can add up the sales numbers of all similar national magazines in other Nordic countries and still T&A sells more in Finland alone.

Why is that, and especially, how is that possible during the times of the dominant entertainment media, The Net and YouTube -fun? Why hasn't it died as a printed magazine? Why do so many people read printed, complex and brain-blowing stories about space-time, string theory, expanding universe, Higgs boson, Mars robots, gravitational waves, magnetic fields of our solar system, adaptive optics, telescope design, and many more fascinating themes and keep on doing so?

The answer is simple: we love the mysteries of the space and universe around us. T&A trusts in this eternal human motivation and in its readers' curiosity and intellectual potential. The sky and the stars are there for us to admire, every night (and day). The readers are the proof that practically everyone in Finland can read and understand when someone writes about space, or any other public topic, in a compelling way - and many are willing and able to do it. About 70 000 curious readers, including me read the magazine. Relative to the population, I believe that on its own field, it is the leading magazine in the world. The platform has very little to do with this.

T&A is not only a magazine: it is a human guide to interesting people and knowledge sources in the net as well. Its writers are specialists and professionals whom we can trust, they can be our knowledge coaches leading us to new and emerging knowledge. Even when they are wrong, biased by their own theories or we disagree with them and their views, they still guide us to the fountains of fresh knowledge. When we follow their footsteps, check their suggestions for relevant sources and find out what are their passions, we become participants on their journey, and learn to read more. The magazine is beautiful on your desk.

At its worst, media interest is created by recursive manipulation: important news is, by definition, what is important in the media game. Due to effective media technology, the formula can be simple: digital media repeats familiar names and topics, and other media conducts the same symbol game, then they immerse into an 'inter-media discourse' and the readers follow this, without knowing the underlying process. The media struggle, especially in US, has become familiar to everyone; some readers even learn to expect for more and so it goes on and on. The first generation of AI will not make this better in news production.

During this strange media discourse, something fascinating is being hidden in the world of technology, science, and art: the amazing human journeys, every day. Somewhere there are passionate people and communities who try to learn new things, every hour and they are not just rock bands, politicians, Nobel scientists, leading artists, or Fortune 500 CEO's. They are on the same journey with us to eternity.

2.   Rotten floors and platforms

The giants in media and technology businesses build platforms to capture us and dominate the markets. Many of them have succeeded, and in Finland, for example, it is practically easier to resign from the Church than from Facebook.

If you are old enough you can remember the time when plastic and other synthetic materials were expected to replace wood and any traditional materials. 'A plastic platform' was being introduced. Similar 'replacement trend' has been seen for wool, silk, tapestry, leather, house roofs, and oil paints to list a few modern developments. It was indeed a struggle for 'platforms' although it was not called by that name then. If you are a child of the digital and mobile scene you probably don't know much about that strange period, but now you can take your turn and follow a similar process happening in the media and communication world.

Today, however, a renaissance of classical materials is taking place in wood building, book design, board games, clothing, retro, furniture, radios, cars, old records, bw photographs and movies, to name a few examples. This has not happened only because it is fashionable, but because it has been inviting and creatively impressive to people who have been attracted to classical objects, their forms and tangible essence. The capital value of the material renaissance has surprised many and the same can happen in media and communication industry. The reason is simple: people don't have any interest in platforms and operating systems as such. We want to lead a good life as we see and experience it, with media as an unavoidable companion of any lifestyle. In the long run, we don't want to be hostages of monolithic platforms although we can become ones by ruthless, persuasive methods and pressures.

In my hometown Helsinki, a great number of beautiful wooden houses were torn down in 1950's and 60's and replaced by modern buildings made of 'new' materials. So important were these innovations that the architects and constructors did not care much about how the houses looked like, they just had to be 'modern'. Looking at them now is painful: we have terribly ugly buildings, spoiling the atmosphere of their environment, and many of them have no future value. But it was easy to sell them as the representatives of 'modern lifestyle'. A pathological optimist might suggest they give Helsinki 'rhythm.'

Sometimes modern and classical technologies have been mixed in a stupid way. For example, wooden floors in old houses were covered with colorful, plastic carpets glued on place. This prevented natural breathing of the houses and made the 100 years old wooden floors rot in a year. Then, because the plastic materials did not breath, artificial ventilation systems were installed, which introduced humidity and mold, making hundreds of families sick at their homes and children suffer in schools.

The reasons for these disasters were not the materials as such – or the 'platforms' if we prefer the present terminology – but lack of understanding of how the classical buildings function, how they live their lives, and what were or are the ecosystems they form together with their inhabitants. Mixing of old and modern is far from a simple exercise. In 1960's and even 70's these aspects had practically no capital value in many European cities. But for people, a box is not a home and a communication platform is not a media. These design solutions became examples of life gone astray on the edge of new technology.

3. Platforms as concentration camps of communication

The ongoing struggle between media platforms mirrors the beliefs in material over meaning and content. Platform and business ecosystem dominance and strategic alliances – forgetting the human ecosystems - are expected to guarantee significant wins while introducing an increasing risk to underestimate consumer habits and life situations. The term 'ecosystem' when we hear it from a digital communication world representative, often simply means 'a concentration camp of communication', a place where 'Communication makes you free' if you keep on paying and staying there. Many media masters don't have a genuine interest in human ecosystems, they want to dominate the economics and logistics: to command their own media camps and scale up.

People get tired, perhaps digitally sick, in an unknown, but modern way, because they typically do not know what an operation system or a platform is and what it does to them, to their children and life. It is almost like the Freudian unconscious, difficult to know it and deal with it but there is no doubt it has a severe impact on us. Psychologists have been slow to wake up to this media-architectural and algorithmic problem although worries about e.g. depression caused by Facebook use have already been voiced. It's like with the plastic carpets: the question 'How can I use that platform?' does not provide the answer to the more relevant question 'What are its consequences to me and my life?'

Own the concepts used on a media platform and you own the minds. It's like what the classic Russian scientist Vygotsky said how language makes up our thinking. Digital platforms and tools have joined this competition for the space in our minds. We can follow a struggle of who will own the next dominant public debate concept on media and personal technology. The competition is not too ambitious, because almost anything that respects human styles and preferences can be better than what we now see in the form of useless apps, platforms, OS versions, thumbs, and searches. Beliefs can be fed to the audience who are under continuous pressure to be experts on new and future technologies. People are bombarded with worries on media and technology developments and parents don't know what is good for their children. Some educational scientists have made things worse by praising children they call 'digital natives', a concept that has dangerous human consequences.

The best-known example of a platform struggle concerns print media. Only a decade or two ago, suggesting that paper media could have a new and better future ahead was a real brain-killer and mentioning it – as I had done several times on various media forums – was taken as a hint of a poor mind, off-the-rocker thinking or it was just an invitation to serious yawns by the 'digital natives'. Now the future of print is under reconsideration and some magazines, indy bookstores and publishers prosper. The future is not about paper its about contents and human life contexts with media.

What will happen to the cultural role of printed objects in our life with media? No doubt, we can expect a sustainable future for oil paintings on canvas and water colors on paper; they have not been replaced by open digital access or huge electronic displays with their immense color reproduction properties or even 3D. The secret behind the persistent value of paintings is their originality, *the material essence* and the visible touch of an artist, with the materials and in the form of the strokes with a brush and paint against the canvas. The object is real for us, with a tangible history. Of course, we can view oil paintings from any imaginable display, even make the classic paintings tangible by AR, but authenticity cannot be replaced.

We might see a media renaissance associated with digitally driven open media cultures. Newspapers are still missing their renaissance future, and have not found out what old and new could happen to them. They can face the destiny of the wooden houses where modern materials and systems were artificially mixed and installed and caused a disaster. Relevant human centered and situationally intelligent media-technologies are needed. To take the analogy a bit further: newspapers covered their journalistic essence with digital carpets and paywalls that can, in the worst case suffocate them. We know why the wooden floors rotted when covered with 'modern' plastic; there is the risk that this will happen to newspapers covered with 'modern' digitalization without humanification.

Paradoxically, the introduction of iPhone, iPad, other tablets, 3D, large and multiple display systems triggered a new and rich multimedia life, and they can give a breath of life to books, magazines and comics. It is not a zero-sum game. The more you read the more you are eager to read. The variety of future media has the potential to ruin any monolithic empires, but it requires that the products, their content, and the way media technology is used will match human needs, life situations and preferences. What I still expect to happen, is that the 'book community' realizes that it's not about what is happening to printed books but what we *decide* about it.

Why I'm convinced on this, with such open and blunt arguments? We took our lessons from RAMI (Rapid market innovations) project where we tried to learn about the ways people in Finland, China and Turkey, for example live with printed and other media. Looking at the networked behaviors within various media and service channels and describing this as an analog to Bayesian network models, was a means to get – at least a first look at personal media ecosystems in these different cultures. Reading is both historically and today a complex non-linear and very dynamic process – socially, culturally, situationally and in human sense – even distributed, not well understood and continuously changing. Every country has its own media-related life style and there are huge national differences in media use cultures.

Media maturation. The major force leading to media renaissance could be a technologically driven but content-orientated maturation we are facing on many sectors of life. Mobile devices and systems are generally available, internet services are standard tools and commodities, digital radio has found its lifeline, home theatres have a high quality for the average size of family homes, high-quality digital printing offers new flexibility for content providers, internet and mobile cross cultural boundaries, and book sales have found new forms in the net and in book stores. Common to these developments is the emergence of high-quality, new and old contents.

The term 'renaissance' may evoke conflicting arguments from historians, but it can be defined as a historical period of a cultural movement that favors originality in arts, sciences, religion, politics, and education in all their dimensionalities. It amends its power from classical sources; it accepts and even assumes different perspectives to human life and to the conceptions of the world as we see it. Global pressure for this opening is stronger than ever and there is no limit to these opportunities for media to succeed and even prosper: it is part of human and social life. Similar pressures originate from Africa, China, and even at the borderlines of Europe and its capitols. 'Renaissance of media culture' means life with media that accepts different habits, worldviews and cultures, both in content and form. Strange enough, Fahrenheit 451, the movie by Francois Truffaut is astonishingly relevant today: many still entertain the belief or even a dream that books and magazines will be abolished and that books are but a temporary historical fad.

9 SOME IDEAS

A short personal story has its place here. Some ten years ago, at a large international innovation event, I led a "Pop-up work-shop", inviting people to join with the title: "Design that motivates to sustainable behavior". I was amazed to notice how the attending participants, a dozen professionals in design, innovation management and even CDOs, did not understand at all what I meant by 'motivation' in this context. I used some ugly design examples of heat pumps to show how aesthetics is a de-motivation factor and it did not help. Then I took up Tesla. It seemed to me, that my audience was searching for direct and voiced motivations and could not see the indirect ones.

1.   Selfish motivations can lead to common good

When the designers of Tesla Motors in Palo Alto, created an electric car – the early Roadster, a decade ago – with a design that was familiar from other fancy high-end sports cars, they joined the designers who broke the psychological barrier caused by the ugliness of design that so often prevents sustainable products from attracting wide markets. Why shouldn't a sustainable product be beautiful and classy, and even more inviting than its less sustainable competitors? Why couldn't it be good business to help building sustainable world with the support of high-class aesthetics, and to help the people in need?

The imaginary 'rational consumer' still looms in the political, ideological and the our-story-is-the-whole truth - movements, writings and commentaries and on the pages of media. It is often used as a direct or hidden blame for us who behave in 'improper' ways. We should just 'change our attitude' and save the planet. This false theory of the human mind and motivation is losing its position as a thought model: the well-funded and popular cognitive-rational emperor has barely even virtual clothes.

Without living motivation everything dies. As pessimistic as it may sound and to claim this today, when the world is shattered by the threats of climate change, the main motivation of people is not – and will not be in the foreseeable future – the promotion of sustainability. Indeed, practically everyone is for sustainability, but that 'attitude' is not motivation although sometimes it leads to tangible actions. Despite the progressive trends, in most parts of the world, nothing remarkably sustainable will happen without inspiring human and social incentives. Luckily there are plenty of motivations that lead to positive environmental and social behaviors and outcomes. We should learn to know them all and cultivate them. The connected world makes this easier than ever before. We need motivational platforms for people to think, act and enjoy – spiritually, aesthetically and practically. It does not happen by instructions or by political rhetoric.

Gloomy and de-motivating counter examples to Tesla exist. When we want to improve the energy efficiency of our homes by installing heat pumps in houses we typically get terribly ugly designs which spoil the aesthetic atmosphere both inside and outside our homes. You might argue that it is 'wrong' or 'selfish' to refuse to use such products just because of their aesthetic properties, and that 'nature is more important'.

Why should people, who are willing to protect natural resources, be forced to – or at least be ready to – sacrifice the beauty of their homes? It is a basic human characteristic, almost an instinct, to create an atmosphere of comfort, beauty, and style at home and in its immediate surroundings. Appearance and aesthetics have their roots in functionality and they are not meaningless decoration. Human history is crowded with beautiful objects and spaces. Why not respect this need, and even make a sustainable business of it?

Quite recently, I visited a beautiful classic-style European hotel where in its stylish restaurant I noticed to objects, side by side: the shining white, but ugly heat pump box that spoiled the style of the room, and a beautifully formed large vase, made of cement beside it. The aesthetics of the vase had not carried to its neighbor.

Figure 1. The facade of an old beautiful building in Helsinki which used to host our Opera.

Many of us take bottles, paper and other stuff for recycling, often into distasteful-looking storage boxes located in an untidy environment. Not seldom, the rest-rooms in public places have better designs. For some strange reason, environment-friendly products, processes, and services typically lack ambitious, aesthetically interesting, radically surprising, or pleasing appearance and architecture, as if it would be better for them to appear shabby, dirty, and thoroughly non-inviting like the stuff we take there. Perhaps they serve as a conditioning signal showing us and other people that 'I'm giving up so much for the good of the world. You can see that I'm even ready to use these ugly and dirty spaces'.

The human motivational system is not a simple hierarchy, but a complex entity of the mind where everything has a function; it is based on rich connectivity of psychological elements. Individuals and cultures have psychological backgrounds that differ, and so do their motivational structures. There are good economic, cultural and educational reasons why most of the plastic waste in oceans originate largely from the same part of the globe, in Africa, China and India. To blame individuals or to put a burden on them does not help.

Here are some simple examples of motivations that support sustainable behavior. They can be used as motivational design requirements as well:

- Creative representations of compelling knowledge can motivate to wise acts
- Beauty rewards and motivates
- We are energized by the joy of sharing the experiences of helping and contributing with our close ones.
- We are empowered by the sight and experience of change happening
- Being in personal contact & control encourages us to take initiative
- The use of our sense of beauty makes us perceptive
- Novel and ingenious solutions maintain our faith in possibilities
- Incorporating positive practices into our life context makes them a natural element of our life

Motivational design finds its place when culturally sensitive business models support it. It is not a trivial task to figure out what these models might be; they must be invented and improved. There are promising developments under way that change the way business innovations will have their impact on sustainable behavior, help the poor, and support peace and non-violence. No wonder then that 'impact investing' in the form of green bonds and their emerging relatives, for example, have become a significant trend in investing. However, it is not about doing good only but doing it so that it is profitable and can support further investments in important impacts to scale up good.

A gloomy local example has it place here. At the writing of this in 2018-2019 in Finland, the privatized businesses of elderly care have made huge profits which has been possible with the cost of terrible malpractices. There has been forgery of the number of employees taking care of the elderly, sky-high pricing of even simplest activities, and politicians finding their economic futures by first participating in regulatory activities of elderly care, then taking positions at the top of these unbelievably arrogant and greedy firms. Some of the immoral firms have now been exposed and there is an intense political discussion on what to do about this. Politicians cannot avoid dealing with the problem and many of them are now suggesting there should be regulation preventing such firms from making profits. There is lack of models where it would be possible, *at the same time*, for firms working in elderly care, to make profits *and* produce quality in a sustainable way. Money has run them astray. Healthy impact models are missing.

Banking business has always suffered from greed problems, especially when it comes to dealing with the poor or with their customers in trouble. Grameen Bank, however, has had numerous followers and there are other related activities as well. "The Net" alone does not accomplish it – the real forces behind such innovations are people and the clever, out-of-the-box business thinking, relevant capital, and all this combined with a healthy motivation to help and contribute. They deserve benefits from this activity but only when they improve their service quality. Some impact models support these activities, but problems do exist.

Clever motivational design of products and services can produce a behavioral-social platform for people to help, support, and invite them to act in a sustainable way. Here 'design' is not related to the surface of a product, a brand, or a service instead it refers e.g. to the consideration and support of inherent human culture, interest in the source-of-origin and meaning of objects and things. Such a design also helps people to find ways to motivated behaviors and it can build bridges between people, be they citizens, craftsmen, public servants or consumers living in their own cultures.

2. Helping people to be motivated

Some years ago, a friend of mine, Irene Wichmann tested a campaign and a business to find "ethically produced, beautiful products ... and their producers" from various parts of the world. Through this process, she wanted to make it easy for us as consumers and global citizens to help those who can design, produce and offer products of beauty for us, but who don't have international connections to sell their work.

We were offered a simple way to do good, in a fair way: to compensate for the work, time, and skill of distant people who had produced the objects and at the same time we could show genuine respect and admiration to their skills. We could enjoy beautiful designs and work of art and craft from the world. Irene helped us to enjoy style and function in a way that was important to us, to our friends and families and to our own culture. We could care about other people, but without a platform we could not have shown it and make it real. What I especially liked about Irene's thinking was that she did not lecture us to restrain from our needs for beauty, style, and comfort. She respected our motivation to be aesthetically curious, demanding - and to help.

The either-or mental model becomes diluted. We are learning to live along parallel individual-social and local-global dimensions, to move towards the epoch of both-and. We can call it complexity of the world, but it is just a classification of the phenomena in our world. I do not share the idea that complexity is somehow a new phenomenon, while some aspects of it clearly are, like the speed and scope of communication, the masses reacting in social media and some other, practical aspects of it. Complexity is a natural challenge to us and to our animal friends but we have always found ways of framing the world so that we can survive.

3.   Your future car saving the planet, cleaning the air

Only three years ago (2016) I wrote in my blog "Imagine that our Fords, BMWs, and Toyotas and their electric and hydrogen versions - instead of having only a low or even a zero CO_2 emission – would fight the climate change by removing CO_2 from the air. The car on the road and in park with its engine running would be transformed from a climate change threat to a global asset and virtue in protecting the atmosphere. 'You cannot do that! There is no such technology! Cities are crowded already!' are the expected comments to such an unorthodox idea. But the thought experiment is fuel for thinking about the nature of human mobility."

Today, the emerging technological advances are fast changing our ways to imagine solutions to serious pollution problems. Removing excess CO_2 (or any harmful substance) from the air is a realistic dream as the MIT report some time ago told us. Scientists have imaging and worked with novel ways to transform CO_2 to valuable materials such as carbon nanofibers or into methanol for industrial uses. Bill Gates invested in a system for sucking CO_2 from the air to transform it to harmless carbonates. The global pressure to succeed in these innovations is almost as high as in fighting cancer. No surprise then that there is an incipient trend to imagine and work on revolutionary methods that clean the air and the environment, instead of just preventing pollution.

Amazing technologies aim at protecting our environment. There is a prototype bikini, as amusing as it may sound - designed by the engineers at UC Riverside - that cleans the seawater from various pollutants that reach the sea, cf. Huffpost Science, 10/2/2015, "This Bikini Of The Future Cleans The Ocean As You Swim". Another invention from University of Sheffield and the London College of Fashion offered air cleaning clothing that removes nitrogen oxides from the air - about the same amount produced by the average family car each day! A research team from China (Shan Gao et al., 2016) described in Nature how it is possible to convert carbon dioxide gas into a fuel having no toxic byproducts when used as energy source. New solutions emerge and it is time to take a second look at the future roles of cars and other transportation vehicles, including the potential of self-driving cars.

According to the United States Environmental Agency (EPA, 2015) in US, the CO_2 produced by human activities originates from electricity (37%), transportation (31%), and industry (15%). In transportation the 'on-road vehicles' produced overwhelmingly more CO_2 than other forms of transportation, e.g. on-road vehicles: 1,442.7 Teragrams of CO_2 vs. aircrafts: 148.7 . In EU, Cars are responsible for 12% of total EU emissions of carbon dioxide and the law requires that new cars should not emit more than a certain average amount of CO_2 per kilometre.

Cars have appeared on the road, having zero CO_2 emission like Tesla and Nissan Leaf (EVs) and even the hydrogen powered from Toyota and other early models. The critics referring to the life cycle analysis of EVs, know that almost half of their CO_2 emissions come from the manufacturing and mining of the raw materials for the batteries and from the primary energy sources utilized for making these cars. The mining and manufacturing related to energy sources – coal, nuclear, solar, wind - vary considerably around the world and depend on the total energy demand. Battery technologies are advancing fast, too.

Opinions differ on how to exactly estimate the total burden on the environment caused by the production, waste processes and the energy sources. Nevertheless, a fair question remains – what if we *could* make air-cleaning cars capable of removing excess CO_2 and other harmful substances from the air? Would it be possible to aim at a car manufacturing model where it is obligatory for any car maker to guarantee that its cars are not only fun to drive but they also clean at least as much air as its cars on the road and the manufacturing process together produce? Could the charging of a car be connected to a grid of air-cleaning systems so that every time it is charged or refueled it would directly –and not only via overall taxation - participate in the air-cleaning process? This would be a revolution in the way we think about transport, logistics, urban architectures and the health of our environments. The question remains, how to motivate people to wise decisions when choosing a car.

The alarming fact is, of course, that not only the increasing number of cars but the whole car manufacturing industry, including the production of electric and hydrogen powered cars, is producing excess amounts of 'bad stuff' right *now* and fast solutions are needed. Even if the car industry and the road traffic would be effectively cleaning the air, many would still resist this development because the cars crowd the roads, cities and public spaces. More cars would remain a genuine nuisance and cities and motorways cannot take more than already now dominate the scarce public spaces. Many cities have made long-lasting decisions to provide space for pedestrians, public transport and biking and to prepare for self-driving car generations. It is not realistic to assume that cars could be removed from the planet within the next thirty years, a long time in developing new technologies. It is highly likely that future global economies will produce more cars when the new middle class enjoys the fun and comfort of driving and owning a car. Globally, the situation is serious as indicated by the health-threatening pollution in Delhi, where a driving-ban was issued to get a million cars off from the roads.

The International Transport Forum estimated that the number of motor vehicles in the world will double by 2050 when it will be roughly 2.5 billion. So, even if we try to limit car use, diminish the car ownership and increase sharing, design self-driving cars and their traffic environment, it is wise to consider cars as major assets in fighting climate change. An optimal strategy is needed.

People will always be moving and commuting even when the best VR systems have matured so that information sharing, collaboration and even social presence and manufacturing have become everyday practices. We want to get together, touch, shake hands, bow to and hug each other, feel the closeness, joy, and share the spontaneous, physical presence and participation at work, entertainment and in any human relationships. When commuting becomes fast, easy, cheap and acceptable, people can adopt new roles as modern nomads, different from their classic predecessors who also had to move from one place to another. The future nomads can arrange their model of life and living by their values on the run – and to contribute to clean air. We are a physical species.

4. Virtual action heroes doing real good.

Massive action and war strategy games can offer gamers a chance to promote real non-violence and peace, while participating in the virtual violent acts by shooting, killing, raiding and conquering their virtual-imaginary enemies. What if we had means to make the games create economic profits that are explicitly directed, by the gamers, to promote peace and nonviolence where they think well-guided money has the best chances to do good. A simple imaginary example makes the potential clear: a minor sum, perhaps 0.1 cents, could be paid each time by a gamer who gets shot in a combat or who kills 'an enemy'.

Figure 2. Navigating in CAVE

Millions of players could do amazing things with such accumulated funds. This activity could be based on impact models having their specific funding aims, pay systems, bets, fees, and profit sharing, even bonds for example. There is no need to further explain this huge potential for good. Gamers could invest in preferred targets, initiatives and activities that they think best promote good. Together, the members of the game community could follow, in real time, like in their games, how they help people and what they accomplish in Africa, Middle-East and other places suffering from violence, war, and poverty, for example. They could enjoy a game of real life aside of the virtual ones.

The discourse on the potential harmful effects of action games on young players is often painted with stereotypical thinking by worried academics and journalists. There still looms the belief that somehow the players are victims, helpless people, indiscriminate and even inhuman personalities who have no higher or spiritual interests, values and motivation in life. But what if they - exceptions excluded and those with real addictive problems in gaming - are just like you and me, except that they are skillful gamers and enjoy participating compelling dramas? We can respect their motivation and skills and think of their potential in other contexts as well.

A generation of boys, and more often also girls play computer games daily. The stereotype that gamers are different from the rest of us makes no sense but it has been repeatedly present in numerous articles dealing with the relationship between violent (real) behavior and violent (virtual) game playing. If games would cause violence, the world would be a battlefield: playing is now part of everyday life of hundreds of millions of young and middle age people all over the world. The numbers just don't match.

Games provide a chance to promote non-violence and peace, even and especially while playing war, combat and action games. This would offer a natural way for the gamers to express their genuine human side, to be *caring* human beings and to enjoy the specific privilege to do good, against all odds;

to give something back, give something to think about to the journalists, academics and other one-eyed analysts who are convinced about the negative effects of game playing and see the gamers as victims of technology and game industry. Why war games, why are they so popular? Well, that is something I don't understand.

5. Genomic games – gene play.

The amazing advances in behavioral genetics and personal genome analysis have taken most of us by surprise: you can purchase a profile of your personal DNA and even receive reports on your medicine-sensitivity and health-related risk factors – some of these with a price of a visit to a doctor and less. Serious problems and limitations remain in these tests and we must be careful with any simplifying interpretations, but they improve fast and more is to come.

An amazing parallel technological and sw progress has occurred in the design of computer games and in gene technology. No doubt, these apparently separate developments will meet and make possible something wonderful. The following is one possibility, combining game and gene technologies: Computer games where each game character has a specific (modifiable) personal genome, real, theoretical or imaginary! Such games would be both entertaining and educational and could have even research potential in e.g. simulating complex consequences of the genome pool in a population or a community, with variable environments and any other conditions. They could be used for massive scientific simulations to study the impact of certain human genome features on human behaviors in specific game worlds and plays, natural or imaginary.

Genomic games could shed light on the interaction of the individual genome with any of the virtual environments where they are played. And of course, time is a flexible variable in such games so that growth, evolution, mutation, gene expression, and any other developmental factors can be included, modeled and studied. Anything that gene and behavioral genetic scientists can imagine can be implemented as a computer game.

Games can be designed, where either the genome of the player or the genome of any of the characters, which the player controls has a personalized genetic, hereditary or environmental background. The genome can be as realistic as possible, based on current research data or it can be just theoretical or imaginary, even and especially grossly overemphasized. All other characters in the specific game world would have their specific backgrounds as well. Innovative operators could offer their services for integrating science and game data, perhaps even open platforms for this.

The implemented gene/environment/interaction variables affect the capabilities, tendencies, vulnerabilities and other personal characteristics of each gamer or a character. However, because games can be hugely massive, it is possible to follow the consequences of certain gene pools or types of genome in any large-scale development – and in any game world. Then of course, it becomes possible to follow individual behaviors and performance of such genetically profiled individuals, having a real, theoretical or imaginary genetic properties and history. We could test our own, real or exaggerated genes, for example in a game environment we see relevant.

Computer gamers could join open projects like the Personal Genome Project http://www.personalgenomes.org, and offer their personal genome data for the scientists to study and to follow them in any of their preferred or perhaps even specifically designed games. Below is an inspirational quotation from the Personal Genome Program (see the link above). Only "Games" are missing there.

"The answers to many fundamental questions about basic human biology, our experiences as individuals, and our history as a species will be illuminated by better access to large datasets that contain many human genomes tied to other forms of personal information, such as medical history and physical traits. Thus far, only a handful of individuals in the

world have been extensively sequenced and studied. The PGP aims to change this by giving individuals a platform to share their genome, health and trait data."

6. Multiple eyes

We have moving and inquisitive eyes. We go to watch a movie with friends and enjoy what we see *together*. That is why the modern 'smart' phone displays are such a pain to use, not only to the user but to her social environment as well. The experience of being attentively encapsulated, alone, socially excluded, onto one specific and immobile spatial location in the world, the display, is a most unnatural behavior and psychological situation to any healthy human being or animal. Socially a person behaving like that spans an atmosphere of exclusion and in meetings and get-togethers it is felt as offending.

We don't yet have multiple, intelligent display devices, like a deck of cards, not even now that AR and VR systems and even bendable displays have entered the markets. Mp manufactures don't offer us several inexpensive displays to be used in synchrony, asynchronously, spatially and temporally coordinated. Why not give a new opportunity to software developers to help us with distributed display apps? This would encourage to shared perception and socially guided activity. Of course, it would not remove bad device quality or bad use behaviors, but with the help of multiple displays coordinated spatially and temporally – and socially - we could become technically one step more social.

We can daily experience and observe the curious catatonia at home, work and public places when people attend to the small displays of their hand-held devices. Interestingly, the UI situation reminds of the early1990s, when user attention was captured by the impossible and stupid user controls, only that now the use factors causing this problem have changed. However, the pathological-psychological form and its outcomes are the same; it is time to introduce transformative changes in these UIs. The adoption of AR and VR headsets can support social behavior and atmosphere but only when their social design requirements are taken seriously. There is a psychological paradox: apparently, everyone enjoys the immersive process, although there is the uncomfortable sensation of being too much focused and closed to the world, out-of-the-world, not-allowed-to-move-eyes-around. It remains to be seen if their future designs take this human side seriously. If they don't they have a serious marketing problem.

Socially it is painful to see people forget their surroundings when staring at their mp devices; it is like observing an alcoholic or a game addict and it is especially sad to see it in parenting. We suffer from observing such behavior but there is not much we can, as individuals do about it; we respect the private pathology of human technology. The same psychological phenomenon occurred in meeting rooms, during old-style phone audio conferences, where everyone fixated at and talked – in a strange and cold tone – to the microphone(s) and to the loud speaker on the table.

Could multiple displays help? In some cases, yes but they have other benefits. We could have them as many as we like for each phone or even for network of phones. The price is not a hindrance, and neither is the near-field or even directed communication technology. Perhaps the first one to do it will again 'surprise' the market. Nobody will be carrying around large displays, even flexible ones, and holographic systems that create images in the air in front of us have some way to go. There is much to improve in the HMD's perceptual-experiential use qualities and many of their users suffer from a out-of-the–world experience and even sickness. See-through does not help when attention is misplaced or locked. The dominating designs have a social flaw.

Figure 3. Coordinated, multiple display set-up.

It is a spontaneous social joy to share objects of interest and sometimes it is necessary for survival. A practical, almost everyday example is a paper map that we look together with friends, declaring a destination, planning a trip, telling about a travel history, discussing global events, for example. Why not have a fixed digital map which can be socially shared in several small linked/connected and coordinated displays? Even better, what if the displays were like in AR, spatially connected so that simply by moving my device (and my friends could move theirs) I could select which part of the key map (defined in the main mp, for example), and even the information linked to that location, I want to observe? I could see what locations others are looking. And of course, this is not about maps only; any coordinated sharing of information and content in many layers could benefit from this. I believe these solutions had not been developed when I first wrote about this in 2011, but today they should be a natural part of social AR.

We could have different display types for use in the same device: one with electronic paper to be read under bright sunlight and another for 3D viewing, one for games. There is no real reason to keep the display in one device only.

Viewing photos in a group would be simple to arrange. We could do many things in parallel: for example, leave one job-device on the table to wait for the next act or give it to a colleague to work on it, while we focus on another task – via another device tuned to that task. This is what we have learned to do with magazines, books and real objects. Psychologically, it is not the same as having a collaboration platform or shared tasks which people can accomplish with any of the digital devices they have at their disposal. This is about having and using meaningful objects with a purpose.

One intelligent display could be reserved for each content entity, like mediating all its associated and specific information, messages, adverts, links, and other stuff relevant only to that content. Using that display, we would know what we get and what is the context, without arranging it with burdensome controls. The difference between magazines and digital devices would diminish and the devices could be integrated with group work platforms. The type and style of the display device would match the requirements of the task and its related information. We could store our displays in a book shelf or any relevant place, each with relevant state, content and specialization, for various purposes. The devices could be re-configured at any time. Price will not be a problem, but new design concepts and architectures are needed.

A specific content could be a person or persons with whom we want to be directly connected with. This would relieve us from continuous browsing, configuration, clicking, and scrolling mania to get to the target. There is no limit to the size and functionality of such visually distributed communities. Bookshelves would become intelligent, direct access storages of life.

It is no surprise to hear the familiar comments to this: "Stupid", "No benefits, we already have apps", "Too complex." "Expensive." "No real business." "We tried it already." "Interesting."

'Multiple Eyes' remains an inspiring concept. Add to this cheap, small, and synchronized cameras and only poor imagination can be a hindrance to a clever future with them.

7. Conquering the audio space

Visual technologies and culture surround us and has made us deaf to innovative audio. Simultaneously, the radio, music channels, and mobile talk have made us blind to other compelling possibilities of audio space.

Noisy visual information overloads us: displays get huge and cheap, 3D, VR and AR are here, flashing, moving, encapsulating, and talking displays surround us, ebooks are trying to conquer our everyday life, and more is to come. It is easy to predict what will happen: we must learn to neglect the visual streams, fight against the visual noise. The broadcasters living on the visual space will be frustrated observing the decreasing efficiency of their visual communications. They will intensify their efforts to reach us with powerful messaging as we can observe today.

Humans are extremely bad in attending to two or more simultaneous tasks requiring vision. Because we are visual creatures and our surrounds have been conquered by visuals, a simple solution is a better use of different sensory channels, which in today's communication practice means, first, expanding the available audio space and boosting its advances. Other senses, especially smell and touch come after that.

Familiar visual and audio §have overshadowed the possibility to use audio space for new forms of communication, shadowing, interaction, on-line face-to-face communication, audio-shopping, and audio-based browsing, audio awareness building – spontaneous talking to each other, whatever.

We could hear what we see. A shop or an object telling its story, a person talking to anyone who wants to hear about his or her life, car drivers telling where they are going, train saying when it is leaving. Practically any object or anyone of us - could have a *directional or targeted* audio transmitter that sends audio that people want to receive (and when) or build interaction. We would have audio connection with everything and everybody we can see and with those who can see us and are interested. There are numerous technological ways, including AI, to accomplish this. I do know that something like this is being developed now, but there is much to do, it's a matter of a major paradigm shift. Alexa, Siri, and their cousins could live everywhere.

Some might think this is just augmented reality as an application with the special AR/VR glasses, for example. Of course, it could be accomplished like this but it is easier without glasses, more fun because we are more efficient and accurate in just pointing at what interests us. We can use gestures, head and eye movements for what they are meant for in our attentive behavior. Eye movement (targeting an object) and a push button would have huge use potential in letting us express what and when we want to build an audio connection. There is no need (necessarily) to have a cumbersome AR system in front of our eyes: we always know the object of fixation and that knowledge we can use in a clever UI.

Audio space can be extended in work, education, business, and in just about any activity in our lives. Anyone interested in the information offered through well-arranged audio sources could then get access - with practically no more effort or disturbance than from listening to music - by simply pointing his device (or eyes) at the source and locking to it: an object, a shop window, a person, or whatever and then start reception or interaction. A shop might want to tell about their new products, campaigns or offerings or just about their own thinking about anything. An advert could tell more than is shown by the flashing visuals to the eager listener. Objects could talk to us. People could talk to each other more, tell their story. And it would not block our vision. But we would be in control – always. A directed podcast of global scale could be arranged in this way by linking it with any moment, tv, display or a movie screen. Sitting down on a park bench and observing the audio-tuned surround would amaze us and we could easily forward what we hear.

As a technology audio tools would be less disturbing than the visual ones that demand our full attention when looking at or reading something on a display or following a trailer or other ongoing story. Driving a car and following a live broadcast from a large display near the road is simply dangerous. We have learned how easy it is to listen to music when walking on the street, at work or engaging with other activities of life. Visual world alone is too demanding, but we could make the best out of it with the help of intelligent and human audio.

Some of these ideas, in various miniature forms have probably been around already for years but a mobile phone or other company will conquer the hidden audio space soon - perhaps starting a new field of technology and its related businesses. Internet of general audio does not exist

10 MANY FACES OF NETWORKING

1. Golden triangle and network behavior

Distributed software production and collaboration intensified near the turn of the millenium and introduced challenges for personal tools, spatial and temporal (synch/asynch) coordination and management. In 1999, working with a Jari Lehto and Pentti Marttiin we studied how to best analyze, organize and support complex distributed project work, especially in sw production. We started with an analysis of an innovative (based on object oriented sw) collaboration platform developed at Nokia, which was used simultaneously by hundreds of sw professionals at different global sites. The platform was designed to support intensive and dynamic sw project work and not only to serve as communication or project management medium. It had a rich set of structures, functions, document models, templates, work spaces, version management tools etc to help engineers in their personal work and collaboration. The analysis led us to serious considerations on what is meant by 'networking' in real work life.

A network connecting people and institutions is not a mesh of connections only, but a living multi-layered human-social-technological creature with its own characteristics, almost like a personality. We needed a sensitive model or framework for quantifying the critical activities and life within such a real, working network community. Golden Triangle was our inbuilt frame: Content = specific requirements and conditions of software production, Human-centered = helping specialists in their projects, at work and in taking care of their responsibilities, Psychologically grounded = several psychological dimensions, explicit or implicit, considered and made measurable if possible. At the time we did not call this 'GT'.

The reasons for the GT approach were the following. First, every network communication instance between parties has its own, specific content. 'Collaboration' is defined and constrained by the *content of the work;* objects with different contents generate different network life. For example, the material communicated can be of technical nature, sharing of important documents, observations, sw code versions, even rumors, or of any other kind of knowledge. Second, each communicating party lives under his or her own *situational constraints* which can be personal, social, cultural, temporal, or technical in nature. Whatever the platform, it should be sensitive to situational factors under which an individual and her communities work. Third, the platform must support personal work in a way that offers best possible resources and *tools for every individual to succeed* at work and in its context.

One aspect we did not include in our research framework was the ability to discard the selected collaboration platform and tools, as fast as possible, with minimum costs when adopting new and better ones. Today, this is becoming increasingly difficult and the underlying business reasons are evident.

Looking back now to the 90's, the most important aspects we underestimated were the personal meanings and deeper purposes of work, the life of the collaborating members, and the impact of all these on network activities. It was a serious neglect. We would be wiser now but the approach, as useful as it was for rational network analysis, was a reflection from the cognitive trend at the time, and it simply overlooked the depth and even fun of human psychology. Nevertheless, I'm ashamed to admit this neglect although there are still relevant insights in our approach which is why I believe it's worth explaining here.

We named our preliminary framework of communication in organizational settings as 4Q, having four major human/social components or quadrants each with several subcomponents. It was tested and studied over several years in different organizational settings and university course contexts – psychology of distributed collaboration. This led to the following dimensions of network collaboration, which we used as lenses to observe and analyze what happens in networked, distributed project work. A fifth dimension on human motivation and purpose would have been needed to complement it.

2.   A look at the networking individual

We adopted the perspective of an individual - as he or she sees the network and collaboration environment. 1. **Work with people**, that is, collaboration – not only work but other activities as well - occurring between people who are not necessarily members of a team or other formal organizational unit, like a project, where the individual works. In other words, they are individuals connected with each other, not necessarily participants in the same project but can share other professional or personal interests. Facebook and LinkedIn, for example are often used in the mode 'work with people' where people communicate on shared interests without working on a same problem or a project. Intranet platforms are forums of collaboration in firms and other organizations. There is much variation in this, but in general, these two example giants have a strong position in the 'work with people' – class although it has extended to numerous use contexts.

Knowledge management (KM) became a popular concept in 1990's, not least due to the works by Ikujiro Nonaka and Leif Edvinsson. As a general term KM deals with practically every sector of business, education, production and innovation, even religion. In our framework, this aspect of project work was represented by a dimension of its own. **2. Knowledge work** in the 4Q framework describes the person's network activities related to the creation, learning, sharing, adopting, using or maintaining any valuable knowledge with others in his/her project or community. The communicating parties can be people or even repositories and why not agents and robots as well, even though we did not include agents in the conceptual framework. There was a good reason to separate these two components in 4Q: remembering the Golden

Triangle, their content, the human activities involved and the psychological basis of communication related to each dimension are very different in the modes and dynamics of behavior they involve. Knowledge work is typically asynchronous in nature, although it has synchronous instances, something we could describe as 'knowledge-exchange spindles', but in general its time constraints are more flexible than in typical scheduled work.

Scheduling, synchrony and relevance of communication and interdependence of work contributions are a must in most project contexts but often they are not properly served by collaboration software systems. As project members, we are interdependent in what, when and how we do and can do things and how our work outcome is made available for those who need it in their own work and system processes. We denoted this as **3. Project work**. It is typically time-constrained and synchronized (temporally, socially, even spatially) activity within the distributed collaboration community, a firm, project or a program. Again, the Golden Triangle view sheds light on the core elements of this kind of network collaboration: *the content*, the constraints of *the individual and the community*, and the *psychological dynamics* of synchronous communication and interaction are rather specific to this dimension of distributed work, communication and collaboration. The negative consequences of a 'difficult-to-see passivity' or bad synchrony - like someone being always late, unpredictable, out of schedule, or even too early – are familiar in collaborative organizations.

Last, we included **4. Personal work** in the framework to emphasize the importance of the individual work and life context. Observing this from the Golden Triangle perspective points out the specific contents and the psychological nature of personal work and its environment, like the tasks assigned, tools available, and the situational characteristics with their specific requirements for successful performance. All these depend on the person, her role, competence and position in the collaborating community. As said, we should have extended this approach to the personal meanings and purposes and ways of caring about others, to the living and its dynamics in a way relevant to the person, his/her work and private life. The deeper, psychological nature of multi-dimensional communication is easy to underestimate and we were not free from this sin then. Today, it is a necessary requirement for any realistic analysis of network behavior.

Often the differences between 4Q factors are overlooked or taken as inherent peculiarities of network behavior, for example when 'networking' activities in Twitter, LinkedIn or Facebook are considered. New-generation groupwork and team tools like Teams and Slack try to improve this. Some of the 4Q features are considered in app design and can become crucial success elements. In our network reality, we live under the constraints of these four dimensions and more, our network behavior mode varying over time and changing, depending on the specific situational requirements. This dynamic aspect of network behavior is one of the least understood human and social behavioral phenomena today, although it's our everyday practice. Much work stress and negative interaction results from this, caused by uncertainties, asynchronous interrupts and network management overhead.

4Q made it easy to see some of the shortcomings in collaboration architectures and functions. Personal, relevant working and communication space capability, the added dynamical, content-orientated features I described above for Facebook and Google, for example, would have been and would still help people dynamically focus on the things relevant at work and life in general, every moment. We live a transitory, technologically and business-driven phase where content, focus and organic human living are constrained by the specific functions and business models of the giant operators and other app and service providers; it's a modern version of Babel. We and our communities are not offered integrated and seamless services that live with us, from moment to moment, from one situation to another, from content to content.

11 STRINGS AND NETWORKS – VERY HUMAN SPECULATIONS

1. Simultaneous, overlapping layers of network life

Advances in modern physics rest on the understanding of interactive and collective phenomena at all scales. No wonder then, that social scientists taking lessons from physics have started to look at computational social phenomena and modeling tools having their origins in physics. With the evolution of sensors, data collecting methods and IoT, masses of data are becoming available for social and psychological sciences. New computation methods are applied to study behaviors and interaction both in detail and in masses.

A novel form of science has been introduced with the ambitious name 'social physics' studying the topics ranging from cultural dynamics, evolution of languages, and to sentiment spread and team behaviors. See e.g. Moss de Oliveira, S., de Olivera, P.M.C., Stauffer, D., (1999) *Evolution, Money, War, and Computers: Non-traditional Applications of Computational Statistical Physics*, Teubner; Pentland, A. (2014) *Social Physics: How Good Ideas Spread* – The Lessons from a New Science, Penguin Press (2014); Schweitzer, F., (2018) Sociophysics. Physics Today, February 2018. See also the Citizen Mindscape project in Finland.

However, the multi-variable, multi-layer nature of all human and social interactions and communication has not led to a research and modeling paradigm that would be essentially based on the (true) observation that all human interactions, however simple they may occur on the surface, always take place at many levels of life – simultaneously, interacting. This observation led me to the following, somewhat speculative but serious analysis and ideas on how to think about networks in real-life human behavior and interaction.

This is indeed a speculative, but potential scheme for applying string theory as it is known from modern physics (http://en.wikipedia.org/wiki/String_theory) to modeling of what we traditionally call network behaviors. Originally, I considered this as an analogy only but after publishing our article "Behavioral Theory of the Networked Firm" and having read Alex Pentand's book "Social physics" it seemed possible that this approach is not at all as speculative as I had thought. There is a need to replace or supplement the commonly used concepts of links, nodes, connections, connection strengths, flow of information with something that better matches the realities of human behavior and life. To put it simply:

Nothing flows between people, but states of both change in multiple forms and scales and in dynamic interaction. No 'connection' between individuals or firms, for example, concerns only one property at a time, like ideas, information, persons, material, input features. Life, in its essence is not only a multi-layered phenomenon but an organic, ever interconnected and interdependent fabric. What we call links are not channels or connections, but forms of dynamic life. It is time to search for genuine representations and models of life and living in network contexts.

The string model is a potential candidate to cover these phenomena, but probably other candidates will appear when computational, even quantum computational techniques become available for this ambitious endeavor. A thought experiment has a place here.

2.   Traveling salesman with a mind

I met my friend Antti at Espoo railway station, some 20 kilometers from Helsinki, where he had arrived on a local train from Helsinki. I have taken the same trip several times, but he had his own amusing story to tell from this short, 30 min journey. Formally we both had commuted from A to B, or in a graph form, A->B, and its representation on a gps-based map would have looked the same for both of us, although our trips had been totally different. We met at a time I had started to imagine a new concept for 'injecting' content and meaning into classic network representations and eagerly explained the idea to my friend who immediately started thinking aloud about the differences between our personal journeys, A->B, our personal trip contents.

Over the years, we have traveled some of the same routes and our global journey maps could be easily compared in the form of a network description just like in the famous travelling salesman problem (for TS, cf. http://www.tsp.gatech.edu/ or try the game to learn about it http://www.tsp.gatech.edu/games/index.html). As a thought experiment, our eye movements during the journeys could have been recorded and find out the maps of our personal interests. Research shows, however, that people can stare at an object without seeing it, so it's not simple. How should we then denote the personal meanings associated with each trip and express them in a formal representation so that we could model the essence of our travels and compare their meaning and impact? In the end, that is what we would like to achieve. There is a hidden potential in this kind of a human approach for the network operators, but as far as I know, the opportunity has been overlooked.

Figure 1. Travelers have minds and souls.

Mathematicians solving the TS problem have not cared much for what might be going on in the travelling salesman's mind, except of course, that the TS might be eager to find the optimal route through all the sales points on the journey. Had they been interested in his genuine intentions, motivations or experiences, they had ended up with a different formalism to represent the complex but very human problem. I'd prefer to call this Traveling Salesman with a Mind (TSM) problem. I could have used even a better metaphor, like Traveling Pilgrim problem because its basic premise would be that the traveling person indeed has a mind and even a soul.

The TSM problem consists of the trip and its personal and environmental context data. But there is no generally accepted or standard way to inject such meaningful, personal data into a typical graphical representation. Map technologies do have related practices but their human content is still rather superficial. This is surprising - we do not travel just to transport our bodies from one place to another. We love specific forms of traveling, taking a rest and interrupting the trip, like when hiking on the mountains or sailing at sea and anchoring in the archipelago. Some trips simply do not take place at all. Psychologists have not heard this mathematical siren calling.

3.   Patterns of compassion.

Rehman Ilyas and his team of Indian and Pakistani university students created the Romancing The Border (RTB) concept and app where people across the Indian-Pakistan border could send their positive, compassionate greetings over the border by using short web videos. The developers believe that this contributes measurably to peace between the two nations in conflict. As an outcome of this, a 'network' of visible positive actions was generated and could be monitored. Another related concept was 'the acts of kindness' map for a Mexican city putting the locations of the good acts on a city map.

How should these behaviors in India/Pakistan and Mexico be formally represented? What is the real nature of these 'kindness acts' and their 'networks'? How are they connected with other matters of the world? Of course, we can count the good and bad deeds or the friendly gestures over the conflict boundaries, map them and derive various statistics, but is this enough to understand what goes on in these positive acts, what valuable human potential they carry and what other consequences they have? We should have access to that kind of data and realistic models to deal with it. It is a huge challenge for future human and social sciences, being transformed by fast technological advances. It's a problem concerning mankind.

More generally we can ask – and there is no doubt about it, that future politicians will be and are exited (in good and bad) about this - what can happen in the world, as an outcome of miniscule individual actions like in the RTB campaign, in the Mexican city and in other similar circumstances of positive behaviors? We should try to find out, follow and analyze that and design means and tools to see farther. New approaches and methods are required. We can set the goals of analysis at a new ambition level in modeling human and social behavior in the real world, on-line when possible. The importance of this has been seen in the form of fake and manipulative news.

The individual and the compassionate acts in RTB may appear separate and weak, even insignificant incidents, below any level of statistical power but why look at massive statistical truths only, when we can search for other impacts, like these single social acts and episodes? Sometimes the statistical view at the world prevents us from seeing significant single events and from imagining what could happen if we had thousands or millions of them. Statisticians have been late in jumping on the bandwagon of miniscule but significant human acts. Many of the analysis methodologies suffer from this and they have taught us that 'true phenomena' in the world are 'big' while in physics they are sometimes assumed to be the smallest of the small. History then reveals how the small acts have turned into big ones.

In business and epidemiology, the statistical view is a standard, but as Malcom Gladwell tells in his book *The Tipping Point* we should have eyes for weak but relevant single behaviors and events. For example, there is no single statistically true answer to the question: how many people are needed to take up a certain type of sports before it becomes a trend? Sometimes one person can change the course of development and – to use a physics metaphor – open a new dimension of life. Indeed, the concept of 'weak signals' is very weak indeed.

4. A string world

The term 'string' wakes up a skeptic in many a theoretical physicist. Despite that I've bravely taken the analogy from the string theory in modern physics: many see it as a real possibility in physics and some ignore it as a dream or confabulation having no trustworthy verification to support it.

The idea to apply string theory to the analysis of general networks owes to the charming *"Little Book of String Theory"* by Steven S. Gubser from Princeton. It is an introduction to string theory with a friendly approach for an amateur and includes lively examples that make it inspiring reading. I will use the 'string' concept rather loosely here without always referring to the peculiarities of the superstring or supersymmetric string theory.

I've had a long-time curiosity and passion for and even studied many forms of network since 1970s, e.g. artificial and realistic neural nets, collaboration and communication nets, knowledge nets, social nets, internet of things, the www and any possible variations I have imagined myself. Some experiences have not been without a related network pain; networking is very human activity, indeed.

Lifeless network representations. There is a lack of life in most of the network models and concepts I've seen. For example, when dealing with human relationship descriptions or with organizational sociograms they typically fail to express and preserve the essential human aspects of the mental: motivation, intentions, joy, excitement, beliefs, love, engagement, reluctance, prejudices, culture, and conflict, everything that makes us human and typically occur simultaneously or in parallel - always.

The little string book suggested to me a striking analogy between the problem of *gravitation vs. quantum mechanics* and that between the *real-world human behavior vs. network theory*. The analogy might appear as far-from-the-real-world, but I see it as a very practical one and indeed worth considering. Not unlike in modern physics we need to learn what are the human forces that create the major global phenomena in economics and social systems and which govern the life and mind of every individual. It is a problem covering more than social psychology, sociology or psychology together. The world of human and social sciences is often split in this problem, just like the physics of natural forces was split in dealing with gravitation and quantum forces.

The web videos in RTB with their peace-promoting content are not only expressions of peculiar, positive connections over a problematic border. They are symptoms of something more profound: the state of the local human ('quantum') world has changed and obtained a new state as an outcome of the minor-appearing RTB acts. Furthermore, something had made this change possible to occur. It may be material or immaterial in nature, we don't exactly know, but a grounding point was necessary. It is a small wonder that such a small event does have a specific impact, instead of being only noise or a random episode of life. The world is not the same after the apparently miniscule change, but how is it different? The forces that made these people across the border behave as they did, was not caused by noise.

Using the string analogy from String Theory: a significant 'string of life' as I call the relationship between two people in RTB sharing the video, has changed its state. This *string of life* with its specific state (and its base) is a material and real aspect of the connected world. By assigning a complex content to the string state this expression can be used as a functional description of a specific human behavior in the world. In this peculiar case the 'sender' and the 'receiver' who had peaceful motivations, introduced this change in the state of the world. Next we can ask what exactly is this 'state' and what are its consequences?

String theory suggests that the way our world exists in its connectivity can be described as a conglomeration of strings each with its own peculiar properties, having its own state of 'vibration'. Furthermore, in the available space (whatever is its dimensionality), not everything is possible and the limitations are set by the properties of the space and the strings. Now, each of the peaceful acts of RTB can be defined as 'vibes' that represent a specific form of good. To make this 'good' happen, the strings must have specific properties and be grounded in a peculiar base of life. In other words - following the superstring theory and again analogically - the strings must be attached somewhere at their 'both ends'.

The friends of physical string theory use the concept of a *brane* (a spatial structure having any number of dimensions, e.g a membrane or a cube etc.) for this purpose. Branes serve the need of the strings to be attached to something real (if I have understood it right). Branes (or bases) are relevant aspects of the string relationship in describing the string states, just like it is relevant to the sound quality and tone of an instrument how the string is attached to its body. Without a solid base, nothing sustainable can take place.

Vibrant string theory. The aim here is not to derive a direct 'strings of life' model or a theory as it is applied in modern physics. The simple motivation here is to prepare for functional, analog models to describe the dynamics and limitations of the content-rich, complex and interconnected world of behaviors. I try to find a way to express life in nets in a way that combines global (in analogy to the gravitational forces in physics) and local (quantum mechanical), multi-dimensional forces of life into one representational framework.

This might sound like a confabulating amateur talking but I believe - just like theoretical physicists think about their own science - that human social sciences need to realize the value of theoretical endeavor and to set the ambition level high. When the physicists intend to solve the problem of matter, space, and energy in the universe why should human and social scientists be less ambitious? The aim is to understand the actors, forces, and dynamics of the behavioral space on earth and why not, even outside it.

Shortly and generalizing a lot, the aim of the string theory in physics (there are numerous versions of it) is to, e.g.:

a) formulate the theoretical basis for new physical space+time+other-dimensional geometries, and

b) to offer a 'string interpretation' of the nature of the elementary particles and

c) to find a correspondence between string states and particle properties. In other words, string theory sees particle properties as aspects of string states.

String theory leads to a larger number than four world dimensions, which is a typical property of the human mind, too: the psychological dimensionalities of man are inherently multi-dimensional. For some reason, however, humanists have remained rather vague on how these multi-dimensional properties like intelligence and personality are holistically built on real psychic 'materials' like mental states, structures, contents, and related biological (all of them, not only the neural ones) processes. There is only scarce theoretically oriented research on how human and social behaviors are determined and constrained by all these spaces together. Personality and intelligence studies aside, so far I don't know of trials to estimate the true dimensionality of the psycho-social-cultural man and what kind of a 'mind and behavior universe' it spans. An interesting question is which of these dimensions have the best explanation value when we try to model and perhaps predict what happens in the world of human interaction.

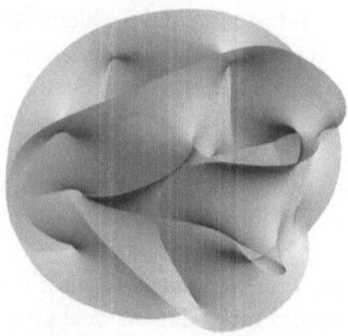

Figure 2. Imaging of superstring theory. Original source, permission/Creative Commons.
http://en.wikipedia.org/wiki/File:Calabi-Yau-alternate.png

Vibes, branes, strings and superstrings of life. Not unknown to hippies the 'vibes' – to be more precise, the state of a string – link the string to the content and meaning that it represents. It is a complex mathematical problem, how to formally (in this analogy) represent these states so that it would allow description of local, collective, and global aspects of behavior and to cover the multi-faceted, simultaneous, potential influences and interactions between human and social behavior and the environment – at any scale.

I will skip the number of string types that might be needed for this analogy exercise or how many of them would be required to cover relevant aspects of human connectivity. I'm also puzzled by the brane concept that refers to a space-time continuum that can have any number of dimensions. But following the analogy, I have interpreted the branes as a necessary, multi-dimensional base of the strings of life: without branes the strings would just float, in a haphazard manner, above or outside our reality with maximum entropy. In other words, the branes extend to all corners of life, as the very basic constituents – a (theoretical) ground - that make up any form of life, be it psychological, economical, or political or all of them together in nature.

It could be argued that the number of strings required for any reasonable representation of human behavior is just infinite. But if we limit the scope to relevant aspects of behavior we can assume it is not so and by looking at simple instances, like real-like toy problems, the string concept could help us think about ways to insert content into nets, to give them multi-dimensional life.

In the following I've imagined two practical cases to explain the logic of the 'string-analogy approach'. First, as an example of far-field human and social connections, we have seen the global political analyses which talk about the divergence of world economy and about the emergence of the new 'multi-polar world.

A *thought experiment. Far field human forces: Multi-polar or string world?* How can we represent the dynamics of far-field or 'multi-polar' phenomena (e.g. impacts, interactions, flow of material and immaterial objects, and even human values) in economics, trade and policies that are characterized by varying activities in different parts of the globe, but happening at the same time and in variable synchronies? Surely the multi-polarity is a field-like phenomenon taking place in a suitable space.

However, there are no general representational formalisms to cover all relevant aspects of these multiple, simultaneous and complex relationships. For example, the concept of 'multi-polarity' can be used in a global and very general sense to refer to strong economically dominating nodes with a new connectivity (like China, India, Brazil) that is different from its earlier state (USA, Soviet, Europe). Numerous studies look at these global phenomena from the perspective of economics, innovations, trade, military, and policies, for example. They all happen at the same time and are essentially interdependent phenomena and hence, using the string approach we can imagine a simultaneously occurring, dynamic 'multi-polarity' where the states of hypothetical strings represent all possible and relevant variables and dependencies between these global systems.

Of course, this is a case of extremely complex, large and even diffuse scale of phenomena and as such useful only as a thought experiment, for now. However, if we want to build a valid representation of a realistic 'networked system' or world, we can try to recognize the relevant 'string systems' that cover the significant relationship information between the nodes. Is there any sense in this and if so, what would be the base of life to which these strings can be attached?

When we replace the 'multi-polarity' view - by recognizing and modeling relevant strings in economy-related behaviors, acts, and relationships – with a string view we can ask: do we gain something real by this change of representation? I believe we could gain, for example, by getting rid of blind statistical models that overlook 'small acts'. It is possible to obtain a dynamic model of the network behavior, by introducing complex contents and phenomena by the string model, by introducing space considerations, and by preserving all qualitatively relevant data in the representation.

Another thought experiment. Near-field human forces: Moments of human interaction. Near-field human interaction happens all the time. An everyday example is customer behavior interaction in service situations. What is 'string life' like in such a simple case of interaction and exchange between the customer and the sales person? Customer experience measurements are conducted daily, but typically, they suffer from the lack of realistic representation of the adaptive, interaction phenomena between the individuals - 'the customer' and 'the service person'. What if we could model this behavior by defining the relevant strings connecting the customer and the sales person, so that it formally describes all the relevant aspects of their relationship and most of the occurring behavioral and mental phenomena at the exact moment of interaction?

One might argue that we already have measurement scales, profiles, and inventories to measure all that. Such measures do reveal aspects of customer experiences and correlations between different outcome measures, but they are isolated and do not connect the customer and the sales person so that all their dynamic, subjective worlds and contexts would be included. There is no formal methodology to do that and often various control variables are used to cover (and typically exclude) the social, economic and other relevant 'background' factors. Emotions are included in the analysis now that cognitive factors have proved insufficient. Often, after acquiring such standard knowledge of this interaction, special education and programs are needed to interpret the data and make use of it in real life. In the string approach, these multiple, perhaps minor appearing aspects of human life are not 'background' factors but an essential part of dynamic human behavior. The *strings of life* can be used to cover the most significant aspects (meanings) of such relationships.

Almost without exception, when we talk about a 'connection' between some units, like the cities A and B in the previous travel example, or between persons over conflict boundaries, what is meant is the following. First, it is assumed that it is possible to know what is irrelevant information, like the clothing my friend was wearing when traveling, or the personal motivations for a newly appointed traveling salesman. Second, the economy principle favors simple explanations and theories of behavior, and third, it is possible to know in advance and choose which phenomena are selected for independent observations. However, the world always surprises the scientists and analysts entertaining simplistic views. Clothing can make a significant difference when traveling.

Some years ago, Rob Cross (http://www.robcross.org) gave a talk at Stanford where he described his studies on the true connectivity (sociogram data) in companies with a certain type of organizational chart. The researchers hoped that by knowing the true network among the workers they could better understand how innovations, for example, emerge and become socially created, in the social reality of a company. In general, the object of interest in such nets can be almost anything from the flow of money and politics to the flow of knowledge and sharing it, to entertainment and communication. But there is no general way to implement meaning and content into these network descriptions although they are a good start. Following the string analogy, we can now ask how to cover the most relevant aspects of the human beings and their behaviors in an organization.

It does matter how you talk and which media channel you use. The persons interacting in organizations studied by Cross could use any form of communication means and face to face meetings to have impact on each other and the organization. Likewise, in the across the border communication of the RTB case the two participants could have had only a friendly telephone chat. However, each form of communication would be an expression of a different string of life with its own limited properties and impact space. In other words, it does matter how the communication is accomplished, it is not a matter of information sharing or transmission only. "Media is the message" gets a fresh meaning in this example. In a general sense, there is a connecting 'ether' in the form of possible strings of life between all people, but its potential remains invisible or at least dormant unless the string states are changed like it happens when people talk to each other f-f or use a specific communication channel.

The communicating parties in the customer service example did not create the relevant strings. Instead, they set their *states* from one of ignorance or passive rest to the expression of willing interaction and communication, for example. More importantly, each string is not about a connection, but about the type of connection (positive engagement, for example) between the interacting people. When interacting in a certain way, they have changed the state of the (pre-existing but dormant) strings into what has then made the essence of their relationship visible as impact on the rest of the world, first only locally, but then, due to social interaction or with the help of technology like Facebook, each of these would have a major or minor impact globally.

People do not live in isolation and their impact on the world and other people are ever present, directly and indirectly.

The state changes between any two people mean that the world state has permanently changed and cannot be recovered, even though from mass statistical perspective the effect might look like miniscule or even unchanged. Within the networks of these specific people this can be a significant event. Its value can be understood if we imagine millions of such string state changes. In the case or RTB, for example, the politicians in both countries would be seriously asking "What does that mean? What will follow from it?" Nobody can accurately explain the emergence of all human and other activities that follow the RTB and similar multi-dimensional events, but such effects do exist and we must try to model this.

5. Injecting life into networks.

Don Tapscott (e.g. Crowdsourcing to Kony 2012: Macrowikinomics: New Solutions for a Connected Planet) has a charming way to express, by drawing, the explosion of content in the connected and networked world. The pivotal question remains, how could we best follow what happens on a large or a small scale in this mass of media, technologies, actors, and the content shared. To do that we need formal tools to help us. Had I the skills of Don Tapscott I would try to draw this same story as a string world – and perhaps learn all the problems on the way.

Future network models need to comply with the increasing demands of content production, knowledge sharing, and meaning management. Novel pathologies have emerged as well, in the form of text and image manipulation and fake news. Fake news for example, are so strong simply because of the weak network representation of the included data; an effective, multiple string representation could better show what is false or manipulated, just like block chain systems would do. We need theories that differ from the classical network analysis that is an idealized – and seriously biased - representation of reality.

Content in the brain. Take a popular example: the brain is typically described as an information processing network consisting of interconnected 'neurons'. Forgetting the mysteries of brain chemistry and the glial cell structures and "the other brain" (see Scientific American for the story) it is generally assumed that the inner and external world has a well-defined representation in these networks. There is a serious theoretical problem in this view: how is the natural (inner or outer) world represented in our brains and how should that be expressed by mathematical brain models? What material is carried by these representations? Even the concept of representation is problematic. Represented of what, by what, and for whom? How can we understand connected brains or millions of them with all their multi-dimensional, simultaneous interactions within each brain?

Even the most impressive achievements using tensor analysis to look inside the brain and reveal its connectivity lack the multi-dimensional content realism. Subjective reality and the related inner personal space remain hidden and it is not even known, what kind of a mental space, substrate, and phenomena hide beyond these beautiful network images. True, with brain damage studies and advanced imaging methods we can observe the activities and the problems in different brain centers during certain behaviors, see individual cell activities by direct recordings with new fluorescent methods, and observe the scary pathologies resulting from minimal local brain lesions. Clinically these methods are life-saving and extremely useful. The multi-dimensional, psychological-cultural contents of the brain system remain, however, obscure.

When is a network representation realistic? Garbage in, garbage out is the alarming truth for the most ingenious network analysis tools and algorithms. If the feature representations of the world fail - as used in these networks or in the Deep Learning models - so will also the models of the brain, world, and behavior fail. Of course, the same problem concerns the string approach. However, in the idealized and, so far, imaginative string model the aim is to represent the simultaneously occurring, qualitatively different relationships between the actor and her environment and between the actor and other actors as string states. The gain from this is the potential relevance of actor data at the source, that is, where interaction phenomena occur.

In the brain example, we could suggest alternative ways to represent the world: as a bottom-up (from sensory pathways to the many cortical projection areas), top-down (from higher brain centers towards lower neuron layers and up to the sensory pathways), or by an internally controlled mix and even a ubiquitous model of these. But there is no exact way to represent (and know if it is wise to use a structural representation at all) the external world with a relevant complexity. Standard models assume that this is a problem of emergence or that we just need to use specialized and rich network models and analysis for each purpose.

What is real in a network? Networks are not only used in neurophysiology but as descriptions of all sectors of human, biological, and social life where theoretical and computational problems are similar and require an analysis of distributed activities. Surprisingly little attention has been given to the 'reality check' of the network models and tools. The reason is simple, the computational, technical and even economic benefits of network models are huge already.

The first influential network applications date back to the late 19th century railway and road systems, and occurred later in logistics, especially in industry and during the times of war, and finally in telecommunication. Psychologists like Jacob Moreno and Kurt Lewin, in 1930s were behind the idea of social network analysis, but mathematicians, especially Euler, had formulated topology problems already in 1730's. The neural network models of learning and the brain, by D.O. Hebb, in 1949, for example, were far from human empiria.

Network representations have now extended to numerous fields. As an example, think about a typical machine learning network: the definition of its nodes and the connection strengths or weights between the units are usually derived by learning and from some well-defined empirical, statistical or other quantitative measures. The phenomenon of 'connection' is modeled by signals and the strength factor (transmittance) of each connection between the units. In the artificial, man-made world, like between computers, electronic components, and media channels there are indeed phenomena that show relatively nice network behavior. Because of that, the economic success stories by Google and Facebook rely on mass statistics, pattern recognition, machine learning, follow-ups, mappings, and continuous improvement in the way knowledge of individual behavior is obtained, used and managed. There is an inviting lure that the current success of these methods suggests that one day, probably very soon, they can be used to model all human mental and physical behaviors and other human phenomena.

Take a simple social psychological network example of two actors, X and Y. The impact of person X on person Y is sometimes expressed by counting the frequency of contacts X initiates with Y, using a suitable scaling in the whole data set. Hence, locally, at the person-to-person connection level the contacting impact can be estimated by simply counting the frequencies X->Y. But of course, a contact does not take place in a vacuum and has always dynamics that concerns the source, channel, content, situation and a human or material ground. More is needed to model X->Y and the question is, how should it be done? We can consider social networks from the 'string perspective' and try to judge if it could lead to ways of importing real-world source data, with meaningful content, and to include real human behavior phenomena in the computational systems that we now call 'networks'.

What are strings and nets made of? Let's push aside the idea of a classic, real-life 'network', the system with connected units and replace it with a string-based theoretical formulation consisting of functional strings that span over complex entities (like between people, businesses, teams, brain cells or across platforms) and having the ability to maintain tangible phenomena by assuming the occurrence of certain possible states of the relevant strings and their sets. Furthermore, we can assume that the strings are attached to bases (branes) that sustain their life. Branes form the layer or ground that supports string life and branes and strings together maintain string states. In this representation, content is a natural part of the string system. It is 'injected' into the system as a state of vibration of a string. The concept of vibration remains here an open theoretical construct.

The validity of a network representation can be checked by the mapping of the real-world state and behavior on the corresponding network model performance and vice versa. Using a string representation, we can view the state of the whole behaving system by looking at the string states and the branes. Emergence considerations are often included where powerful performance like generalization and associations can be born from very basic mathematical network properties and the same is true with the string approach. However, the farther we go in trying to model and understand real world or a human being the stronger become the demands for a realistic representation of the simultaneously present actions, actors and objects (behaviors, individuals, contexts ...) and the higher costs for not having a relevant representation at the source of the data. So, even here hides the risk of misrepresenting reality.

Ashby's excellent analysis of isomorphic machines demonstrates this problem well: we can build two systems with identical input/output functions, while their material basis can be totally different: one machine can be electronic and the other one mechanical but their transfer functions can be made identical by suitable selection of their materials and component parameters. (See Ashby: Introduction to Cybernetics, p 94). In this sense, the problem of realism is analogous to the problem between classical Newtonian physics and quantum mechanics. When we aim deeper in trying to understanding reality there is the risk that the overly idealized network representations prevent us from modeling it. One way to avoid the Ashby trap is, from the start, to inject content and meaning data early into the representation which then serves as an early hindrance to misrepresentations. The string approach rests on this insight.

The 'string exercise' here is indeed pure speculation and general; it leaves many questions open, but I believe it makes a point. The analogy suggests a possibility – the way it gets rid of the standard way of representing particles in physics – to do the same with the traditional representation of network nodes, and their connecting links. Accordingly, we can figure out representations that pay respect to complex, underlying, multi-dimensional phenomena of human life.

With the maturation of network computations, pattern recognition, and sensor apps there will be an overload of 'dumb' information they produce, while at the same time MyData and similar movements are getting stronger in aiming at protecting the individual from the misuse or unconditional use of their data. Future networks need to deal with this: to design organized and analytical ways to collect valuable information about human behaviors (internal and external) while providing data protection to every individual. I believe that it is possible to avoid both the data crowding problem and the security challenge by improving the validity of the representations of reality and the quality of source data in the computations – even without identifying the individuals as sources of big data.

6.   Monkey mind networks and a quick look at content.

The concept of human network has quickly gained the position as every-man's theory but it is not 'holy' by any means - it has a rather weak physical grounding. Culturally, it is a practical concept that probably originates from the times when people became aware of the importance of family and tribe relationships: even monkey colonies have their hierarchic and jungle-functional 'networks' although monkeys hardly consider their herd structures as 'networks'; at every moment of life, they must entertain suitable concepts relevant to their minds and situations and the wild life. In the eyes of an external observer they may well appear to have 'networks'. There is no general formal way to represent these meaningful monkey relationships and typically monkey behavior is considered as a collection of many facets of life, which do not fit into the same representation.

Nevertheless, a valid formal representation of the relationship between individual monkeys should allow description of monkey perceptions, actions, their collaboration, caretaking, roles, interaction and even survival in a gang fight. In other words, 'monkey network' concepts should carry relevant content knowledge and meanings in every situation of their life. We have learned a lot from monkey and especially gorilla life, but it is fair to say that so far, we have no idea what exactly is this knowledge and how it resides in their brains and relationships.

So far, there is no brain theory that would, at neuron-level detail, explain the significant aspects of our normal everyday behavior, like having a lunch, riding a bike, making love, following and enjoying a theatre play. Neurologists know the roles of various sensory and motor pathways and brain areas, and some have even studied the brain dynamics related to reading Jane Austen novels but that is about it. The resolution in these studies is far-far from a single neuron or distributed neuron function and there is a strong assumption that during their actions neurons remain invariant with only parameter changes. Honest neuroscience is slow on these problems and will in a very near future face the need to re-think the representations of natural and dynamic phenomena.

Impressive network work. Lazlo Barabasi (http://www.barabasi.com/) has published beautiful work on mathematical network analysis introducing ways to analyze e.g. network structure, strength, stability, growth, adaptation and 'gravitation' between the nodes. While these mathematical methods help to classify network types, to understand – in human/social context - how networks evolve, and gain specific properties like connectivity, strength, and competitive fitness, they still do not explain *why* (from content, motivation, intent, meaning –perspective) this happens and what underlies the behavior of the nodes and links; what supports their life, what is their exact nature and what is missing from them. There is no general theoretical framework to describe how content and context are related to each net considered.

Twittering strings. Twitter messages do carry content information and their maps have become attractive social information sources because they indeed follow the spread of real and relevant communication and influences in various domains from politics, to sports and activism, even in real time. In other words, they come close to communicating contexts and situations. To know more about what is going on in the life they represent, content information, like the name of the commenting or commented political candidate or other names, key words, locations, and other relevant data are attached to the net descriptions. But even then, the life events don't have a place in the maps and must be inferred somehow from the map data. However, twitter maps do seem like the closest candidates for string theoretical modeling but as far as I know there is no general theory that combines the content, processes and data representations, and the network properties in one, simultaneously functioning representation.

String view - a simple human example. We can return to the Romancing The Borders web videos case and apply the following scheme:

Let's assume that there are dormant strings (links) available to actors I_n (from India) P_m (from Pakistan) to be activated, that is, to tune the specific state of each string – something that I_n and P_m have not done before. These strings are attached to their branes, that is, to an imaginary, but solid base (psychological, economical, physical) that makes string vibrations possible and stable. Positive action between two people is nothing new, it has been exercised and practiced over the history of mankind, but in this specific case it has a peculiar cultural nature, human background, and complex consequences: it is grounded somewhere in material and spirit. We can even assume that a specific class of strings, each with a set of possible states represents this kind of behavior. When either of the actors prepares a friendly web-video, nothing (not much at least) has yet happened, but when the video is sent and made available over the border to receive it, the states of the strings in the specific set between I_n and P_m change. They are now in the state of a 'shared friendly connection'. A mathematical representation for this state is needed but I will not try to do it here.

There are numerous ways to accomplish this friendly connection in the real world and one could simply argue that this kind of an approach requires an infinite number of strings and states and that there is no sense in it. But if we are interested in this specific form of engagement the theoretical number of strings and their states needed can be assumed limited and have a magnitude reflecting the finite number of represented behavior classes, which in this case are the positive engagement behaviors. It is not impossible to start listing the aspects of personal behavior that might be relevant here, but my wild guess is there are less than one hundred significant ones of them in this case and context, each simultaneously active but with different impacts. This is a lot more than would be in a typical network representations showing a 'connection' and 'interaction' between the two individuals.

Why this example? First, the state of each string of life represents some specific aspect of the human world. A set of strings covers complex entities. A new state in a string or string set has impact or is dependent on other strings (world states, activities, perceptions or acts). These changes can be miniscule or large but they are part of the system, not something that should be discarded as noise or background factors. This is not to make the representation complicated but to respect the essence of life. We need a way to represent such consequences and a system to formalize them.

Let's further imagine we have a very large mass of individuals where such string state changes occur, in other words, a large number of 'friendly' connections between the individuals I_n (from India) and P_m (from Pakistan). The string states within this pool of people have a 'mass and energy', a form of 'kindness energy' that was not activated (although potential to it existed in people's minds) before the connections were made. Their personal, potential kindness energies drive the use of web videos and is expressed as specific string state changes between the individuals (or communities) originating it. However, personal kindness energies could and would drive other activity/behavior forms (strings) as well if the space where they take place allows and requires it. No state of the world or behavior occurs in isolation.

The other side of the coin is that the states of all the strings can be imagined to cover all behaviors that we as humans are capable of. There are limitations as well since not any kind of behavior is possible. Hence, the strings – if we can define them – are bound to the realities of life and can take place supported by the available branes.

We can try to rely on traditional psychological theories and models to describe what happens between the two persons interacting in India and Pakistan. We can even include part of such theories in the string considerations but there is no doubt that separate use of cognitive, emotional, social and cultural approaches in human psychology, perhaps even political psychology, would only complicate the analysis and make it fragmented. This is where future theoretical psychology, like theoretical physics will have its integrative place.

7. Some personal remarks on networks.

The roll-out of network theory during the last 40 years or so was driven by e.g. network devices, models and architectures, but the strongest forces came from social applications. The evolution of www and mobile communication rested on this human and social power, but we can imagine an alternative development: what if the networks had remained solely for machine and automated industrial systems to communicate with each other, and not with humans. Had this been the case then the network theory, net apps and their UIs had become quite different. Indeed, it is possible to imagine a totally different chain of actions, even today when 'the net' is something that is taken as a ground truth – which it is not. It has become a dominating paradigm.

I was lucky to closely, as one of the founding members of the Pattern Recognition Society of Finland, to follow this development, due to the pioneering work of prof. Teuvo Kohonen first worked with diode networks and then with the models of associative memory in the early 1970s which later led to self-organizing maps (SOM) and other truly innovative distributed learning concepts. They proved and demonstrated – and are still doing it - the amazing power of network mathematics.

However, even they are constrained by the computational model that maps tangible reality on artificial networks. I believe that most network scientists applying SOM and other learning networks to real-life, even neurophysiological and language-related problems, have become painstakingly aware of the interpretation problem when they analyze the learned maps and input-output functions, trying to figure out what they tell about reality. It comes close to the famous Munchausen problem, since the input patterns are defined by the person observing the SOM outcomes, trying to interpret them. In purely technological contexts this may not be a problem, but in case of human behavior, brain, and consciousness it is a major puzzle.

As an educational example, the road maps of New York and Moscow both represent their own realities but something else is needed if the aim is to understand life in New York and in Moscow: the contents, contexts, and meanings. A popular technological question today is what else do we need besides the road maps for uncovering the life of these magnificent cities. An implicit answer – considering what is happening in the field – is that we need more content, actors, and location specific network models and integration between them. An alternative solution can be imagined: less networks but more and richer content in them, in other words, something along the idea and concepts offered by the string theory, for example.

The problem with the network approach reminds of the Heisenberg's uncertainty principle: true understanding of real world requires high-level concepts but computational economy and accuracy demand focused measurements. The string approach could be one way to at least move towards higher-level representations without losing the computational potential.

Neural Darwinism and related theories, which have occurred during recent decades, suggest that neurons do not communicate, humans do it, neurons just 'try' to stay alive by acting and adapting biologically in their bio-environment, in a reasonable way. Their signaling activity is a sign of this pursuit for survival – their life is not information processing, it is cell life, the life of cell communities, or part of the states of complex biological control systems. It is beneficial to build a theory that describes that life. Communication or pattern recognition theories alone do not suffice; content, context, and meaning must find their rightful places in these models.

In summary, the evolution of current networks and the underlying thinking have their origins in topological problem formulation in mathematics, the cultural basis of social network concepts, and the apparent (and illusory) similarity between artificial (e.g. McCoullgh & Pitts -neuron) and natural neurons (Ramon y Cajal). Later then learning, pattern recognition, and general mathematical properties of artificial neural nets have boosted the development. The next steps after e.g. 'deep learning', 're-inforcement learning', and 'generative adversarial networks' models are still an open question. A general theory of networks of the brain, and of an economical system for that matter, must be grounded in a general theory of life, not in a theory of communication. This is true for any other networks that aim at describing living, human, and/or social systems.

8. The scale of the global brain network – a reality check

Astronomers have repeatedly increased the estimation of the number of stars in the known universe (see e.g. P. van Dokkum & C. Conroy. A substantial population of low-mass stars in luminous elliptical galaxies. Nature, 2010). In this study it was of the order of *3 x 100,000,000,000,000,000,000,000,000*, or to put it into a readable form, 3×10^{23}. While this long line of zeros would not surprise us even if there were 10 zeros more in these numbers beating our understanding, one of the authors had noticed an interesting coincidence (cf. Huffpost Green): a simple calculation by Conroy suggested that the rough number of cells in the human bodies on earth is also of the order of 10^{23}, in other words, the total number of cells in all human bodies together on earth matches the number of stars in the universe. This reminds of the scale of the scientific challenges facing us in studying the biology of life and especially it gives something for brain scientists to think if they happen to believe that we have come close to solving the problem of the human brain and consciousness. There is another inspiring message in these numbers: the neural connectivity of mankind. A simple calculation reveals amazing human potential.

The human brain has roughly 10^{11} neurons and each of them has, on average, thousands of synaptic links to other neurons. It is highly likely that the estimated number of these connections will increase when more is known about the combined hormonal, chemical and electric nature of cell communication. Nevertheless, it is not a monumental mistake to assume that the number of synapses per neuron is of the order of 10000 or 10^4. If we take the human population on earth as 10^{10} we get the astonishing total number of neuron connections (synapses) on earth, in all human brains together: it is of the order of $10^{11+4+10} = 10^{25} = 10\ 000\ 000\ 000\ 000\ 000\ 000\ 000\ 000$. This exhausting number tells that the human neural connections are significantly more abundant than the estimated number of stars in the universe. Why should this matter?

Global synaptic connection mass as a theoretical upper limit for human behavioral, mental and cultural potential? We can rely on the popular hypothesis that learning takes places via and in the neural synapses; they form the neural structures, mechanism and information architecture through which change and learning in life can take place. The huge number of 10^{25} connections in the brains of mankind invites us to consider this (loosely theoretically) connected neuron population in all the human brains as *the potential network that the human global society and all its forms have as a resource for developing now and in the future.*

Figure 3. An entrance sign at Stanford.

While a single brain with its 10^{15} connections has some limitations, the total brain pool has an amazing potential – if it can be used. One cannot avoid thinking that this simple 'neuro-cultural computation' provides an immense call to think theoretically, how much potential we have as a human species and community. In this sense the problem is analogous to the estimation of the number of stars in the known universe.

There is another, a wild one perhaps, but a delicious analogy: stars connect with each other via gravitation and radiation. As a thought experiment, we can consider the gravitational forces in the stellar systems as an analog to the synaptic connections between neurons and between different brains. Gravitation regulates the dynamic and mechanic relationships between the stars, galaxies and other masses and this determines their ways of interacting with electromagnetic radiation. Not quite similarly, but interesting enough, in the same sense there are only a few material forms of communication between different brains: perception of signals (or any reaction to them) is necessary and it typically happens via synaptic activities (other possibilities exist and complement this); the synapses in our brains are used and altered every time we are affected by direct or indirect perceptions generated by actions of other human beings and by life on earth in general.

In this speculative sense, our environment and other people act on us just like gravitation acts on any stellar systems. But neither of these mechanisms is scientifically understood: how and by which exact mechanism does gravitation affect distant objects and how the synapses of our brains are changed via external events by direct and indirect communication. All we can right now do in science is to observe and somewhat also predict the constellations of the stars and the changes in our brains (our behaviors) but the true underlying mechanisms remain hidden.

Togetherness via synapses. A sceptic may claim that our brains are not physically connected and that information does not flow directly from a neuron of one brain to a neuron of another brain and that pooling the brain networks together in the calculations as I have done here makes no sense.

Our brains are continuously connected in numerous indirect ways, not least due to the global communication technology: we transform our environment for others to see, feel, experience and live in and we communicate, create and shape cultures around us and globally. An especially effective way to have an impact on others is by changing the environment.

We can think that the huge human synaptic connection mass of all human brains together is the only (presently known) upper limit for the development of human culture.

This imaginary potential gives hope: it is difficult to see any limitation to our cultural and human development due to this immense information theoretical limit. On the other hand, this makes one wonder, what is the nature of this inter-brain networking? How are we connected with each other's brains?

We can look at this from constraining perspectives: human information processing, human physiology and anatomy in general, development and evolution, food and drugs, environmental changes, even our dreams, and any other factors that continuously alter our brains – and use any speculative model like the string analogy to understand this huge entity. Nothing in the human mental life on earth happens without the presence of these synaptic forces of change and we cannot achieve more than this potential allows even though the context – nature – makes all the difference. In this sense, it is an inspiring scientific challenge to make these calculations and listen to their story to human cultural potential, in good and bad.

These and similar computational considerations can form a basis for looking at the information theoretical constraints that our networked brains provide to the civilization and human beings on earth. Then of course, it is possible and even probable that the theory of synapses collapses and the computed limits will change, just as it is continuously happening in astronomy, but the limits will probably be pushed farther.

The photo above is from Stanford, I thank Sayed Shariq for a peculiar synaptic energy.

12 BEHAVIOR DATA IN THE NET

1. Internet of behaviors

What if we could know exactly when thousands or even millions of people on earth are doing the same thing or engaged with the same plan, content, intention or a wish - at a certain moment of time? What, if we could have this knowledge without knowing who they are or where they are, but we could build an interactive, psychological and behavioral connection with them? That was the trigger to my idea on the Internet of Behaviors (IoB), about a decade ago. Excited, with an engineering colleague of mine we tried to get funding from relevant Finnish firms and funding organizations to promote and pilot the concept, but with no luck or even interest. They did not "understand what it could mean", so here is the explanation.

We don't know why people behave in certain ways and show certain behavior and thought patterns. Even with the best of AI and ML it is difficult, often impossible to guess this. Take an artist, driving to her studio, admiring the landscape, getting ideas and inspiration on what she sees. Getting to the studio, the impact has not left her, but it stimulates and motivates her work and life; it is her private, emerging, dynamic space, difficult for others to access but easy as a child's play for her. For an outsider, it is sometimes possible to get a glimpse of this intimate personal world by letting the person express the subtle psychological elements in it. It is not enough to know the observable behavior or the identity of a person. If we want to understand her mind, we must listen to her. AI can help but at best it makes artificially educated guesses; it is helpless in front of these private human mental states.

In everyday life, to say nothing about politics and the use of management power, we spontaneously build *situationally relevant contacts* with people. Big data and AI tools are getting better in doing the same, and predict something of it, but typically they touch only the surface. Of course, even that can be enough to make masses of money and indeed help us frequently, but it does not mean understanding people.

Living with modern communication practices we suffer from a relevance-mismatch syndrome. Very few would argue that future businesses and governmental services can survive without having ever better knowledge of human situations and behaviors, internal and external alike, especially in future work environments, which are becoming increasingly intelligent and abstract in nature. Relevance of communication is crucial.

A flow of tools, methods of analysis, statistical frameworks and mappings of everyday behaviors are used to reach the human soul and to get in touch with the acute meanings and contexts of individual life – and to manipulate it. However, personal (changing) motivations, their individual character, and multi-dimensionality of thinking and feeling, the personal intentions of individuals remain mostly unknown universes. Computationally, it is not possible (yet) to detect the drivers of individual, mental acts and their personal meanings even though we, as persons, can easily provide some of this information, if allowed to do it in a wise and compelling way.

A good definition of Big Data is that it *overpowers any available computing systems*. Curious enough, it has happed almost without notice that the amount and diversity of personal and human behavior data seems to increase faster than any other data in the net. An educated guess is that data about individuals and their relationships increases exponentially and the question arises, can something be done to alleviate this computational crowding? Relevance of data and situational intelligence are becoming more valuable than 'new oil or gold'.

There is a paradigmatic 'search, follow & thumb' hindrance to this new development: the underlying assumption that relevant behavior patterns are simple enough to model, and that to get access to their meanings, clever data processing schemes or objective (physiological recordings) are sufficient. Many seem to think that it is expensive and cumbersome to collect data directly from individuals, the way we have learned to communicate with each other. This is far from truth: why else would we talk to each other, read what we write to each other, use simple gestures in life? We could do more with human technology that enhances, instead of dwarfing our human communication.

In Finland, Dr. Timo Salmisaari has constructed an extensive architectural-functional description, consisting of dozens of social and health care service processes, needs and overall situations where citizen engagement would be of significant value when improving the targeting of critical services, avoiding misdirected and crowding communication and helping people and families in acute need. Such an architectural scheme is a gold mine for a clever, human-centric and situationally sensitive service design that uses the power of human technology.

Future service technologies must reach human beings at the right time and with relevant content. The depth of this challenge has been understood now that there is an explosion of apps and services competing for the attention of their potential users. The winners will rely on relevant guidance and information directly from individuals and communities: they will have situational intelligence, that is, they know – they do not guess it with AI or ML – the situations of their target audiences. Some weak signs of this insight do occur already, but it requires a major paradigm shift where individuals are given the control and initiative and the means to provide situationally relevant and timely information about their own mental, physical and even culturally biased world to the technology operators, who can then serve them properly. There are major steps to be taken and the following offers one such step.

Imagine first, that it was possible for us to provide a means to indicate – in as much detail and style as we like – our acute situation at home or at work, for example, and what we are doing or experiencing. We could have a specific knowledge need, a housing problem, suffer from an acute social/family/health problem, or are planning to buy a new apartment, moving abroad, or preparing a specific item in the tax declaration etc. Further, we could also indicate any need for knowledge, help, contacts, or guidance. Imagine then that as individuals we allow external access to these significant instances of our life. The access (service offer, help, guidance, contact) could be related to specific, exactly defined behavior patterns, be they external, like doing something or internal, that is, planning, imaging, creating, daydreaming, but we would be in control, anonymously when we so want. We could get only situationally relevant offers and knowledge.

Internet of Behaviors (IB). IoB is a human-technologic framework or a platform that offers individuals and/or communities an accurate and systematic means to indicate their selected and meaningful, ongoing behavior patterns (internal or external alike), or situations exactly when they occur, dynamically, and with as many and natural variables as they like. This is achieved by assigning a specific IoB code/address/indicator (analogous to IoT) to each occurring behavior, act or thought. 'Behavior' can be purely a thought pattern: "I'm afraid that we are divorcing", "I'm planning to quit my job and find a new one", "I'm dreaming of an electric car". When this assignment has been done, semi-automatically, by individuals themselves, by external observers or with the support of machine learning systems, and accepted by the individual as a relevant code, it becomes possible to use it and allow external operators or even individuals to approach the person engaged with this specific behavior. This happens by connecting with their personal digital gear, or by providing the immediate environment information about their behaviors - when they allow it.

Naturally, a compelling and new kind of future UI is a crucial part of IoB design and IoB users will not directly deal with 'codes', but relevant contents and support. Note that the focus is on situations and behaviors, not on identities, that is, not about who these people are. Relevance matters: when we communicate with our close ones, we only rarely make mistakes in interpreting the mutual situations while it is an everyday, disturbing experience with present digital apps and gadgets.

The idea of IoB is simple: often (crimes, some public and financial services etc excluded) in society, the first priority is to know the occurring human behaviors and situations and serve them - not so much who these people are. Of course, it is practical to know a person's identity since identity is a natural part of our social relationships and it is a powerful, personal 'data management tool' that binds together everything typical for and done by us as individuals. However, identity knowledge is not the only option when we want to serve people; it is a double-edged sword. Due to historical-bureaucratic and now bureaucratic-technological developments, identity has become the dominant link to a person's behavior and because of it, analytics, spying and any possible means are used to locate and know the person as accurately as possible. GDPR tries to protect us, but IoB could help find another way to do that and still aim at situationally relevant services.

It is easy to reveal the identity of a person when we know the behavior, have some additional information like location, videos and other imaging data and behavior history knowledge to help in this. However, for a responsible operator it is also possible to use valuable behavior data without exact time or location tag in it; often exact time and location information can be scrambled or shifted in a random manner, without affecting the value of the behavior data. Frequently, absolute time is not even relevant for individuals using digital services but contextually right timing (situational relevance, contact building, offers, messaging, etc) is of huge importance. Anonymity is finding its place as people have become aware of its value. This is a complex issue, and there would be much more to say about this; generalizations are problematic.

Figure 1. Entering my favorite bar, with 'X' on my mind.

Individuals, communities and service providers could design the coding schemes related to any behaviors that they see interesting and relevant. A simple example, based on my personal experiences, as a patient at home after a surgical operation: at the hospital, they know well what are the typical patient complications and how the recovery proceeds. Their coding is not a complex procedure since systematic and well-structured printed and digital documents have already been prepared for the recovering patient. There is a problematic asymmetry across this service boundary today. On one hand, patients are worried and uncertain, wanting relevant help or knowledge immediately; most of the time they only need simple advice and support from their doctor or from other personnel; they call them or send email. On the other hand, each of these events (a call, an email) triggers a burdensome data management process and crowds the health care personnel. Who is calling? What was done? What is the situation? Is this a high-priority situation? At the hospital, they lack situational knowledge – or intelligence in their systems and the reason for any approach from the patient must be checked.

Some of this can be automated but a major improvement would be if there was a direct channel via which the doctor could see immediately what is the situation with the patient, what was happening before the call and what is the 'intention' of the patient. IoB serves such needs.

Patients have often difficulties in memorizing and describing what they were doing when they had an attack or how they recovered over time in various every-day activities. In addition to real-time physiological, gps, emergency and other recording data, many mental-psychological moments and episodes of life or patient histories can be most valuable for medical purposes. Today, the coding of natural behaviors and episodes at home and at work, for example, is not a technical problem and could be accomplished in number of ways.

There is a major opportunity for service providers to help their customer/citizens. Public and private service providers can offer a specialized IoB gateway for their clients to approach them during significant life events or when they are engaged with thoughts, plans, situations, and behaviors related to the specific service need. Of course, IoB is a major communication scheme because it means that we can become aware of other people's activities, situations, behavioral and mental states, in a very detailed but relevant way, even without knowing who they are – and at a global scale with no limits, if needed.

2. Some examples that could fly

Below I have listed only some simple examples which are by no means perfect, but I hope they serve as inspiration to think about the huge potential of IoB.

Sports behavior and experience tracking. IoB can be used by a sportsperson and his/her coach who have designed a scheme specific for each of the exercises, the exercise moments they see relevant and which they want to systematically map and follow, in real time and synchronized with other recordings, timing, data collection and sensor devices. Video is now commonplace and recording components of various behaviors and bodily processes have become standard in QS gadgets. However, for complex, repeated behavior and especially mental patterns they are not very effective. It is possible to target any aspect of natural behavior, physical or mental alike, when it is properly represented in IoB.

The coded behavior patterns can be as complex or abstract as needed, the main thing being that each of these patterns has a unique code assigned to it and its meaning is known. IoB data can be integrated from individual behavior sequences or from several persons and be compared, contrasted and analyzed in any valuable manner – in real time and globally if needed. Having such an open system publicly available would make it fun material to viewers interested in any entertaining behaviors, too. For example, if thousands of sportsmen of the same sports would share a coding system (for a selected set of behavior patterns) it would be possible to collect, compare, compute, and map large amounts of interesting behavior data for numerous purposes. This is possible today but the recording and analysis systems are still a modern version of Babel, for evident business reasons.

Figure 2. Sharing my moments.

IoB points always to a meaningful (often ongoing) aspect of behavior, which can be anything, a large or small detail, significant to the person. There is no need to use artificial intelligence data mining and try to guess these behaviors because data has been coded on the run already and is 100% accurate and relevant. Computational power can be used for more ambitious tasks like identifying relevant behavior patterns to be targeted by IoB.

Small children could have a mobile IoB system. Every time they move from home or from the school it opens an IoB address (only) to the parents who now have access to every coded behavior related to the school trip, if there is a digital system (camera, gps, mobile phone, microphone etc) using the IoB addressing. How the parents want to and can use this knowledge is a matter of practices, needs, ethics, regulations, and imagination. Any aspect of behavior could be in the focus of the selected IoB service.

A journalist working in a dangerous conflict area can indicate his or her actions and intentions, at any level of abstraction, when travelling and collecting material on his subject. By activating the IoB system he opens his personal digital environment to those having a permitted and secure access to it and he can get relevant, real-time support, materials and even protection and guidance from trusted parties. With this he can be behaviorally, in real-time, two-way contact with partners, service providers and help.

Today it is possible to know *when we read* a digital magazine article, but this is not so with the printed ones and books. With IoB, publishers could know how, at that very moment, you (or an anonymous version of you) are 'engaged with a magazine' and reading its article with the aim that only you know. They could know *'the why'* everywhere on the globe, like 'Fifty thousand people are reading article X right now, with the same aim or interest.' It is more than 'the act of reading' that IoB reveals. The address/code declared for this behavior by the publisher or other actor lets the publisher offer any supplementing service and content related to this moment of reading, be it journalistic or other relevant material. The publisher does not need to know who the reader is because her known behavior and intention is the significant trigger of interest and guidance to anyone willing to approach her, based on that knowledge. It remains the task of the person to react to any possible message or offer received on the base of IoB targeting, but the initiative is his. There are a number of ways, public and commercial alike to arrange for this type of mindful mediaspace to be used by those with an acceptable motivation to serve the readers – and to support them in any endeavor, be it education or whatever pursuit.

Travelers arriving at an airport can share the information about their travel intentions and current situation (schedule, shopping intentions, needing rest, meeting someone, working, etc) to relevant parties who could then offer services, support, information and help to them. Knowing the intentions and personal activities of the airport visitors, the service providers can be better prepared in advance, to use their limited resources and improve the accuracy of the overall service targeting. This would also free the travelers from excessive search and would function like a navigation system only that the 'map' would be built on the personally relevant environment and situations, not on locations; IoB data can be used to produce a behavioral navigation map of a probable future. The gain of this is the advanced, reliable knowledge, a relevance-based, expected behavior map, based on human data at its source: the person. AR and IoB together will boost this by creating suitable overlap information on the views of the physical world.

Activists could share the address of the next 'behavior operation', like a predetermined way to act in a demonstration. When everyone participating opens the IoB gate to the specific occasion there will be thousands of coordinated eyes, ears and recording devices to know what happens at the sites. Address & code traces will be left of any activities on the spot so that vast amounts of eye-witness and other data can be wisely collected afterwards, when needed. Identity problems aside, this has numerous potential uses – and problems, of course but the problems are nothing new.

IoB can be used for dividing any *problem solution* into sub-problems (with IoB codes) like it is done in Microtask. When solving a specific, large problem, it becomes possible to have access to anyone who, right now, happens to be engaged with solving one of its coded sub-problems. We could then have direct access to the solutions these people are producing or have produced earlier and to the materials and documents used.

In entertainment, a popular band could maintain an IoB-based gateway for the fans intending to attend their gigs, or simply listen to their music, wherever they happen to live on the globe. It's a matter of imagination to find out how to use this fan-behavior information to delight the fans. Notice that it's about human intentions, not about something the music apps could record by their systems which try to guess what might interest people next. There is no explicit digital trace of intentions outside IoB, except for the Spotify- type of intelligent guessing systems that indeed have rather good expressive power within music genres.

We use *bank apps* for managing our weekly, monthly, even daily money affairs, the accounts, payments and mortgages through the Internet and mobile. To guarantee security, some banks offer ways to secure the connection, but whatever the nature of the apps and the security tools they always open a private bridge between our everyday life and the banks.

Over the coming few years, these apps and services will evolve, but one thing is certain; we will be communicating with banks or other financial operators, mobile or over the net, using these systems and personal devices in a way that marries us with them. Surprising enough, banks have not realized – or they have been very slow to do it – that many of us, their clients have these daily or at least weekly intimate 'mental contacts' with our banks, directly and indirectly. Even more interesting is that at the specific moment when using the apps and managing our economics at home and in our businesses, we discuss it with our spouses and colleagues, and are fully tuned to the world of personal finances. No AI can exactly guess what these thoughts and discussions are in detail and when they happen to conquer our minds. IoB knows.

Market operators try to guess our state of mind and approach us at the right and relevant moment with their targeted offers. Usually they fail because even with the best, current and near-future machine learning systems they cannot know how busy, open or motivated to engagement we happen to be. It is not untypical that we use bank apps under other significant pressures at home or at work and have no time or interest to make it more complicated by paying attention to the interfering market messages and offers, as lucrative as they might be, received from the bank and other service providers. Only seldom we discuss financial matters in isolation, without a connection to other significant aspects of family and personal life. IoB can help coordinate this.

With IoB, while making a connection with your bank, you could, with a push or two of a button, express your any, acute economic interest, wish or worry, or simple curiosity, that is on your mind right then and you believe your bank, or some other source, perhaps a partner of the bank from public sector, could have something to offer to you, even give valuable advice and help. You would inform, without significant effort, the bank about this peculiar 'state of your mind'. This was sometimes easy to do in the casual, 'old-time' face to face contacts and receive timely information and advice. Chats and chatbots are adopting new roles in this now but they are psychologically stupid psychopaths.

You could have your private and shared coding system that over time, as a trusted customer of your bank, you build with them and of which only you and the bank know what each IoB code (behavior, situation, thinking) represents. We can call these codes as addresses to your (ongoing) behavior that only you fully know, be it internal behavior, e.g. planning, thinking, imagining, day-dreaming, worrying or external, e.g. buying, selling, calculating, going or being somewhere, whatever relevant to you. It's a private code between you and the bank.

You could have a set of personal IoBs that have been reserved and implemented during the occurring, *'specific work behaviors'* in your work environment. When you 'turn on' the IoB system to let it monitor you and what you do, then everything (coded) what you do, including behaviors related to your mobile phone, computer, or to your colleagues, becomes stored as consistent behavior sequences which knowledge can then be used in numerous ways. It's up to you to decide how, where and with whom you want to share it or do you want it shared at all.

For example, when you approach a meeting room, your car or your computer, it is prepared to receive you for that meeting, journey or a task. IoB is a situationally intelligent magician that allows you to be received according your situation, mindset and interests. It does not guess like AI does. *It knows.* The most basic property of IoB is that it produces a map of and remote access to individual behavior patterns and their history any time that this history is available.

Future library - a simple service example. Knowing that a person is at a library, especially at a modern one like the fascinating Oodi in Helsinki does not tell much *why* he is there and what are his intentions. This is especially true about Oodi since it is based on a new, modern and unusual library concept. A typical library does not offer a service by which you could have everything you need ready for you, from books and other activities to your relevant knowledge and news sites, open documents and the work space you plan to use – and not only the spatial-physical space – and that you need when you enter the library. A journalist could have his last manuscript exactly in the same state, with all the related documents, as they were left last time and have even fresh announcements about potentially interesting new information or comments to the story at hand. Some new tools support this but part of it used to be easy at home: you just left books open and the manuscript and any drawings or sketches beside them and continued from that; when you told your colleagues about your doings, you learned from them. Now we typically arrange the work space configuration every time we start working on something, even very simple assignments and manage our networks.

With the simple message, and a unique IoB address related to it: "I'm going to study and work on X", a place (library) and time tag, the student could announce that she is a client, ready to enjoy any possible service and data targeted to this address. If she happens to live far away, public transport info could be of help. On the other hand, when she would express this same intention to "study and work on X" at home, in her own ict environment the same service could be available to continue exactly where she last time left, in the texts, with open documents and net connections - anywhere in the world; it is situational intelligence which would allow travelling with personal context.

The library case is simple: today the library does not know us and even with the best of AI it cannot infer our individual, acute reasons to be there; only rarely it asks. This is quite different from how we behave with our friends; we just tell them indicating a real and simple intentional act. We tell it because it is good for our co-existence and typically it is useful and triggers relevant communication.

... and then there is the unimaginable app potential for cars, games, new media, research, and mobile phones, health care - everything where people are engaged with and have plans, intentions and real-time needs and situations which they can easily express but which are difficult to compute and predict from the available behavior and other individual data.

There is no one system of IoB codes or addresses to cover all our behavior domains - it would make it an unmanageable mess. However, a service provider and we as clients can easily learn what these aspects of our everyday life are – and how to best benefit by coding them. AI and ML can support this, but alone they cannot do it. It's an adaptive process, a new kind of a learning journey between the two communicating partners; it is a new human-centered design challenge.

A note on identity protection. Despite the EU-GDPR policy aiming at protecting people and helping us to be aware of our personal data, there will be an increasing amount of such intimate data that computational and AI-based systems keep producing about us. This will continue and multiply; no doubt, they learn better to guess our interests and even some of our future behaviors. The problem with most, if not all intelligent services is that they want to know our identities, who we are and everything they do is based on following, computing and targeting each of us as individuals with identity. GDPR is built to fight this.

Underlying the IoB approach is the assumption that it is not always wise to build intelligent services on the identity knowledge of the individuals, the primary data sources and service users. For example, it is possible to know when one million people, anywhere in the world, are engaged with the same type of behavior or situations in whatever they do. Based on this situational (source) intelligence people can be approached with a nearly 100% relevant content and timing related to what they are engaged with; they would not be disturbed by irrelevant messaging which of course has extra value for traffic safety. Targeting such a large mass of people with such a high relevance provides huge benefits. Based on the knowledge of various behavior and situation distributions and their timing a lot can be done. All this could happen without knowing the identities but in case of emergencies, identity knowledge of course, can be crucial.

3. Address space and behavior space

Originally I thought that IoB could use IP addresses to make behavior data in the net accessible, but this is not the only option. In IPv6 there are 2^{128} available addresses, of which people can be offered thousands of addresses for personal use. Imagining my own life, if I would like to cover the most relevant aspects of it with IoB codes, the number of addresses for my most frequent behavior patterns and their components (taking my medicine, reading a book or an article, exercising at the gym, meeting a colleague, intending to visit our local organic farm, buying a product, planning to write an article, on my way to a concert etc.) would not be more than 10000. If they had a compelling form and UI, and organized contextually and dynamically I could use them for variable purposes and invent new and useful ones on the fly, with a push of a button. AI could indeed help me in accomplishing this. Accessing any of my IoB coded behaviors would open a communication channel to and from any data, devices and tools I would be willing to share and use during that specific behavior. I could even have a specific 'portfolio' of data and services related to IoB only. Sometimes privacy is crucial. That is why in IoB the subject decides what, how, what and when she is willing to share and receive any data and channels of communication.

In the demo photos shown above I was thinking of my personal history in Fisterra, Galicia where I spent a fascinating time at Bar A Galleria and had many non-recorded, memorable experiences there. What a great help IoB would have been for recording my 'behavior patterns' there with IoB and to be able to return to them like to an active, mental diary, when I wrote a book of my visit there. I could have shared my life there with my (distant) friends and companions. It could be like psychological record of my mental history there. This will happen soon – and with the increasing use of audio/video, it becomes a fascinating way to record external and internal behavior history, simultaneously and in a manageable way. It's the next generation digital diary.

Of course there is the challenge of introducing the use of address/codes into everyday life, but there are simple ways to start and do it - some are straightforward and can be made automatic and some are complex. Recurring routines, for example, can be easily coded and produce supervised and even unsupervised learning systems to help build the personal coding systems for the elderly, for example. Looking farther in future, we will have innovative human UI solutions and wise machines 'programming' that for us. They will free time for more human activities than staring at, manipulating and being locked into our mobile phone apps.

There are unlimited possibilities for IoB to be used in business, personal finances, education, work, collaboration, co-ordination, service providing, marketing, personalization, you name it. My long lasting idea since working with the Stanford Peace Innovation Lab has been to use of IoB for mapping positive behaviors and any behaviors related to promoting and following of non-violence and global positive behaviors. But of course, IoB schemes can be used for coding of any observed or monitored behaviors, from good to bad.

4.   Problems of resolution, complexity and detail

Relevance is the key in IoB, not the exact accuracy; it's like human memory and mind space. This is where it differs from standard technological systems.

Stephen Wolfram has collected an immense amount data of his daily activities over a couple of years. He is a creative character and we can imagine how much we could learn from him if he had an IoB-based system to record his critical behavior patterns, intentions and situations in doing what he does? It would be a gift to us all and not only of his life, but there would also be others who could innovate IoB schemes to share their creativity and knowledge and make it well-organized historical data.

AI and IoB. Current discourse on AI typically underestimates the complexity of the intimate, forward-looking and difficult to measure individual mental phenomena and knowledge. Big data, machine learning, sensor and scanning technologies, face recognition, and even brain signal measures are expected to reveal the essentials of the individual mind. This will not happen in the near-future. AI is sneaking closer to us, perhaps to our doorsteps and into the domestic equipment, but not much further; it has much to learn in having an intimate touch with the experiencing, motivated, and intentional, even a spiritual person.

Systems approach is not only needed in building services but also to understand the dynamics and content of human life and behavior, where new dependencies emerge, especially with the new technological tools. One way, and the best one I know of, to relax the computational complexity of the problem in trying to serve these multi-dimensional, human behaviors and experiences is to let people express their relevant behaviors and states of mind themselves, securely, either semi-automatically or by communicating it voluntarily and to do it in a compelling and easy way. It is not an impossible task for modern technology to design such systems and people learn quickly new habits with technology if it serves their life well.

Many behavior monitoring, tracking gadgets and systems, have turned to AI schemes to improve their performance. My guess is, they will sooner or later transform into IoB-related systems which will then significantly extend, boost and widen their use scope and help develop standards that further improve their human compatibility which is not too good today. I believe this is the next generation human technology (digital) challenge and expect it to happen within the next ten years within the health care services, especially in patient follow-up and monitoring of medication where the pressure for such solutions is growing.

5.   Intentions and the internet of behaviors

The intimate human background of IoB makes human intentions tangible and it becomes possible to know what is *about to happen* in the connected world. IoB is an easy technical concept but psychologically a complex one; it has risks and uncertainties, but offers huge potential if it is, in one form or another, implemented wisely. At minimum, it's a thought experiment that cannot go wrong.

Not so long time ago, only a fool or an idealist would ask and expect a real answer to the question "What is happening in the world, right now?" Today's knowledge companies are making mountains of money by answering to it. We can turn to the next question, "What are we intending to do to the world?". There is no 'Intention Google' to satisfy that curiosity.

As an example, at the writing of this, my gotepoem blog has had about 15000 views, not a big number in today's blogsphere but I would like to know what were some of the true intentions of my readers when they met my texts. Knowing that I would understand a lot more about the world and it would teach and touch me; the spirit of my texts would change and I could be prepared for the future. Intentions occur without leaving a trace in the digisphere.

When we are blind to the intentions of people, we are doomed to be blind to part of our future that could be known. It is for personal pleasure and benefit that we want to know the intentions of our trusted friends, loved ones and fellow citizens, even our enemies. In everyday life, we simply ask, listen and trust what we hear. We do this at individual and organization level and use the acquired intention knowledge, or human guesses of it, to be prepared for our near and far future. Parents, company executives and medical doctors mine intention data routinely from children, employees, and from patients. All this happens automatically, but we do not call it 'intention knowledge', and strange enough, the term is not used in cognitive psychology.

Learning to perceive intentions. Psychologists use the word 'anticipation' which describes how a person prepares for any incidence while intention perception refers to the integrated knowledge of the intentions of someone, a person or persons, whose behavior is relevant in the situation. As an example, imagine walking on the street and someone approaches you aggressively, threatens your child or your spouse. You get automatically defensive and tensed and you prepare to defend yourself and protect your close ones. What is this 'perception of a bad intention' *before* there is no bad act? Clearly, it is a peculiar form of human perceptual intelligence, similar to opportunity perception that immediately reserves and integrates specific mental structures in our minds to prepare for action, while pushing other ongoing mental and physical processes aside. We assume the state of anticipation and construct, quickly, our own intentions.

Similar situations, in a less dramatic form occur frequently in everyday life when we feel that someone – a person in a street crowd, in a sports event, in theatre play, in an organization or even a leading figure of a nation – reveals intentions to help, serve or harm somebody. What is common in these instances is the power by which the knowledge – or better, the assumptions – about the intentions touches us automatically, with full force and it launches a vigorous mental organization, relevant to the situation.

Intention perception is more than just recording or guessing an event in the world. It is not only opening the gate to the emotional meanings and anticipatory energy but it contains all these psychological phenomena, integrated together in the form of specific type of knowledge, proactive in nature. Intention knowledge integrates our available, relevant psychological resources. Scientists do not know how this happens in the human and animal mind. Like animals we must react quickly, not to what we see as the world state, but to perceive what someone is intending to do, what is about to happen: a ball thrown at us or an aggressive animal approaching must be immediately perceived and the behavior predicted. Any deep psychological analysis is time wasted because all this must happen in less than a second, even within hundreds of micro (not milli-) seconds as we know from the fast sports like ice hockey, boxing, karate, squash and tennis. Had the goal keeper in ice hockey no idea of the intentions of the shooting player he would have no chance to catch the puck coming at the speed of 200 km/hr. It moves at the speed of about half a meter a millisecond (1/1000th of a second). The human reaction time at its best is about 100 msec. The goalkeeper must correctly perceive the intention and predict its consequences.

Figure 3. Subjective worlds have barely no limits.

Sociologists and politicians teach us that the dominant powers in the world are structural and ideological in nature and that individual behaviors are but direct reflections of these main forces. Accordingly, individual intentions are but buried noise masked by the sociological power fields of human masses. Psychologists on the other hand, are often trapped with the academic and 'context independent' personality and intelligence constructs that have practically no predictive value in normal everyday life, some diagnostics and specific disabilities excluded. It is not of common knowledge that, for example, the most popular personality factors 'The big five' have close to zero % explanatory value in predicting future success in work performance.

We can learn to deal with intention knowledge and accept that several drivers exist simultaneously behind intentions, which are pure subjective phenomena. It was almost impossible to understand what made the Norwegian mass murderer to act as he did. There was no one explaining variable, not even a complex set of them like intelligence, mania, political view, or personality, while there was no doubt that he had intentions, clear and explicit, with different time scales, that integrated all his inhuman psychological forces, whatever they were. This, and the fact that nobody knew them, made him dangerous. In the connected world individuals have new potential in good and bad: the acts of creative souls and stubborn maniacs have repeatedly surprised us; first with their intentions, which typically have been recognized late and then by their revolutionary and transformational actions that have surprised us and changed the world and its structures.

Intention is more than wishful thinking and self-deception. Imagine that we could know more about the intentions of individuals, organizations, or even about artificial systems? Wise parents have always been sensitive to the acceptable or questionable intentions of their children, just like civilized managers are interested in the intentions of their personnel and their competitors, to interfere and to provide support early. Perception of intentions requires situational and dynamic intelligence; an important aspect of this is 'the grace of intelligent mistakes', meaning that humans don't make any possible, haphazard mistakes in perceiving intentions. 'Intelligent' machines fail in this, especially when they misunderstand the situations.

Our behaviors are constantly being addressed by the knowledge giants. They have ways to represent our expected behaviors (traveling, shopping, work, hobbies) but as we have experienced it is often shotgun style, with a very coarse aim. They do not call this 'intention knowledge' although that is exactly what it is, only that it is typically only 'intention guessing' because we, the target individuals have not been asked and don't have inspiring means to express ourselves. All this happens invisibly and typically we are not informed about the data structures that point their finger at our assumed intentions.

Each behavior we show, can be driven by different intentions and their multiple, simultaneous variations. Not unlike the admired and feared giants, also pirates use our data without us knowing it. Because their data is inferred (relative to mass profiles) it is only superficially based on what we have directly told or otherwise expressed. This is a peculiar inverse problem of human behavior: *as individuals and even as communities we do apparently same things but for completely different reasons.* IoB can make this human, behavior-driving background visible and to declare this knowledge our own property that only we control.

Why should we let others know our intentions? Having a means to express them – before we act – is a most valuable, human knowledge skill we master; it is meaningful for our physical and mental behaviors. A fresh couple, learning to know each other practically lives on the delights of intention knowledge. Between lovers it is a fascinating human asset but for libraries, intention knowledge would have another role.

Intention knowledge is useful; monkeys signal their intentions to each other and even reindeers have systems to share intention knowledge when they move in flocks. For a fascinating lesson (in Finnish) about reindeer 'team behavior' by Esa Kirkkopelto, see "Erään poron tunnustuksia. Laumaeläin esityksen toisena." (Confessions by a reindeer. Social animal as the other in the performance. Näyttämö ja Tutkimus 7: Esitys ja toiseus: Thuring, A., Koskinen, A. And Kokkonen, T. (eds.) TeaTS 2018, 29-46).

Science of intentions? There is no real empirical science of human intentions although for philosophers it is familiar from many perspectives of intentionality. It has remained a poorly charted territory in psychology while the intentions and motivations of politicians, criminals, entertainers and other public figures have remained endless material for media speculations and yellow papers. In psychoanalysis, intentions have been buried into the mystery world of the subconscious. Modern cognitive psychology as known from the works of Kahneman and others, have described basic interpretative, choice and decision making behavior and thinking which, however, do not have much to offer for predicting real-life individual, complex behaviors like criminal acts, political career choices, and individual or corporate economy behaviors to mention a few.

Intentions remain hidden and objects of guessing and post hoc speculation – unless they can be somehow revealed, which is not always the case and typically happens afterwards. Our everyday intentions have become ad hoc and guessing material for big data and AI analytics.

Some research on the psychology of life strategies has come close to the science of intentions. For example, studies have looked at specific and general problem solving and planning in life (cf. the classic book like Miller, Galanter & Pribram, 1960: *Plans and the structure of behavior,* and the article by Smith, J., 1996: Planning about life: Toward a social-interactive perspective. See also B.F. Malle, L. J. Moses & D.A. Baldwin (Eds), 2003: Intentions and Intentionality, MIT Press, for a cognitive and social cognitive analysis of intentional and unintentional behavior.

I return to the false belief among popular brain scientists and marketing professionals that it is objectively possible to know these hidden human phenomena of the mind. Sometimes it seems that there is more trust in our sweat glands and face muscles than in human talk. I want to be clear about this and distance my views from these 'objective' beliefs about human sciences:

Based on research experiences with thousands of people in the lab and at their homes or as clients I believe we can and should learn to know how to trust people for the benefit of developing truly human future technologies. This is possible when we allow people to be spontaneous, to stay within the limits of their 'own' mental space, and don't assume that they are fully coherent in their ways of 'feeling and knowing things'. We can use proper adaptive methods in interviewing and approaching people and analyzing the acquired, especially qualitative data. There is promising future technological potential in this trust paradigm.

On a January morning, some ten years ago, reverend Smith, in his Harlem Church in New York, preached to us "Trust your data! Trust your qualitative data!" He did not know it but he touched on the key discussion topic we had during the journey when we happened to visit his church.

6.   On the gaps in human knowledge

You might still wonder if the IoB approach is any different from the already available customer inventories and other means to collect client and any other human data? It is: it puts emphasis on the quality of data at its source, it is dynamic, general and can be standard like, it is fast, real-time, focused on data relevance and timing, and relies on acute intentions and acts of people, it scales tremendously, it can be quickly re-oriented, it is easily scalable, it returns the lost control to people and it is cheap.

Gap of human knowledge

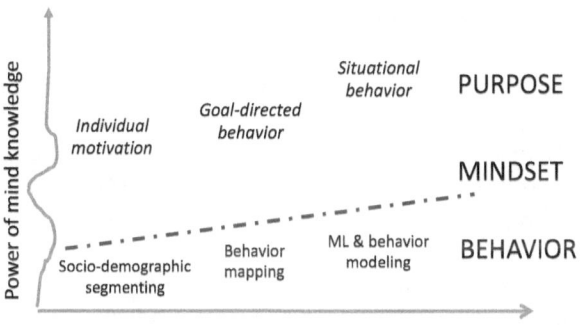

Figure 4. Mind- vs AI knowledge.

In the figure, I've summarized, the knowledge gap between two current computational paradigms: a) the increasing power of computation and AI, aiming at learning more about individuals and b) the potential power of what I call 'mind knowledge' which is the knowledge all humans and individuals foster and live on, but which is not directly available for any external sensor or recording systems, AI included; it's our private mental world and life.

As human beings, the very basic skill we spend our whole life learning, is to generate, manage, and express our personal intentions and situations. It makes future-oriented behavior possible. This skill is the backbone of any social community from homes to nations. We have learned ways to express intentions, often before taking actions; we have learned to understand and guess other people's intentions. We do not express the intentions only for selfish reasons but also to help our friends and community members to be prepared, to join and interact with us. We need them in learning and organizing our mental contents and physical behaviors. Of course, we have become masters in hiding our intentions.

We can collect massive real-time and near-historical intention data, from the whole world if we so want. Surprisingly few operators and services are doing this at a global scale. Psychologists are uncomfortable with the intention concept; many refer to decision making. However, decision making and intentions are psychologically different: intentions are integrative, cultural, creative, social, and internal mental phenomena that frame and organize the decisions and the preparation for them. We know that (cf. Daniel Kahneman's or Herbert Simon's work, for example) intentions do not automatically lead to unique behaviors. Sometimes we do have 'good intentions' but accomplish something unexpected. Explicit and voiced intentions have a strong impact on audiences as we so well know from the current politics of threat.

"Knowledge is power" has become the lame symbolic statement of social optimism, social revolution, transparency, crowd sourcing, and empowerment. A better expression would be: "Knowledge without power is only data". Seeing the avalanche of the world knowledge it is astonishing how few innovations have emerged for novel data mining and representation. Visualizations and open data improve fast, and massive search, classification, source tagging, and pattern recognition schemes are used but relevant meanings and significance continue to evade these. It is possible that GDPR becomes the human driver for the renovation of current paradigms.

At the writing of this, Facebook faces trouble with its data use, computational models and practices. Google defends its position as the knowledge search and social knowledge sharing emperor and is fast becoming the master of future AI-based services. Media world lives under an intensifying turbulence and any speculation in the media about how to best reach the audience is welcomed, entertained and then soon cast away. Competing knowledge companies hit the same wall of dynamic world knowledge because the pool of meanings and human behaviors underlying any data multiplies as fast as the amount of data collected, or even faster. Intention knowledge can offer a valuable 'relaxation' to the problems faced by big data and AI, but it is essentially very private data.

When something goes seriously wrong it is natural to look for reasons or psychological predecessors to these events and to speculate about the intentions behind them. Journalists and public servants, for example, conduct *post hoc* discussions on violent acts in society, searching for motivations, political or religious reasons or personal histories of these violent persons. Only rarely they refer to the direct emergence of intentions in these acts, as if no such knowledge existed or it was difficult to obtain.

Consider the following curious cases of intention. A clerk in the Vatican office stole documents from the papal office and was charged for the theft of secret documents, which allegedly revealed corruption in the Vatican. His explanation was that he *intended* to reveal the misconducts and corruption there. But intentions did not seem to matter, not even in the papal system, and he was treated as a thief and punished accordingly.

In Sweden the court in Göteborg freed two suspects (the men were from Somalia and Irak) who entered a galleria, looking for the artists who had drawn a cartoon of prophet

Muhammed. There was no proof of *intended* murder although the men had knives with them and they were looking for the artist, who luckily was not present then. What was their intention? They know it, of course, most people have no difficulties in guessing it, and maybe also Muhammed knows it, but the court was helpless, it was not able to deal with the critical intention knowledge and let them free.

The system of law has problems in dealing with intention knowledge, and only recently, in Finland, for example, it was not a crime to prepare a theft or a robber and you could even arrange an effective crime exercise to fulfill your criminal intention, to get properly prepared for something that looks like a theft, killing or other crime. The law was changed only recently.

7. The power of intention knowledge

Without intentions, we would be reactive machines. It is amazing indeed how the nature of intention knowledge in our minds, the awareness of our own or of others' intentions, has remained practically an uncharted topic in human technology. Although it is inherent in almost any design, explicit, functional intention process models are rare if not nonexistent.

Intuition, on the other hand, has become a popular topic in the present management and decision making literature and research (cf. Hodgkinson G. & Starbuck W., (Ed.), (2008) *The Oxford handbook of Organisational Decision Making*, Oxford University Press, Oxford). One reason to this is that basic cognitive psychological knowledge and decision making concepts do not have explanatory power over psychologically complex and contextual phenomena like intention which has led to the use of concepts like 'intuition': we don't know what went on in a decision maker's mind when he made his choice because we cannot look inside him.

Sometimes the lack of intention knowledge is demonstrated by environmental and technical designs that fail to serve our simple needs to act according to personal preferences. We are guided by intentions and try to find relevant opportunities. Parks, especially in Finland have often geometrically orientated paths for walkers but people just take the shortest routes across the lawn. Earlier here I described 'opportunity perception' as our constant habit to look for (to perceive) ways to proceed in life, be it external (acts) or internal (mental processes), to fulfill our intentions. Bad technical or architectural designs present a temporary hinder to this.

Watching a movie, we associate subjective feelings with the intentions of the characters we observe and follow. We have learned how strongly the knowledge (which is an assumption) of bad intentions of a character in a play or a movie touches us. In extreme, real-life conditions when life is at stake it gives us the power to kill. No wonder then that painting the picture of 'bad intentions', making people perceive intentions or assume them, is so efficiently used in political rhetoric, yellow paper journalism, and in various forms of propaganda. By revealing or communicating imaginary bad intentions the audience is made to react intuitively, inviting them into the drama and then to internal and often external actions. Fortunately, we are also profoundly moved by perceived positive intentions: seeing or experiencing that someone wants to care, help, love, support, save or conduct simple good acts for us.

Intention is a psychologically energizing force. Animals have it as dog owners know; dogs are marvelous in perceiving your intentions – and to react accordingly - and sometimes even better than many humans are. Konrad Lorenz, the Nobel laureate, had a parrot which could recognize who would be the next one from the seminar participants to leave the session: the bird would approach the person even before she had announced her intention to leave. The bird observed the human signs of the emerging intention.

Intention perception and knowledge processes do not occur at individual level alone and it has a significant role at corporate and national level as well. In organizations intention perception (managing the intentions of the organization itself or recognizing the intentions of other organizations in the environment) is an essential part of the mission-vision-strategy process.

8. A few steps back: knowledge that escapes us

Contrary to the common optimism about the knowledge society, significant knowledge escapes us faster than ever before – not in the absolute sense but relative to what there is and will be for us to know. This paradoxical knowledge explosion (I don't know if it has been formally shown) is an indirect consequence of the human side of the big data phenomenon.

In the spirit of big data definition (Wiki: "Big data is data sets that are so voluminous and complex that traditional data-processing application software are inadequate to deal with them.") we can characterize the Large human data:

Large human data pool originates from human behavior and experience data, which in turn is transformed by humans interpreting the data. As a result, human data increases faster than the continuously improving data-processing systems can follow, quantum computing included.

It would take a story of its own to accurately defend this claim, but the main reasons for introducing the Large human data concept are as follows: technological innovations reveal new aspects of human behavior with increasing accuracy and detail; human data becomes irrecoverably distributed, dynamic, interactive and fragmented so a large part of it becomes irrecoverable, even with the strongest methods of decrypting; human behaviors and ways of relating to the world and data change with technology, generating new sources of human data; human perspective to human data as a concept will change; humans will run – in a multitude of ways - the most powerful computers systems to generate and interpret new human data. It is an endless circle.

A pervasive challenge will be how to best compute meaningful knowledge from the clouds of human data. A corollary to the human data explosion is that all potential meanings underlying the observable data escape even faster because of the increasingly wicked inverse problems: recorded phenomena will have a continuously increasing number of alternative explanations and small mistakes made in data capture and coding introduce large mistakes in source estimation. Similar-appearing things, acts and behaviors happen in numbers, for totally different reasons. Some have suggested that we are approaching the time of revealing all meanings of data, that 'the end of theory' is close (cf. Richard Bookstaber's book with the same title). They better think twice.

Classic and relativistic worlds of knowledge. The concept of 'knowledge' is transforming from something to be discovered or constructed to something that evolves and self-organizes (socio-technologically) with the help of knowledge technologies and hence, continuously escapes us by being transformed by humans and by itself.

This is nothing new in cultural history and natural sciences. In quantum physics and cosmology it has been an essential aspect of theory building. To use a brave analogy, we can consider the knowledge of today as *'classic knowledge world'* as opposed to the *'relativistic knowledge world'* emerging. Relativistic knowledge includes, as its essential elements, situational knowledge, interaction, continuous learning, and changing domains of intelligence - all these varying dynamically, and being interdependent. In the relativistic view the basic assumption is that the limits of the observable knowledge world are defined by the relationship between the available computational capacity and the accelerating speed of knowledge space expansion. This is a somewhat wild analogy to the geometrical space-time problem in the general theory of relativity.

Why not borrow and use the analogy for a thought experiment and apply the concept and role of the maximum speed of light in physics: it prevents us from seeing as far and deep into the universe as we would like to. Similarly, we can imagine a maximum data processing speed and capacity that we have available for accessing the evolving and expanding data universe. Because of this assumed and profound speed obstacle we are bound to use our cultural imagination and mathematical tools to model and comprehend the distant universes of knowledge (and stars).

Is it indeed possible that valuable knowledge is already escaping us? Many of the querulants on AI threat indeed seem to think so and predict that AI will conquer us. The situation in knowledge processing is not as hopeless as it is in cosmology where we will always have serious problems in trying to make a direct contact with the distant data sources (far-away-stars, galaxies and universes).

Here are two strong hypotheses concerning the causes of accelerating knowledge escape.

The number and nature of data sources in the world increases faster than we can improve the available data processing power and make it match this development.

The most significant limitation is the human factor in developing and implementing the best technologies.

The quality of the data content obtained from the source (world, our minds) cannot be improved fast enough to narrow the large human data gap even by using better and more efficient computing systems and algorithms.

The latter hypothesis is based on the observation of data sources that increase fastest in quantity, due to e.g. dumb use of wide bandwidth, increasing amounts of real-time data, sensor applications, human interaction data, the Internet of Things and many more. At present, the standard solution to the problem of bad quality of the source data is to increase processing power, to apply better pattern recognition schemes, to rely on statistics and learning approaches, data triangulation and by collecting suitable contextual data to relax the solution frame. A serious problem is that as humans we have the 'computationally problematic' but very human habit of changing our mind on the fly and we do it often, it's what makes everyday life different from army life. It is not noise, it's genuine human data. Things being like this, why not assign relevant meaning at the data source, as early as possible?"

The 'source data interpretation problem' can be turned upside down: by acquiring relevant, situational knowledge of the aims, goals, interpretations, and intentions directly from the people (or of artificial systems, robots) of whose behavior we are interested in. This is not typically done in any depth. With situational intelligence, it can be accomplished, for example, by tagging the meaning of the human data and any of its components as early as possible at the source. Digital technology is starting to evolve in this direction.

The later in the data creation or in the sense-making chain meanings are introduced the more knowledge value escapes, drips away from the objects of computation and the inverse problem gets worse. The data becomes irrecoverably biased, making computational problem increasingly difficult. There are no self-correcting codes that would recover the lost knowledge of intentions and meanings that are dynamic in nature.

As very simple examples, when I step out from my house I know exactly why I do it and what I have on my mind. I could easily tell, but typically, nobody asks even though it would be easy for me to tell. Further, saying 'hello', and 'goodbye' to our friends and loved ones carries so much psychology, always. Speaking to a robot, Siri, Alexa or Google Assistant is possible today and they will improve fast, but they need to learn to perceive our human situations and intentions.

It may not always be possible to get to the meanings early, but often it is. Perhaps the worst obstacle is that there are no relevant data structures, or even suitable programming languages (thanks to Paul Suni, I found an inspiring, related talk by Rich Hickey: "Are-We-There-Yet") for expressing the meaning of sensible human data, especially when it concerns natural behaviors and human characteristics. This is somewhat surprising considering the development in AI where the need for AI-specific programming systems are being introduced at MIT, for example.

The complexity of the inverse problem in recovering the meaning of human data at its source is increased by the computations applied to it after its coding at the source.

The walking pilgrim with an intention. To summarize the views above, let's return to the story of the pilgrim walking. We would like to know why and how she is walking her Camino, perhaps hundreds or thousands of kilometers, and chooses her own specific trail. Because this is an open problem it is not a general case of the traveling salesman problem: we want to know *why* she has taken the specific steps and movement patterns on the pilgrimage. Pilgrims on the famous Camino de Santiago all have the same goal: to reach the Cathedral de Santiago in Northern Spain. They take a long walk that can be anything from 3000 km to 50 km long from east or south. The motivations behind the nearly identical movement patterns are, however, totally different. When starting their journey the pilgrims are asked, by the church clerks, about their intentions or motivation: "What is your motivation: religious, sports, spiritual?"

To solve the problem of pilgrim motivation we could use an accurate gps system, find out about her previous religious history and activities, and map the pilgrim's location on the Camino at every point of time to describe the individual route *(x, y, t)*. From the data recorder's point of view, a dense sampling and rich contextual, even social, supporting knowledge would help to reveal the motivations underlying the observed walking behavior. All this is possible today. Knowing the constraints, like the knowledge that the pilgrim can be a tourist, a priest, a sportsperson, a reporter, what time of the day it is, is he hungry, or does she live somewhere nearby, relaxes the problem and allows the exclusion of false interpretations. We might arrive at reasonably good interpretations of average walking persons and their intentions and motivations on the Camino, but for an individual pilgrim this is not so; they take personal journeys.

Figure 5. A Map meets human (pilgrim) intention.

From the pilgrim's point of view, the walk is simple, driven by intrinsic, emerging and transforming motivations: what it means to be a human and not a robot. Like any healthy person, a pilgrim or not, it is likely that her mental and spiritual drivers are dynamic and change continuously. Every time the journey motivation changes, the analysis of the walk data becomes irrecoverably problematic: an intentional pilgrim walking does not remain a stationary system and the meaning of her history knowledge changes. After all, for most pilgrims this is the spiritual *idea* behind the walk – to change as a spiritual person.

Walking a Camino is not about transporting the body from point A to point B. It is even risky to consider the pilgrim as a physically stationary system and certainly it is not reasonable to make this assumption about her mental states. As a consequence, it is practically impossible to recover the original meaning of the (x,y,t) data without accurate and dynamic pre-knowledge of the pilgrim and her evolving intentions. Mind knowledge is required. It is necessary to talk to him or her – and listen.

Figure 6. Tools, stuff and intentions as partners. 790 km to go.

What if we could have relevant and true behavioral (mental including) meaning data at the source? What would it be, how and when could we record and use it?

Curious enough, in the geographical mapping of the pilgrim's trail we in fact lose context knowledge each time a computation is performed to calculate the distances, velocities, accelerations, turnings or other aspects of the walking pilgrim's behavior patterns. For example, two dots on a map can be computationally connected but there is a high probability that these simple computations fail to chart the internal mind-space trail of the pilgrim walking. The relationship between the computed movement patterns and the dynamic internal states of the pilgrim remains fuzzy.

We can use clever movement pattern characteristics like entropy, for example, to model the movement types (cf. Särkelä et al., 2009) but every computation introduces significant noise to the meanings of the movements at their source and it becomes unclear why these movement patterns occurred the way they did.

Preserving the meaning at the data source may not be a mainstream idea (I do not know what exactly has been accomplished in this field), and I've been repeatedly puzzled why this view has received so little interest even with the presence of clever sensing systems and other data collection innovations. The loose term 'small data' has been suggested to implicate something like this. It is as if the computing systems were designed to accomplish just the opposite: most of the computing power is devoted to clean up bad data. Mathematically this can be elegant and a necessity because we do not know more about the data itself and its exact origins.

Real-time operating systems declare significant events so that when an important external or internal event takes place the system program reacts to this by an interrupt or 'a flag'. However, within the human and social sciences this kind of thinking is not mainstream and it has not been used to model human behavior and its control. There is no coding system for significant human events although practically all important places on earth have been coded in today's digital navigation tools. Innovators are realizing the benefits of improving the quality of the data at the source. Some use tagging of data to provide relevant content information to the viewers.

I summary, IoB aims at tagging the essential meanings of a specific behavior pattern at its source, as early as possible (related to the behavior of a human, machine, organization or data processing chain, for example). By doing this IoB points to that specific behavior pattern to be used for beneficial purposes.

The beneficiaries of the IoB addresses/codes (individuals, communities, designers, engineers, artists, journalists, firms) can expect that it is somehow useful and safe to express their specific behaviors and receive relevant and timely services and information based on this.

Helping and supporting people at a large social scale is a significant potential of IoB. However, it does not do that alone, and a holistic, functional-architectural description of the intended social and health care service sectors and contexts are need to point out the instances where relevant and timely support and help is needed and can be arranged by the IoB model.

13 HUMAN-CENTRIC PHYSICS

1. Foundational considerations of technology: human perception and physics

Above I have described, somewhat superficially, very practical approaches in different human situations and contexts and focused on the nature of human experience and ways to 'measure' it. Working with these problems I became aware of the monumental and classic problem: how are human experiences and reality related? Ever since Fechner, basic psychophysics has quantified many such phenomena and new paradigms in studies on sensation and perception and consciousness have emerged. However, the problem extends deeper than that and concerns all studies of human experience and practically all sciences – especially physics.

There are two unusual but strong insights to start with. First, physics is a *human-centered science*. This may sound strange to those who see physics as the major science of nature, universe and everything related to these. Second, there is no well-established theory of the *general observer* in physics. Considering this, the problems of what is the nature of human visual experience, and any other experiences of the world, and subjective image quality, as an example, in their deepest human sense, are simply magnificent.

The implications of this kind of thinking are only shortly introduced here but an interested reader can find an introductory analysis of this view in my article "On the construction of a psychologically based, general theory of observation: an introduction" (arXiv:1309.3633 [physics.hist-ph]).

Imagine, for example, that humans (and monkeys, for that matter) had an extremely accurate 3D stereo vision system that allowed direct visual perception of the relative distances of the moon, planets and the stars in the sky. Such an exceptional capacity would have changed the history of classical and modern astronomy and physics. Simply by looking at the sky, even the prehistoric men (and monkeys) had seen that the moon is relatively near to us, compared to a few other close-by celestial objects, the planets, of which only two had been seen to come between us and the sun and the rest of them always further from the sun. Most of the stars would twinkle somewhere far, far away and it could have been everyday knowledge that we travel around the sun. These perceptions would have led to another kind of development in physics and in natural sciences. The first telescopes would probably have been stereoscopic, different from the present ones.

Figure 1. A classic stereoscope.

One could take this as an insignificant, imaginary story of science fiction or a fairy tale. However, some may know that 3D stereo maps of about thousands and thousands of stars have been produced from the observations conducted by the Hipparcos satellite. A printed 3D star atlas was created so that with stereo glasses you can directly view the (scaled) relative locations of a number stars and galaxies (cf. Monkhouse & Cox, 2000). A specific 3D atlas of the universe has been published using parallax effects to make the 3D perceptible (https://in-the-sky.org/ngc3d.php).

There is more than meets the eye in this specific example of 3D stereovision. We can now ask, what if our other sensory-perceptual systems were totally unlike they are now? The mechanistic idea of human perception is so deeply engraved into our minds that it is not easy to imagine what a totally different sensory system could be like. Most if not all physical paradigms and models take it as given that a wisely selected human observer is good enough to represent any observer, and what we cannot directly perceive we can accomplish with ever better and clever physical instruments. Other species do have different sensory-perception systems and they can be compared against the human senses but even their performance has been studied using human-centric physics as a 'grounding point'. A theory of the general observer does not exist in physics.

How had a different (human) perceptual system affected the development of physics? What kind of instruments, measures and theories of the world had been designed for intelligent living and clever science? What about aliens having totally different sensory (if they had such properties) systems?

Realistic biologists and opticians would argue that the kind of a 3D stereovision system mentioned above is not simply possible in the human head where the eye separation together with the diffraction-limited optics is just too small for perceiving large 3D distances. Indeed, we use stereovision for rather near observations in our personal space and for accurate manipulation of objects. But we can imagine a biological system with an extremely accurate visual (iconic) memory and a 3D stereo processing capacity that could have an effective depth perception even for stellar relative distances (just like the Hipparcos satellite does). It would combine the image sensed when the earth is at one extreme position on its trajectory around the sun with the image of the same object observed at the opposite side of the trajectory. This would function as an immense stereoscope with an artificial between-the-eyes distance of about 150 million kilometers that would provide a magnificent celestial 3D stereovision through space. Possible or not, the thought experiment is eye opening: any kind of sensory systems can be theoretically constructed. The stereoscope in the photo is from the early 20th century France.

Had we possessed this valuable capacity for 3D vision, our knowledge of the universe had certainly progressed faster. Ptolemy, Copernicus, and Galilei had been puzzled by other celestial problems; perhaps totally different skills and talents would have been valuable in natural sciences. Giordano Bruno could have survived, or at least be murdered for some other reasons by the Roman inquisition. Indeed, the capacity limitations of our senses have had significant social, cultural and even religious consequences.

2. Sensory determinants of physics

A thought experiment: what were the consequences for physical theory formation that distances were measured with stick standards? What about the impact of other 'natural' standards constructed and used, for example, for estimating the weight of objects or passing of time? Originally the 'sticks' were invented to compensate for our sensory limitations. Can a physicist forget these simple human constrains and assume that they have not guided physics at all or that it is only a matter of transformation from one domain to another or that there is no risk of being seriously biased by them?

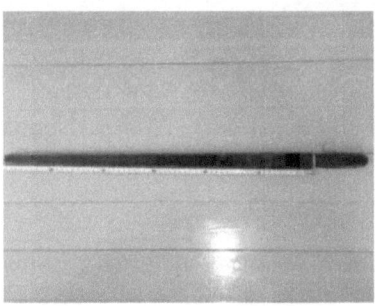

Figure 2. A Finnish measurement stick from the early 1900.

Such thought experiments have not been too popular among theoretical physicists. A delightful story is George Gamow's *Mr. Tompkins in Wonderland*, published in 1946 where he entertains the idea, considering all its relativistic consequences for our world, that the speed of light was only 30 miles/hr. It would be creative fun to write a fairy tale of a physics professor in a world where human vision had an extremely accurate spectral sensitivity, visual-spatial resolution better than an electron microscope, and 3D vision with a better depth resolution than that of the Hipparcos satellite. This physics professor would not lecture about the discovery of the spectral redshift in the stars, everyone would know the phenomenon. He could go directly into its interpretation with the help of the basic astronomical 3D-depth knowledge.

We will always need a grounding theory of observation, not only in the form of fairy tales but because when taken seriously, it is one of the eternal tasks of mankind, trying to understand our perception of the world and ourselves. The knowledge building in classical and modern physics has been profoundly constrained by the limiting capacities of the human sensory perception; measurement systems have been invented to compensate for this human lack of objectivity. Hence, all physical measures and the theories derived from them are inherently human-centric, and direct outcomes of our human 'observation mechanics'. The measurement stick in the photo is from my grandfather, originally from his father.

It is no accident that pointers have been found useful as indicators in measuring instruments: human ability to discriminate relative visual position/location is one of our best sensory abilities. While these considerations may sound like superficial perceptual speculation or ungrounded philosophy, it is possible to show that they have serious consequences for any physical theory building.

Frogs and the theory of the universe. Had the frog a brain like ours, but still possessing its derivative eyes that are sensitive to spatial and temporal changes in the environment, it would have created another kind of physics from what we have today. For example, for a frog, a meter stick 'is not there' unless it moves, vibrates back and forth or it is visually flashed on and off. Human vision has similar limitations since images stabilized on the retina disappear within a few seconds but luckily our eyes move constantly and prevent this peculiar kind of biological blindness. If they (or our heads) did not move, a stationary meter stick would have little value as an instrument for measuring the length of a fabric, unless it was waved back-and-forth to keep it visible, which would make the measurement of the fabric – also moved around – very difficult and unpractical. Without moving eyes, we would see the pointer of a voltage meter when it moves, but would see only a glimpse of it where it stops.

Frog's eyes are derivative or transient sensors and they are by no means linear instruments. Hence, the theory of the universe created by the frog (with a human brain) would (most probably) not be a simple linear transformation from ours. It is an exercise of high ambiguity to try to derive a physical theory that is testable by instruments and measures that are relevant to the frog, and then to build a theory of the universe based on this minute difference between man and the frog.

We can use the frog or some other 'model animal' in the same way that pharmacologists and brain scientists use their animal models in trying to understand human mind. But above all, we need a theory of observation that includes a general observer (even an alien).

In the following I have shortly speculated how the human sensory properties have constrained the theory formation and practices of physics. This has carried to all other aspects of natural and human sciences where physical measurements are used directly or indirectly. The development of physical measures was an evolutional, human and social-cultural process which included at least the following steps:

a) Cost/benefit analysis was probably among the first steps in the invention of any human measurement system, typically based on economical, ecological or any practical considerations like securing minimum losses in measuring the amount of materials sold or minimum 'engineering' cost of the errors made in its use.

b) Sensory amplification is used in most forms of physical measurement, for example in the use of measurement sticks, scales, compasses, and ammeters. Showing the position of a pointer relative to a suitably marked background makes the positional reading accurate: our visual system is extremely good in such comparison tasks. A standard measurement stick functions in the same way. For a scientist frog, however, the pointer would disappear when not moving.

c) Perceptual transformation from one sensory domain to another. A fascinating example comes from China, in about 200 BC. A system to measure the amount of liquid filled into a barrel of fixed size and form, was accomplished by using a set of reference barrels filled with known amounts of liquid. By hitting alternatingly two barrels with a bat it was possible to get a subjective estimation: hitting first the one being filled and then the reference barrel, and listening to the sounds generated. Equal sounds meant equal amounts of liquid, wine for example. This was a case of deriving a physical measure based on perceptual transformation from one sensory domain (perception of volume in which we are not very good) to another (perception of sound differences in which we are relatively good). The gains made by the measurement system boosted its use and standardization. This mode of physical measurement is not untypical for modern physics either. The famous Wilson cloud chamber was used for detecting particles from ionizing radiation as visible tracks that could be photographed and measured. Again, a scientist frog had not been happy with such poorly visible measures and it would have invented dynamic arrangements, which of course, would have led to early consideration of complex temporal dynamics of the observed particles. We can also ask how different other chamber inventions – compared against the presently available ones – would have been created by the brainy frogs?

d) Combination of sensory domain information. The speed of sound was difficult to measure during the times of Newton when suitable chronometers were not available. Newton used a simple 'walking with a pendulum' method that you can still try today in the same corridor in Cambridge. He attached a nail, like a thumbtack on the sole of his shoe. Having the swinging pendulum with a known time constant hanging from his hand, walking in the corridor towards its distant wall, he listened to the sound from the nail hitting the stone floor and then the sound returning as a delayed echo from the wall. He observed the phase of the pendulum when hearing the echo sound and based on this he could then estimate the speed of sound when he knew his distance to the wall. He made a measurement error of about 10% by this creative subjective method. It relied on sensory transformation by combing the sensory observation between sensory domains: visual position, timing, and the sound. In this case, comparison across sensory channels made an accurate physical measurement possible. With the speed of light, something different was needed.

A question now arises: could novel physical theories be invented by changing the way basic physical entities and measures are defined? Is it possible to build a physics of alternative realities that are as true as our present ones, but from a different perspective, the perspective of a known or general theoretical observer, a frog, even an alien, or someone only slightly different from us? Why not include the 'general observer' in the wave equation? Would it make any sense? Can these human-centric thoughts about our physics knowledge offend mathematicians and natural scientists? Perhaps not, they might even inspire them.

14 PERCEPTION AND ORGANZATIONS

1.   Perception as a master strategy

In their short discussion "The Art of Strategy" (October 2013) two McKinsey strategy specialists did not refer to strategic perception at all, although their comments touched on physics, resourcing, analytics, rigor, and even psychology as important concepts and metaphors in strategy discourse. Their view on perception was quite different from the famous Japanese swordsman Musashi's who had the saying (my very free translation): *"Seeing is weak, perceiving is strong"*. In his dangerous world, a misperception at a critical moment would cost his life and so it is with organizations – a difference in time constants perhaps. Vision without intelligent perception was fateful for a samurai. Indeed, it is not rare to forget 'perception' in strategy considerations although 'vision' is ever present.

I will here take up some familiar problems of classic organizational vision-strategy processes and relate the two worlds that mostly are related by words only, not by their meanings: those of strategy and perception. This may be an unorthodox approach but I have been fortunate to live in both worlds during my academic and not-so-academic career, and Musashi is no stranger to me either. You might wonder why I take up this topic in the contexts of human technology. The reason is simple: human technologies will guide the development of our future organizations' life and technology makes the eyes, ears and memory of most organizations.

Intelligent perception should be an essential component of any organizational, vision-strategy model, but typically it is not. Indeed, 'perception' is not a standard concept in organizational studies and it is often misunderstood, hidden under trendy disguises like sense-making, sensing, framing, or awareness, for example, its relevance underestimated, or it is used in a popular-psychological sense and as such of not much use.

Perception is not an easy topic: theory of perception is an evolving and moving target itself. Earlier here I argued that there is no general theory of the general observer (perceiver) in classical or modern physics (cf. my introductory article related to this at http://arxiv.org/abs/1309.3633). Even Einstein used layman ideas of the observer in his famous thought experiments on relativity. No wonder then, that a serious observer theory does not exist in the organizational sciences either. Superficial and verbose models are abundant. No doubt, observer models will soon evolve because of the fast increase in the complexity of organizational environments, where perception skills and capabilities (by humans and organizations using special technologies, especially AI) are necessary assets.

Perception is not about recording the world or oneself. It is acting <u>in</u> them. The 'in' here is not a spelling mistake, I do not mean 'on' – I hope I use the language right: perception-action cannot be separated from the system consisting of the world and the perceiver, not without distorting the knowledge about either of them. Further, perception is directed outwards and inwards – simultaneously and in various forms of synchrony. Because of this, intelligent perception is a most intriguing capacity and has huge 'strategic' value when it drives the internal and external 'behavior' of an organism, human experience, the behavior of a machine or a firm.

The perceiver/observer constructs internal images, scenes, scenarios, spaces, models, and other, mostly unknown mental structures and their inherent processes that relate the observer (subject) to these representations of the internal and external worlds. She aims at recognizing potential invariances in both worlds. Every time an invariance is learned or adopted, the system saves time, energy and processing power and it becomes better in surviving changing and complex internal and external events. It becomes intelligent.

Take a simple example of invariance: in a city, a constant flow of sounds reach our ears: from cars, people, electronic gadgets, echoes, and material sounds of any form. At the ear, we receive a sum of these audio waves. However, we practically never make strange interpretations about the sources of these sounds: we keep hearing cars, people etc as if it was natural that they are unchanged audio sources. In theory, it is possible that we could hear strange combinations of these entering sound waves so that at any moment we would hear a new 'source' and next another one; the world would appear as a continuously alternating, creative mess. As an analogy, it is not rare at all in organizations to hear such multiple interpretations of the world or of the firm from people 'perceiving' identical data, especially during turbulent times. In natural life we have learned the invariant properties of sound sources in our world even when the sources undergo changes (cars in summer and winter, for example, new engine types) or our situations (weather, echoes) where we listen to them change. We can experience a well-structured, kind world. With the coming of electric cars and bikes having their own sounds or practically no engine sounds, the importance of consequent audio will be understood.

Invariant data relationships are, behavior-strategically, the most important and informative 'measures' of perceived objects and perceived mental states. By obtaining knowledge of these invariances, the observer can make intelligent assumptions about the world, and guide his attention, plan actions and become willingly entangled with the objects in the (assumed) internal and external worlds. Intelligent perception means being sensitive both to the opportunities and obstacles when reaching for something of importance.

The perceiver must adapt to the environmental changes and generate intelligent perception structures (hard-, soft-, inherited or culturally wired) that help automate further perception and action processes. This is necessary for survival. Intelligent perception makes it possible for the actor-observer to use its limited resources for ever higher-level functions, and finally – it allows the organism's full trust on its perception so much that actions can be accomplished with full power and accuracy. It may be good to repeat here that perception is not directed to the outer world only. Beneath all this hides the internal world of pain and pleasure, shades of mental life, aesthetics, culture, and love – which I only can imply here.

We can admire the amazing perceptual abilities in human sports and performance arts and in animal flight and fight. Often we miss to notice that we enjoy similar amazing skills in our everyday life and activities, but most of these wonders remain hidden from our awareness because we *live our perceptions*. Even the best robots are ignorant: in war they can accidentally kill anyone and they are practically useless in trying to recognize peace. Having said all this, is there anything in this description of perception that should not be an essential aspect of any strategy consideration? Could this insight be used in the analysis of strategy processes and perhaps inform their design in organizations?

2. Strategy discourse – problems and opportunities

Some strategy researchers discuss the 'demand or consumer/customer side' of strategy research (and practice) and others look at the resource-based view emphasizing the production side (cf. Priem, Butler, Li, 2013, for example). A practical question remains in any approach, how to best conceptualize and organize the strategy process of firms, large companies and even nations. The vision-strategy process as it is typically applied carries an increasing number of problems, one of them being the neglect of strategic perception.

The most amazing property of a typical organizational vision-strategy process is that it is practically never impossible to formulate a vision! I have not met an organization that would openly say that it was impossible to build a vision. Every firm has a vision, even the third sector communities, universities and minuscule departments have it. What a wonderful tool that works everywhere, in any conditions, and by anyone?

Not so long time ago, in Finland, we had several national vision-strategy documents – and they were of no help, we got into economical trouble for a decade. We even had the national brand vision and the Team Finland strategy for 2014 and after that, a futures document from our Government (which totally underestimated scientific views). The documents had no national impact, except for the irritation they caused when it became evident how useless views they were. Nobody remembers these visions now and they helped none.

Vision can make a strategy process blind. Because of the way a firm or a national government decides to look at the world and perceive it through its vision, it runs at risk of masking crucial information and patterns in its environment. Hence, it becomes biased in its strategy formulation. Indeed, it would be more realistic to talk about 'directed attention' than 'vision' in these cases and we know what happens when we direct our limited resources at a distorted or a false target only.

Under changing circumstances misdirected attention can be more typical than not in many of the present-day organizations, especially the large ones. We Finns could sense something like that after the collapse of Nokia – practically blind to its evolving market life: the Finnish Government Program from June 2011 led us, as a nation, to a slow but determinate deterioration of production and finances. Again, like Nokia with its "connecting people" vision, the Government's vision described our wonderful national vision to be a "caring, open, responsible, globally aware and prosperous well-fare society." Economic suffering was not mentioned.

The way our national vision was defined in the Governmental program and was guarded by various stakeholders and situational factors, fixated the national vision on business-as-usual targets, blocking perceptive, smooth, adaptive and novel ways towards a realistic national vision in the fast-changing world. The outcome was that during the improving global and European economy we suffered for years from the lack of intelligent perception inwards and outwards and even for today's Government it is a difficult task.

Figure 1. A strategy puzzle.

3. Strategic tools as weapons of organizational destruction

Like all strategy programs, the Finnish one included an analysis (perception) of the current environment and the foreseeable futures, and then looked at the politically agreed strategic means for reaching the goals. It was a standard process, based on difficult party negotiations and hidden lobbying after which compromise policies were chosen to work towards the vision.

The worst strategy formulation and processes I have seen implemented is almost identical to the Government case: the experience is from the higher education and university context in Finland. Still about a decade or more years ago the strategy processes at universities were mostly harmless. An academic, eloquent discourse and documentation could go on in parallel – having only a mild interference – with effective real-world work and activities. It was a strange form of virtual activity within the academia. Now with new and tangible power structures at our universities the situation has changed profoundly and the vision-strategy process has become a powerful tool of management and it has impacts – especially disastrous ones. Today there is research data, showing how terrible the situation became because of this, but the problem remains nationwide.

It was disturbing to see how the strategy process became a de facto *internal weapon of academic mass destruction*: the power relationships dictated how different organizational units, dominant individuals, and research groups would struggle for resources and their 'strategic position', to guarantee survival. It is not a local national problem only, but occurs elsewhere in Europe and in US. Those who make it and succeed, will be the ones defining the new vision and strategy weapons and gain more power – not much interest is given to the rest of the resources or the organization.

Many in the academia and higher education management seem to think, in accordance with their vision, that the 'fittest' will survive, but the question remains, 'in what sense the fittest' because after destruction the weaker ones have no voice to begin with and nobody perceives them any longer. Perhaps the main reason for this strange development is that self-perception had no role in these organizational considerations: perception was fixated at external and formal outcomes. Businesses are no different, the metrics used and the weights given to different measures only vary. The sense of reality makes all the difference, especially if it is economically grounded and understands the critical role of human commitment, purposes and competences.

Of course, the classic strategy models are meant to be fast, dynamic, sensitive, relevant, creative, and adaptive by using intelligent data, analysis, excellent leadership, and modification and re-evaluation during the vision-strategy cycle, every year or so. However, all these wonderful aspects are relevant and reasonable only when perception is intelligent.

Change and volatility challenge any strategy model. Our Government case was no exception among the organizations suffering from the unstable environment and massive changes. The financial crisis in 2008 happened too fast for many. From the beginning, it was a challenge of perception – but it was not recognized as such. In Finland, already by 2010 we could perceive, by looking at our falling export data and its trend that something was seriously wrong: the export did not show any signs of recovery, unlike in Sweden and Germany, our two best reference countries in this context. The relative data looked scary – we did not perceive (our leaders did not turn their attention to it) the lack of invariances in this dangerous development. There were strong signals all around us – but the observers in power were reluctant or weak and the relevant observers had no voice.

Returning to the US financial crisis we can now assume that it was, most of all, a problem of intelligent perception but this became clear only after the crisis. Earlier here I described how Charles Perrow showed the real predecessors of the 2008 events and confirmed the problem of biased and weak organizational perception (Perrow did not use the term 'perception') that had prevented many from seeing what was coming despite the warning signs that were not weak at all. It was about a true lack of intelligent strategic perception. This was an excellent example of the difference between the concepts of perception as recording and perception as an intelligent, architectural process, linked with action.

Strategies are meant to meet any positive and negative futures any organization can face. Our Government's perception remained separate from its action; it had the vision and it did receive the environmental information but lacked the perceptual intelligence to interpret what was visible and hence its perception did not support action. Furthermore, there was a grounded strategy, produced with difficulty and in addition, the backing parties were willingly or unwillingly freezing it. The Government remained not only blind but also a hostage of its own public vision-strategy process: there was no quick way out or even a chance to perceive and share new strategic opportunities which would have been desperately needed.

Media and the public have learned to 'know' what a classic strategy means. Hence, the situation was not made easier by the media that loves to remind of the strategy (plan) and its 'promises' made in 2011. The same kind of political discourse on strategy and 'political promises' continues still today, it's a political-social practice that media loves: in media, 'strategy' equals 'promises' and targeting of national attention. The Finnish Government had and has effective and willing guards in the media – and opposition, of course. As if to strengthen the friction effect, the visible public opinion in the news-hungry and social media have together become powerful means in treating the national strategy and its vision as promises and together they have obtained the power to inhibit any strategic changes from happening. In the discourses produced in this way, the strategy adaptation process is transformed into a 'breaking promises' discourse.

I could closely follow a case on how our dominant media were unable to turn their perception to the export and innovation problems in 2011: research data showed, without a doubt, that Finland had been unable to build economically large-scale firms during the last 20 years. For a distinguished colleague of mine, Professor Eero Byckling, it took nearly two years to get published a serious and well-founded analysis based on this nationally scary perception. Our leading business magazines and the main newspaper were not interested to write about it: they could not perceive what Eero had clearly perceived. Finally, he could publish his analysis on the Finnish export and innovation system failure in a journal focusing on cultural matters (!) (cf. Kanava 1/2013). Today, these topics have become public knowledge in the media discourse, but we lost valuable time and money in billions. Why does this happen in 'broad daylight' and when we perceive the same 'world'? Who or what prevents intelligent perception?

The standard explanation to the national-level problem is that we suffer from the same ideological and democratic crowding problem as the US. Democrats and republicans block each other's way to what the opponent sees as progress: the two parties perceive totally different and divergent worlds and opportunities to reach for a national vision.

A well-known cognitive-theoretical explanation to poor organizational perception is the notion of cognitive dissonance. Accordingly, denial and distortion of perception or even blindness can be caused by a person's – or an organization's –

observation and experience that reality appears to challenge her deepest and most established assumptions and beliefs about the world (e.g. Kessler, 2010, in real-world economics review).

One is tempted to claim that due to cognitive dissonance, our (public) national perceptual architecture did not include sources, which would have revealed such negative phenomena and we remained partly blind and passive, as if waiting for an external and forceful attentive signal or even instruction (from economists, EU politicians, rating organizations etc.) to include such perception sources – had the situation become undeniably threatening. After that, the new perception mechanism would be spanned and opened for public use, but time had been lost. Fortunately for us, our national economy improved and now in 2020, some years after the previous Governmental visions our public actors have been 'forced' to adapt. Surprising enough, a poll in Finland, already during the troubles in 2013 showed that about 50% of citizens were ready, unlike most of the politicians, for significant policy changes related to taxation and retirement age, for example. Can a strategy process be weaker than this, frozen, even in front of its perceptive audience, willing to change?

4. Lack of passion for the vision

Only rarely does a formal organizational vision evoke a vivid passion among its audience, in the employees or citizens, in those responsible for reaching it. It was no surprise that our Government turned to a national 'guru' who had the rhetoric and media fame and was expected to re-formulate or translate (perhaps even transform) the formal visions and programs so that the citizen audiences could become enchanted by it. Dr. Himanen and his co-author, Manuel Castells published a book in November 2013 on our national vision where they lifted 'dignity' as a core element for our national vision. Of course, nobody is, or can be directly against such a valuable thing and many seemed to accept it as a promising vision. The process made the governmental strategy process a mess.

It is not rare for companies to invite charismatic speakers and showmen to ignite the audience which has become tired of boring visions. In Italy, a clown became a significant political actor. Such performers and gurus are hoped to act as apostles with the ability to offer an inspiring vision – or a criticism of it – which is derived from the organizational situation and documents but to which they are hoped to breath signs of life.

In Finland this led to a strange episode, now called 'The Himanen case' when it was found out that the questionable national strategy-project application had been accepted without open competition by the Head of Finnish Academy, the Head of Tekes, and Sitra, our leading and the most prestigious organizations for the national management of science and technology. The process was against all standard evaluation practices and ethics in Finland. It became a double failure of trust in the strategy process – even before the final report of the work became public. When the report appeared, it had a chaotic reception and it blocked any reasonable, new national perception for a year or two. Now it's been forgotten.

Organizational vision is not perception. Recently I browsed through a list of popular strategy tools in a local business magazine (Optio, 16/2013) introducing their core elements: scorecards, swots, blue ocean, lean systems, neo-taylorism, scenarios, weak signals, co-creation, change management, vriq, benchmarking, portfolios learning organization, and so on. While they do include a plethora of means to observe, analyze and model the environment, they have no serious interest in organizational perception. 'Vision', however, remains the core component.

The term 'vision' as used in strategy discourse has nothing to do with human or any other vision system or perception. It is a definition of what an organization wants to see to happen to it, internally or externally, and it is not a matter of perceiving something. A better term would indeed be organizational imagination, dreaming or attention, sometimes even confabulation – with the requirement that it must be, in some acceptable way – grounded and realistic in the eyes of the presenter or the audience.

Below, I will explain my view on why I believe the classic strategy process paradigm fails and suggest alternative, opportunity perception-based concepts for supporting an effective strategy process that can match the demands of the complex and changing world. This is where human and social technologies become elements of organizational perception; most of the suggestions require specific technological environments and implementations where human, artificial and organizational perceptions occur.

5. On strategic perception

What could a perception theorist tell a strategist? I put the perception implications in a question form and as you will see I keep repeating – on purpose – the word 'perception' instead of measurement. Often I use the term 'observer' in exchange with 'perceiver'. In addition, I use the term 'firm' when I refer to any form of organization, public, private or other.

I do not make a separation between cognitive, emotional, motivational, experiential and contextual aspects of perception in any way. I take it for granted that they are always tightly inherent in perceptions, integrated and inseparable, otherwise what we assume to be perception is simply accumulation of fragmented data. Narrow experimental and brain science paradigms typically separate these essential aspects and the result is dwarfing of psychological phenomena. The problem is not that such focused studies would not be needed but it is in the way the obtained results are generalized. In everyday organizational life, these multiple psychological aspects of perception are permanently 'entangled'. The core questions emerging from the perceptual system theory to strategy considerations, are the following:

a) How does a firm understand the meaning of *intelligent perception* in its business/behavior environment? What are the firm's domains of perception?

b)   What is the *observational architecture* (measurement, observation, participation, action) through which the firm relates to its environment and to itself? Who and what objects and processes in and outside the firm are at the center of this architecture and why?

c)   How is *intelligent perception-action* implemented in the firm?

d)   How does *perceptual learning* and related actions take place?

e)   How are perception processes linked with the strategy process and decision making?

f)   How are the *critical invariances* recognized (e.g. on the market, competitor activities, customer behavior, in technology development, business environment in general, financial developments, internal practices and interactions and development, management culture…) in its environment and within itself?

g)   How does a firm find its own *one-world interpretation*? How are the alternative and changing worlds derived and dealt with in the perception processes?

h)   What is the firms *operating system* and the bandwidth of solutions in connecting perceptions with action? How are the perception processes given the right to action and system control when something critical happens?

i)   How does the firm secure the efficiency of its early (immediate) observations and the intelligence of the high-level processes in interpreting the perceived information?

j)   Is there a cost/benefit analysis of the firm's perception system?

6.   Spanning the observational architecture

Intelligent, biological perception systems are not designed to observe and react to everything. Relevance is everything, more important than signal quality. Hence, biological perception systems have the capacity to form a relationship with relevant external and internal events and adapt dynamically to changing conditions. They direct their resources: perceptual, neuro-hormonal, evaluative, and motor ones accordingly. Furthermore, perception systems are multi-dimensional (cognitive, emotional, motivational, forecasting etc.) in nature and involve both the pleasures and pains of perception; they are always intimately linked with behavioral preparation and control. Artificial perception systems have many weaknesses in these characteristics but they improve fast.

We humans don't know how much of the world we can perceive and it has been a matter of popular discussion on how much of the environmental visual information we can, in fact, 'see'. Due to the eye movements, we are blind about half of the time, that is twice a second. Furthermore, I believe we see less that 1/1000 000 of what there is to be seen in the whole visual field – even if it is within the sensory range or our senses. These aspects of perception demonstrate the amazing 'strategically clever design' of the human perception system and its architecture, by which it optimizes between the system economy and functional relevance. We are blind most of the time but do not suffer from it and we don't even notice the blindness. On the other hand, a curious biological detail is that some brain cells can follow a visual flicker which the observer does not see as flickering indicating there is always more going on in the brain than we can see (e.g. Gur and Snodderly, 1997; Vision Research 37(4):377-82). Strategic perception is no different: in the middle of continuous blindness, intelligent perception is necessary for survival. For firms, this is perhaps news, as an analogy at least.

Perception is spontaneously agile. Perception without action is nothing: when we accidentally burn our fingers, the incoming signal pathways do not have to ask for permission from the 'brain management' or the 'human resources center' to recruit the motor system. Or when you triple and are about to fall down, your sensory-motor balance-maintaining system not only reacts to the surprise but it is 'allowed' to take full control over your whole external and internal behavior – for the moment – to regain balance. After that, control is swiftly transferred back to the base behavior and the relevant context is recovered.

We can characterize this smooth perception-action behavior 'agile' as is fashionable in talking about 'fast strategies' and agile development projects using scrum and other modern methods, for example. In scrum, as in the above human examples the full (distributed) project control is momentarily transferred (planned and interactively allocated) to individuals or teams that have a relevant task to accomplish at that specific phase of the project. This is accomplished and secured by forming a holistic project entity, including a dynamic team structure and multiple-level feed-back system. In this way, continuously interacting and evaluative collaboration projects avoid the pitfalls of rigidly applied waterfall methods.

As a system, the scrum model resembles the human perception-action system: it includes specific actor roles (purpose-driven) and continuous interactions among the participants, and it proceeds by following fast, effective, and planned sprints (during a week, for example), guided by the continuous feed-back and evaluation processes. At its best, a scum organization is perceptive, fast, adaptive and can orient to new situations as required by the internal and external project events.

Later below when I explain the core principles of the perception system behaviors, it becomes clear how they closely tangent the scrum methodology principles. But even scrum depends critically on its ability to gather relevant perceptual information about its distributed environment. This is challenging when the participants come from different disciplines, having their own background, stakeholders and operation domains with their limitations. The true observational architecture is span by them.

I'm not an experienced scrum master, but my experiences from formal scrum projects is that from the start it can be unclear what is the perception architecture and how it is spanned. Of course, everyone in a scrum project has a saying on the 'perceptual background' but not everyone is aware of its relevance in what is to come. Over the exercise this can become evident when conflicts of interests occur and hidden problems are revealed and discussed: this happens when the perception/observation architecture has not been optimally spanned and shared and it does not fully serve its purpose. Scrum-like approach could benefit from some of the perception lessons.

Organizations relying on the classic strategy model – mission-vision-strategy-resourcing-implementation are slow and have much to learn in trusting their perception sources and in avoiding the risks of giving full control to its sub-systems. Indeed, a firm trusting its perception must secure access to organized action when the perception system so indicates.

7. The lure of a kind strategy world

We are destined to rely on strong assumptions about the world. Only rarely can we hear CEOs and other high-level leaders and politicians to explicitly describe what, in detail, these assumptions are in their own strategy contexts. In everyday life, we expect the world to be relatively kind to us – so that we don't have to observe and double-check everything. It would take all our efforts and would still not be enough if we had to assume that anything in the world can change, any time. Sometimes intelligent perceptions or measurements can warn us of a coming dangerous change.

We do have moving eyes, which we could whirl around, but luckily we have developed the swift ability to shift attention based on target relevance, and using focal visual capacity without continuously moving the eyes; we move them when we don't get any better information by fixating at a selected target. This is a wonderful challenge to any firm, trying to get rid of its bureaucracy: to build intelligent perception systems that can direct attention by using the existing resources optimally and furthermore, by relying on such systems, to avoid excess 'organizational eye/people movements' but instead, observe (measure) the significant events and objects with relevant accuracy. Together the selectivity of perception and its ecological success show how valuable intelligent perception is for any system, biological or artificial. Current AI systems are still in their infancy in attentive intelligence.

Organizations, public and private, orient to their world and are guided by a strategy, which includes their de facto perception system and observation-action architecture – although firms do not typically use these terms. In classic strategy processes the perception system is used for collecting relevant internal and external forecast and other information and the current situation is analyzed with the purpose of making the best possible choices and decisions for the foreseeable future. Information sources are many and can be anything from cash flow, competitive performance, competence, market, financial, and competitor data to the technology situations and trends. SAP and other integrated systems are trying to provide the technological implementations of organizational perception: in extreme cases (imaginary only, I hope) such systems can become the only eyes to the world by an isolated manager or a bureaucrat.

Although the managers don't not talk about 'perceptions', their way of collecting data is a direct expression on how they think about the organization's perception mechanisms in scanning the external environment and the firm. Typical strategy building cycle starts with the declaration (either by designing it or conducting an inventory) of this observational architecture and perception resources are then spanned accordingly. This includes e.g. knowledge acquisition, measurement, and analytics, and can be considered as a part of the firm's knowledge management process. In this sense the firm defines the relationships it has with itself and with its environment. Often this is a tacit phenomenon, a reflection of the organizational culture and the way it discusses its environment and itself. This may sound like vague philosophical talk but it is not: in designing and building artificial vision systems, for example, the observational architecture is a most critical factor constraining the system performance.

Organizational perception can be directed at the customer, markets, sales and forecast data, various data representation forms, discussion forums, person-to-person interactions – on any big or small data process and it can also occur in various knowledge and customer relationship activities of the management and the personnel. However, it is not an extremely complex task to map and model this observational architecture in a company, or a government, for that matter, and to describe the basic components and the inherent perceptional relationships. It is rare to see it done properly.

8.   Scorecards as perception bureaucracy

Balanced scorecard (BSC) models come close to the perceptual approach in how they define the metrics for a firm's progress on financial, customer-, growth, and business process sectors, for example. The BSC system spans a 'measurement architecture', but it can differ from the perception approach where the emphasis is on intelligent and 'strong' perception. I use the concept of 'perception-action lens' as a tool for looking deeper into the nature of the measurement and at the observation architecture. Perception is more than measurement as it has its own domains of activity and forms of engagement. No physical or organizational measurement happens without some form of human engagement.

A simple example is an employee responding to a questionnaire probing the firm's atmosphere. It is not rare to hear complains on how workers lack means to express their relevant feelings and observations at the right time, for example on quality, coordination, or management communication, even when it would be of utmost value for the firm. The problem is not lack of data, or lack of personnel inventory - it is a failure in timing, relevance, content and impact of the perception-action system. For company strategists, the design of measurement metrics is crucial: ignoring the perception mechanisms can entertain unfounded faith in data sources and measures or simply make the firm blind to relevant information.

Distorted perception architecture is disastrous. A curious example of a distorted perception architecture is the work of the investigation panel reviewing the Challenger accident in 1986 where one member of the panel, Richard Feynman, the famous Nobelist could not get his strong and clear message through and had to find clever ways to open the eyes of other committee members and the media when expressing his opinion about the accident causes. The panel did not accept his simple and practical views, at first, which inspired him to demonstrate his hypothesis on a televised hearing.

Feynman took a glass full of ice and water and put a real O-ring from Challenger into it and then showed how he could break the cold ring by hand; it was impossible to be blind to such a strong observation and his arguments and their timing were perfect then. For an unknown reason, the panel had spanned its perception mechanisms in a way that made Feynman's observations and thoughts invisible or insignificant to them. His arguments had remained weak or silent signals but the demonstration changed the situation. It is a good question, why this happened, even in the case of a terrible accident, and the view of an exceptional physicist whose problem solving skills were a legend. Not unlike in the 2008 financial crisis, various explanations, political, social-psychological, institutional and others were offered post hoc but the outcome was the same: the distorted perception architecture determined which perceptions were included, 'interesting' and accepted. As is now well known about the economic crisis n 2008, several firms had active short-range, economical reasons to hide their knowledge and data and make the risk factors difficult to perceive. Distorting the perceptual architecture on purpose is nothing new and it is today an explicit form of interference in social media.

Like the Challenger case, the perceptual architecture of the US Government and its analysts' network was biased, for several reasons. It did not include the players, especially banks and insurance companies, the main actors who were in continuous lobbying contact with politicians and other stakeholders. Information about the subprime problems had been visibly accumulating and a few specialists had explicitly warned about it, but they were excluded – perhaps on purpose – from the perceptual architecture. Indeed, some of them later complained about improper treatment and behavior they received to their warnings (cf. the texts by Keen, Roubini and Baker). The forbidden observations on these actions and behaviors were left out from the relevant architecture.

9. Failure in perception - why?

Is it a matter of sensitivity? Yves Doz, for example discusses strategic perceptions in terms of strategic sharpness. As the Governmental crisis examples show, there is much more to perception than meets the eye: clarity is not the same as accuracy or sharpness. There are at least two, almost orthogonal ways to interpret these architectural perception-problems. On one hand, some futures researchers argue (Ansoff, Hiltunen, for example) that it is a question of weak signals, which are difficult to observe. Because of that, information gathering tools like the Delphi method are needed to probe the best imaginable information sources (people).

I have earlier here questioned this weak-signal concept by suggesting that it is rather a matter of distorted perceptual architecture, which does not include relevant perception mechanisms and processes. The observed signals may appear weak, but only because the sources have not been properly understood, identified and included in the relevant perceptual-observational architecture. Of course, it is possible to combine the Delphi with the architecture approach but there is the challenge that the best sources may not be included within the set of a priori relevant sources like the stereotypical members of the establishment or those having fame as recognized visionaries or as other knowledge sources.

Another addendum to this criticism is related to what a colleague of mine Professor Leena Kasvio once described: an unusual accident where a landing passenger airplane crashed against a car driving on the runway. Her interpretation of the causes was that the air traffic controllers had a distorted (she did not use this term) idea of what was their core task and consequently, what to monitor. However, their core task was not only to manage the air traffic and to find the right landing window and maintain related communication and safety procedures etc. for the planes; their core task was to secure a safe landing for the planes. The latter view would span the perception architecture accordingly and it would naturally include all runway traffic, be they cars, cats or bulldozers.

At SimAnalytics Ltd Finland (http://simanalytics.com) where they design and build massive scale Machine Learning and automated systems for e.g. industrial environments, with thousands of data sources and complex environments, they have seen the explicit value of the observational architecture concept. It is useful in complex environments where the implementation of human-machine-AI interaction solutions is a hard challenge and it is necessary to look at all the critical data sources, processes and human-machine interactions that must be covered and modeled within the implemented ML systems. By doing so, it is possible to cover any relevant, even emerging data sources, human or artificial, to be used in the AI and ML design, testing and implementation.

Distorted perceptual architecture can sink ships. Disastrous consequence of a biased perceptual architecture is not a modern phenomenon only. A most curious historical example of the dangers of perceptional distortion is the stability test of the famous *Swedish Vasa warship*, which sank outside Stockholm on its maiden cruise in August 1628 (http://faculty.up.edu/lulay/failure/vasacasestudy.pdf). It was built in a hurry and with the largest investments ever to make it the most glorious warship in Sweden. King Gustav had hurried its building and put the shipyard management under royal pressure. By doing this, he seriously distorted the perception-action mechanisms at the shipyard.

The construction process was problematic from the start and there were early doubts about the ship's stability. Aware of these problems, the shipyard management had Vasa tested at the harbor by ordering a group of 30 men to run from side-to-side of the ship: already on the third run Vasa was rolling dangerously. The warning signal was strong enough for the test team and curious enough, the test was halted. No information of this result reached the critical, perhaps close-to-royal decision makers and Vasa was prepared for her celebrated maiden cruise. One could say that from the perspective of the top management the warning signal remained 'weak' – certainly this was true from the King's perspective. For the running test crew the signals were scary and strong. Then on the first celebrated cruise, a mild wind outside the harbor was enough to heel Vasa over and she sank after a 1300 meters cruise, taking 53 seamen with her. Today the well-preserved Vasa, raised in 1961, can be admired at the amazing museum in Stockholm.

One could consider Vasa either as a simple case of bad communication or a combination of bad management, fear for the Royal power of the King and his subordinates – and a communication failure. But there was more to it; the catastrophe bears a close resemblance to the preceding events of the financial crisis and it is not much different from some device, product and service tests. Theranos is a sad, holistic example of that. In both cases, the Vasa and the US crisis, many seemed to ask, after the disaster: "Why didn't we see it coming?" It is a wrong question – it should read: "Why didn't we tune our perception-action architecture right from the first place?"

A relatively recent study on how Nokia lost the mobile phone 'battle' is like directly from the case of Vasa:

"Top managers were afraid of external competitors and shareholders, while middle managers were mainly afraid of internal groups, including superiors and peers. Top managers' externally focused fear led them to exert pressure on middle managers without fully revealing the severity of the external threats and to interpret middle managers' communications in biased ways." (Vuori & Huy, 2015)

10. Strategic inspiration from perception

This is not the right place to make a detailed 'correspondence analysis' of all intelligent perception-action systems (very little is known of them in humans), and their strategy process elements but I assume it will happen in the future strategy research. Here I introduce some aspects of perception, which have fascinated me over the years and try to explain why they have implications or can at least serve as inspiration for strategy thinking. Furthermore, I assume that all perception-action processes are inseparably tuned and tinted by feelings, experiences, and emotions. We cannot live without all these 'properties' of human perception acting in chorus. Of course, not all phenomena described are new or novel.

I chose the following themes to consider for their strategy-relevance: *functional structure of perception, invariance-based perception, and opportunity perception.* The last one is a relatively novel concept and practically non-existent in perception sciences. The point here is to consider how these aspects of perception could refresh strategy thinking.

Figure 2. Beautiful humans inside, masked by technology.

Functional structure of perception. Human perception system is the best example of a successful strategic architecture I know, but it is not as well-known as many seem to think.

No species can survive without well-integrated perception-action; it is a vital capability that supports our development as primitive or cultural organisms - simultaneously. Of course, each species has its own advantages like the extended spectrum of vision in birds and insects, the amazing skill of birds to 'compute' the time-to-target measure in their flight, the infrared sense of snakes or the zoom-like properties of the eagle eye. These exceptional qualities have provided them with real, perception-based strategic advantages. Here I use a few metaphorical views - derived from the analysis of intelligent perception – for the architectural analysis of strategy processes in firms.

Ascending centers of intelligence. During the development of biological organisms, the increasingly intelligent processes have been progressively drawn or pushed upwards in the (neural/sensory-perceptual) system. There are upper limits to this, and because of that the most developed species like some birds, mammals and we humans have even learned to outsource parts of the perception-action architecture (by adopting tools, writing, crafting, any technological and cultural objects). These intelligent resources are then refined and incorporated into the perception-action system – it is a very slow process - while the early object and pattern recognition processes are made fast, reliable, and automatic; they must be efficient, without wasting the resources of the high-level processes. Today, AI is finding its role, both at the lower stages and in higher level perceptual outsourcing.

There are two parallel development streams in the evolution of the perception-action architecture: towards faster and automatic early processes and towards intelligent higher levels, including the adoption of tools. A continuous evolutional pressure makes the higher-level processes faster, too. Opportunity perception for example, has characteristics, which have made humans extremely skilled in visual scene analysis (cf. Oliva and Torralba, 2006; Prog Brain Res. 2006). When humans learned to produce language, cultural objects, symbols and learned to write, development did not stop there (cf. the works and theories of J. Fodor , L. Vygotsky). This 'outsourced' material became then available for the internal processes as well, in the form of thinking, imagery, creative acts and imagination. As a result, human intelligent perception has been a continuously evolving system with interacting external and internal components. In the long run, new functional forms of intelligence have become inbuilt in the brain and the nervous system structure. These are now finding their place in the evolution of AI.

It is not straightforward at all to define any upper limit to the quality and kind of tools that we as humans can adopt. It is possible to speculate about the neural processing limits of mankind, but we simply do not have enough scientific knowledge to support this analysis.

The human retina, for example, does not deal with the most complex visual processing and has allocated this aspect of perception to higher or 'later' layers, at the thalamus and the cortices, for example. Frog and rabbit eyes, on the other hand, use significant resources to record movement direction already on the retina in a way that (probably) does not take place in the human eye. The 'bug detector', the early pattern recognition and intelligence system, is a term originally used in the study of frog retina where such useful, intelligent detectors exist.

The bio-evolutional process may appear like opposite to the prevalent organizational development: modern firms shift their decision power from top to bottom and praise the value of low-hierarchical and distributed organization. Serious strategic questions remain: what kind of intelligent processing is valuable enough – and why - to be shifted higher up and transformed in the command chains or system network? What exactly is good to implement at lower levels, in what form and for which purposes, contents and contexts? It is not only division of labor between the lower and higher level processes but a genuine change in the quality of both. The environment and context are the critical constraining factors. I do not use the expression 'should be left to' - I want to emphasize that it is a matter of intelligent resourcing and long-term learning in the organism's strategy.

With complex, emerging value network environments of future firms the distribution of different resources becomes a difficult strategy problem. We have outlined some of the behavioral aspects of this challenge in "Behavioral theory of a networked firm in value network environment" (Nyman et al., 2013) where we considered the significant role of 'network perception' – the way a firm perceives its environment and itself as a network - in value network analysis. Despite its long history this is still a relatively new form of organizational perception and established concepts barely exist to model it.

Humans and rabbits face different landscapes in their worlds; nature keeps experimenting with their biological strategies. Our higher brain centers are specialized in the analysis of complex, neurally computable object relationships (related e.g. to spatial analysis, numerosity, scene structure, color relationships, sound source recognition, among many others) of the external world. Surprisingly little, however, is known how the brain perceives its internal (mental, mental space) environment and it is not rare to see a neglect of formal analysis of the internal perception in firms. Strange enough, a similar tendency is evident in psychological and brain sciences, too – there is scant interest in the formal-theoretical study of internal/mental perception. This is not the place to go deeper in this topic, but it is more than just subjectivity when referring to the problem of *strong form of internal perception*.

There are signs in psychological-technological literature suggesting that in a very near future many of the internal perceptual phenomena we now call vaguely 'experiences' or 'conscious processes' will be treated as specific forms of pattern recognition and decision making; technologies are being tested to monitor and manipulate these mental processes. Brain stimulation has a long history dating back to 46 AD (cf. A. V. A. Sironi (211) Origin and Evolution of Deep Brain Stimulation) but its modern AI/ML based intelligent versions are only arriving on the stage as I have understood from the work by professor Risto Ilmoniemi from Aalto University.

Assigning bandwidth and priorities. Connectivity from lower level sensors towards higher centers, from the sense organs, especially the retina, limbs and face is arranged so that the most relevant information from the sensory 'radar-field' (the center field of vision, sensitivity of fingertips, and lips, for example) is assigned a significant information transmission and pre-processing power. There are also 'fast lanes' that carry relevant attention-grabbing visual and other sensory information along special pathways somewhere higher in the system, where it has special value. In the Vasa ship case, there was no fast lane to carry the perception data to the King who could have stopped the mad maiden cruise.

Foveal information from the visual field with the diameter of only a few degrees uses most of the fibers carrying information from the human retina to the primary cortical areas which also have separate, large cell masses reserved for hands, fingers, lips and the tongue. Frogs have a different retinal organization and their eyes are more uniform, roughly reminding of camera sensor-cell systems.

Considering firms, we can now ask how should information-action relevance be defined and how to assign the bandwidth within the whole perceptual/observational architecture? It is a strategic resourcing question and with the increasing importance of dynamic, networked environments it is becoming a wicked problem. Hence, whatever the answer to this will be – or was in the case of the financial crisis, Vasa ship, Challenger investigations, Nokia, the Finnish Government - it is a most profound matter of strategic analysis and discourse in any organization. However, it is not uncommon to rely on strategic conventions and measures that together with a rigid power structure can hinder and block important perceptive processes.

Purposeful feed-back. Division of labor, feed-back, and functional organization in biological organisms starts as early as possible in the sensory pathways, already before the higher centers are reached, where it then continues throughout the system and is probably the most complicated aspect of the dynamic brain system. All human sensory systems (already on the retina, and in the auditory pathway) have strong feed-back (including lateral feed, either inhibitory or excitatory) at all levels. This helps the system to adapt fast to changing environmental conditions and to tune its selectivity to certain, hopefully relevant sensory patterns. For the artificial neural network and Deep Learning models the discovery of these physiological features led to what are now called convolutional neural networks which have both a neurophysiological and computational history since 1970's.

Feed-back has different functions, depending on at what level of the system it happens. In the early processing, sensory feed-back can serve e.g. cleaning of noisy incoming data and help reveal the relevant signals from other stimulation like overall luminance and shadows in vision and the noise background and echoes in hearing. At higher levels, feed-back can have a role in complex state control and world model updating, for example. Negative and positive feed-back have totally different functions and I will not deal with that here.

Feed-back is not always valuable or even possible – its system properties like time constants, parameters, purpose and processing cost determine its value – which in the natural, dynamic organizational context is difficult to model and quantify. Sometimes like in fight and flight a slow feed-back is useless and can be dangerous. Ballistic and pre-calculated movements and the bird's time-to-collision (proactive) computations are examples of fast, non-feed-back based and executive processes. Even we humans would break our bones by simple throwing movements if we did not have the extremely well-coordinated ballistic ways to execute powerful movements like throwing a ball. It can be amusing to recall similar episodes in organizational settings, of which most of us have experiences: what happens to employee behaviors when the top management forces through initiatives that do not allow any feed-back control or when a fast, 'ballistic' movement is suddenly interrupted. In case of a sport performance a misplaced interrupt can break bones.

Elinor Ostrom has vividly explained in her studies on the management of commons, how important relevant feed-back is for optimal problem solving and performance of people who have different interests and personal preferences but who must collaborate as communities. In modern organizations, technology in its various forms provides the means for feed-back but the use of technologies varies considerably along the dimensions of contexts specificity, synchronicity, targeting, and many others.

Cross-functional connectivity. Very early, rich connections are made with functionally different centers (senses, motion systems, emotion, attention and arousal control, orientation processing etc.) in different parts of the cortical and subcortical brain. All senses feed to the brain centers responsible for the control of sleep-wakefulness, orientation, and alertness. In other words, they have access to the vital functions of our bodies. It is not well known how and why these connections have developed but of course it is easy to speculate that they provide – what is now known in organizations – a possibility for the bottom-up and top-down information to cross functional boundaries which makes possible any relevant state-related behavior required by the multi-dimensional world. Extreme specialization and functional separation (silos) would be inefficient, costly, and probably disastrous.

Early relationship processing. This is probably the most foundational aspect of sensory and perceptual processing but it is rarely discussed in popular texts on perception: as soon as possible, perception becomes relational (relationship computations). Information about signal feature (and object) relationships – not of the features themselves - is carried to or offered for further analysis by higher centers. As simple example, there is no exact or unique point-to point mapping between the optical image on the retina and the visual cortex. Knowing that a visual cortical cell is active does not allow (without experimentation) back-wards computing to decide what and at which exact location on the retina stimulation has caused the observed cortical cell activity. The same is true for all sensory data.

We live in the middle of an inverse problem of the brain and life. Top-down connectivity makes this kind of a system complex – but also adaptive. The relationship extraction starts already at the receptor level. In the eye, a single receptor cell does not sit there quietly waiting for photons to arrive and to excite it. It has a hidden biological engine that supports it (trusts it, using organizational rhetoric) by keeping its membrane potential at a suitable level for survival and sensitivity. When photons then hit it, it is prepared, and a biochemical process with strong ionic feed-back is initiated; the membrane potential changes: this is called the cell response, but in reality it is a cell *system* response and intimately connected with the surrounding biochemical systems. The physical world as we interpret and experience it, has already at the receptor layer lost its 1-1 mapping on our senses. Hence, it is impossible to exactly and objectively perceive what we call 'the world'. There is sense in this strange fact: without such a relativistic process the brain would be overloaded with stupid but accurate information - copies of the optical images or sound waves and the system just would not work. It would be like a standard digital computer memory and a perfect bureaucracy.

An inspiring thought is that the measurements concerning the outside world, as conducted by an organization are not much different from measuring what goes on in the retinal cell systems. It is basically a relationship extraction process by an active recipient (a worker, analyst, researcher, engineer) who extracts (locally, but dependent) meaningful relationship information from the received stimuli (clients, partners, contractors, networks). Then there is the inverse problem in trying to interpret the data: what exactly has caused that data to be available? What systems underlie it? How are the early processes supported?

In simple situations, the relationship perception by a firm happens without problems. Monitoring well-known (with fixed or relatively fixed set of underlying assumptions about it) phenomena or conducting straightforward measurements can be done without errors and the firm has learned to make the right guesses and behave accordingly. However, as soon as the objects of observation become dynamic, complex, dependent on other objects, or just show unexpected but significant behaviors, the characteristics of the observer and the observing system itself start to affect the 'measurement'. This is nothing new to theoretical physicists. The observer characteristics are affected by system variables, like the royal pressure in the Vasa case, the middle management fears at Nokia, or the limited field of view of the financial analysts of the US Government in the crisis.

When a significant event becomes measured or perceived, the priority-one goal for the organism, or a firm, is to guess what has caused the event: the same percept or measurement result can occur for totally different reasons. Only a tested or otherwise reliable theory or a good model of the world can help the perceiver to interpret the measurement data and do it fast.

Integration of pattern, object and scene information. All incoming sensory information is integrated and sensed together: the perceptual system makes holistic and relational inferences about this mass of data and ends up in one plausible and possible interpretation (object vs. background, for example) about the world perceived. That is why flight simulators (vision, sense of acceleration, tilt) and 3D movies with various augmentation features (tremor, water puffs, sound surround) work so fine and we are led to feel as if living at least for a moment, in one world only – it is a miracle performance how we accomplish this since other alternative world interpretations do exist always, both in our reality and in simulators. Sometimes a unique interpretation is not stable and we can see alternating versions of the same world. This happens in the well-known figure-ground perception demonstrations (Necker cube, for example) but it is not rare in firm contexts where the management can disagree whether they are facing a threat or an opportunity. There are numerous eye-opening visual demonstrations of these phenomena (cf. Colossal or Gizmodo demos) and especially on how much perspective matter.

Attentive mechanisms guide perception and efficient action. Priority mechanisms govern the perception processes and have the capability to orient us towards relevant sources and hence, help allocating the best resources to signal analysis, pattern recognition and to react with relevant perception-actions. Amazingly, the attentive system is capable – almost hardwired – to take full system (body and soul) control for a limited amount of time, when it is necessary to gain immediate understanding of the environment or of the organism itself and to act accordingly. However, it is not only a catastrophe processing protocol, it is a most natural part of our everyday life and behavior during any simple task we perform. It can happen hundreds, even thousands of times an hour.

Shared resources for internal and external analysis. Partly the same higher processes start dealing with both the sensory information coming from the environment and the information generated within the system (imagination, memory, attention, experiences, dreaming, …). It is not well known how all this happens in the brain and in our senses although a popular topic are the mirror cells believed to demonstrate just this kind of resource sharing (cf. the famous work by Rizzolatti).

Perceptual invariance. This is a most fascinating but not well-known aspect of perception. Contextual invariance refers to the perceived relationship between the elements of the world, or certain parts of it, that remain constant or similar under variable observation conditions – when the world undergoes changes. When we perceive a stable world or our own internal state, despite major variations in the external or internal conditions, we are not directly aware of the underlying dynamic mechanism that make this perception possible: it is an automatic, inherent and inbuilt process in our mental life and determines what we perceive and experience. It is perhaps the highest level of pure human intelligence: we remain ourselves under extremely varying conditions, in the world and in our minds.

A popular example from human vision is instructive. The retinal image size of a person you are looking at from a 2 meters distance can be about 14 mm high. When she then moves to the distance of 4m from you the size of the retinal image of her is halved and it will be only 7 mm. Amazingly, and as we all experience it, we do not see the size of a person to shrink (with the size of the retinal image) when she moves away from us. This is called *size constancy* and it is based on a perceptual size invariance: the brain has detected something in the world, a *relationship* between the image of the person and the image of her environment (room height, perspective cues) on the retina that remains relatively the same in both situations. This makes it possible to make an interpretation, a guess, that the person's size has not changed: we perceive the object size as practically constant. We have no subjective experience of this 'computational' process happening, it simply happens as a percept but it is very intelligent and extremely useful. If we did not have that sensory property, the world would appear as a continuously changing chaos where the size of the people and other objects passing by us would increase and decrease in size and shape all the time. The famous Ames room prevents the observer from having natural relationship information of the scene and then the size perception mechanism can be vividly fooled.

When firms measure their objects of interests they face the same challenge that some call the context of data: having the measurement data is not enough for unique interpretation and can be misleading if it is not known against which scene or environment the measurement (observation) has been made. Market data, for example can be highly sensitive to the cultural background of the consumers which makes comparing the purchasing behaviors in different cultures problematic and can introduce a risk of misinterpreting the data. On the other hand, having relevant data about a 'background scene' or environment can provide significant added value to computations and make interpretation of the data more intelligent and reliable. It is not self-evident what in each situation is 'relevant' background data.

If you remove the environmental information totally, leaving the object of observation alone visible, then the invariance of perceptions does not hold any more. Perception experimentalists testing the size constancy in vision know that if the subject observes a target person totally without her environment, the constancy effect disappears or becomes weaker. Through the invariance phenomenon we have gained the knowledge that the observed object (the target person) has not changed although the image (information) of her has shrunk or increased in size on the retina. It is a most intelligent and valuable (learned) ability to perceive objects and phenomena in the world as the same even though our sensory mechanisms record significant changes that are caused by us, by the environment, the behavior of the observer or by the target itself. Perception is not a straightforward physical measurement process; it is very weak in measuring anything (physically) objectively but it works for us in this world and at the scale of our living. This is a delicious topic to consider as a metaphor for organizational considerations, disputes, and disagreements about their world.

If we did not have this wonderful skill to recognize invariances we would be exhausted. There is a story about a small fish – the article reference to which I have lost - that does not have the size-constancy ability. It has been reported to attack anything that produces a certain size of a retinal image on its eye: sometimes the object can be an edible, nearby bug but sometimes it can be a large fish away from its reach. You can guess how such a creature behaves in clear water: it wastes a lot of energy but can survive under the mercy of kind statistics. Maybe it lives in murky waters, where it just cannot see far which saves it from futile attacks, maybe its myopic from the start, I don't know.

Any organization should be interested in the internal and external object relationships that remain invariant in its living context. When an invariance is about to break down it is a sign of a significant change in the state of the world or in its objects or in both. An analogical, a bit far-fetched perhaps, example is the popular media discourse on print vs. digital magazine and book consumption. Not so long ago, some analysts entertained the assumption that media consumption is basically a zero-sum phenomenon: an invariant total number of printed plus digital magazines are read per customer or that people devote a constant amount of time to media from their personal time budget. Hence, because of this assumed invariance (without considering the context and various human/social aspects of 'reading'), the fast increase in digital magazine consumption was expected to cause a fast death or at least fast disappearance of print. This did not happen – there were other human invariances behind the media-use evolution but the sources of this context data were not known or seen as relevant.

If the 'perception system' of a firm is tuned only to direct measures and metrics it runs at risk to miss important relationships. Market data did not show the magazine and book reading to fall with the same speed as digital reading increased. Neither has aggressive behavior increased with the speed by which war and fight games have entered the lives of our children. People are not dying in masses by eating meat. Similarly, the number of car accidents has not increased in direct proportion to the number of mobile phones used in cars – indicating that mobile phone use in cars is not directly causing car accidents. Such relationships are complex and finding invariances is puzzling. But they are hugely important for understanding the world through perception.

Other current examples where analysis of invariances can be valuable are Facebook and Twitter, for example, and the type of networks people (unconsciously) build there. There are many business-, technological, and economic reasons to be curious about what in these behavior networks remain structurally invariant even when their size and connectivity changes. Having this knowledge can help reach the intended audiences when planning campaigns, estimating ROIs, distributing any information - commercially or otherwise. Basically, it is a matter of recognizing the invariances in human communication, relationship formation and activity patterns – and what underlies them.

It is a most strategic perceptual decision to select between two or more alternative world-views. The famous works by Kahneman and Tversky demonstrated this, in the specific decision domains or spaces which their test subjects spanned in their minds when faced with the given tasks. The experiments showed how people make different decisions depending whether they have a vision of sacrificing or saving people. Such a vision would, on average have an impact on the behavior of an individual – when forced to work unnaturally alone and in isolation – and determine how he perceives the problem at hand. This would then have a significant impact on the perceived problem solving opportunities. On the other hand, there is a good reason to ask how often do we perceive the world in such a clean arrangement? We have our friends, colleagues, tools, cultural practices and even prayers to help, support and challenge us. Further, sacrificing people is subjectively painful and triggers mental load, but Kahneman and Tversky did not have a control situation where the pain and mental load would have been introduced by other means, by inserting splinters under the nails of the test subject, for example.

Figure 3. Navigation is a game with opportunities.

11. Opportunity perception

Every now and then organizations are surprised by a competitor perceiving the world in a totally different - productive or disastrous - way. One of my own educational experiences is from 2000/2001 when I tried to encourage the technology management at Nokia to open their device systems for software developers and to create what some years after that became the dominant ecosystem run by Apple iPhone.

My talk to Nokia tech managers included the explicit and well-formulated idea of a Nokia-run, half-open ecosystem, but I could immediately see and feel that they did not perceive any opportunity in what I saw and offered. After one of the two sessions, each with about 40 high-level participants, only one attendee approached me – she had a psychology (!) background - and commented on the huge importance and relevance of the idea for their future. Surprised by this overall lack of interest and reaction I wrote a letter – which was then untypical for me - back to the head of technology, even put it in English (and suggested it to be shared) to remind of the importance of the topic:

Dated on 5h January, 2001. *"The issue concerns the degree to which mobile phone products (or other related or similar products in general) should have an architecturally open structure for usability components".*

Then I continued:

"There is no doubt that some major player in this area will open up their devices and at some phase get a status as open standard and start an avalanche of usability applications from personal to very specific ones and even technical..."

Nothing happened, no reaction. Anyone who knows or remembers what was going on in the mobile phone industry then, understands that this was a very early suggestion or a strong signal of an opportunity for Nokia. Now its history what Apple did, it perceived its opportunity differently – and right.

The question arises: what prevents a firm or an organization in general from perceiving or reacting to a most vital strategic opportunity? In this specific case, all ict professionals in Finland already knew Linux and everyone could follow the Mac/Apple use culture; there was a stable background and strong signals available; the evidence was there for everyone. What I and probably a few others were seeing were no weak signals – but they were not perceived by all, in the proper sense of the word. I know there were reasons to this at Nokia, but the blindness has kept me curious for years. I've been reluctant to talk about it openly but over the years when experiences accumulated I became certain about my (then) conviction and have seen the significance of this failure in opportunity perception.

Engagement aversion causes a peculiar type of blindness among management. Immediate threats are easy to see, to recognize the opportunities for being damaged or hurt and to react because it is imperative. It is a very basic biological requirement for survival. Positive opportunities, on the other hand, mean an invitation to a voluntary engagement, perhaps a change in the current world view – and it requires extra time, work, re-orientation and re-thinking. It is a tough strategic requirement, creative in nature, and especially when the dominant ways to perceive the world seem to work well. Then it is not rare at all to observe what I have called 'engagement aversion' in managers who already are overloaded by responsibilities and tight schedules. It is a way to negative criticism as well.

Opportunity perception and entrepreneurship. 'Strategy' in a firm relies on the perception of opportunities to achieve the vision and to reach for the related sub-goals. In cognitive psychology, chess is often mentioned as a popular research model of strategic decision making and players have been studied to understand high-level strategic perception and action together (cf. e.g. de Groot, A. D. (1965). Thought and choice in chess. The Hague: Mouton & Company; Hartston, W. R. & Wason, P. C. (1983). The psychology of chess. London: Batsford). Opportunity perception and its underlying observational architecture precede personal and organizational intentions and the pursuit of opportunities (cf. Stevenson, H. H., and T. M. Amabile. "Entrepreneurial Management: In Pursuit of Opportunity." Harvard Business School Press, 1999).

However, even in these studies on chess the concept of perception is rather vague and researcher like Simon and Chase (1973), for example, were skeptical about the possibility to obtain relevant verbal information about perception at all:

"The player's perceptual processing of the board is so rapid (and probably unavailable to conscious introspection) that it is impossible to obtain an accurate verbal description of the process from him."

They focused on the rather primitive concept of 'chunk' in perception and memory. It refers to a meaningful cognitive storage and perception entity (the exact nature of which is practically unknown) – a kind of human knowledge package or data structure - that the players use in various chess-related tasks. A simple lesson from the well-known study was that *chess masters perceive and pay attention to meaningful game structures and relationships*, not to individual pieces of the game; in this sense, they differ from amateurs. Professional wine tasters have a similar ability: they use a rich and systematic vocabulary for classifying and differentiating complex, even relational wine tastes, which allows them to perform better than amateurs. It is my understanding that it is not yet known, which chemical aspects in the wines exactly and in combination produce the most informative taste perceptions which the tasters use for evaluating wine quality and its potential for aging.

The exceptional skills of wine tasters are not rare aspects of intelligent human perception in general, and from our lab we had numerous similar findings from the studies on perception and evaluation of camera and print image quality. Similar approaches can be found in the study of subjective perception and evaluation of the quality of acoustic spaces like concert halls. In other words, efficient perceptual (subjective) processing is a human core competence in complex environmental situations. It requires proper personal systematics and a language of its own.

Opportunity perception as a concept occurs in the study of entrepreneurship (cf. Shane & Venkataraman, 2000; Eckhardt & Shane, 2003, Zolin, 2013). Most of the studies use the terms opportunity identification, opportunity recognition and opportunity pursuit but with much conceptual variation. However, as far as I know, they do not include any real theory of perception but instead rely on everyday concepts of perception. Hence they have remained descriptive, and conceptually superficial.

Among these studies there is an interesting approach concerning the need to speed up the strategy process. Eckhardt & Shane, 2003 have introduced what they call "The life cycle of opportunities" by which they refer to the risk of transient advantages – just like in any strategic choice – in capitalizing on a new opportunity. Their view is related to the classic work and ideas of Schumpeter (1934) and suggests an approach to manage the temporal risks of quickly emerging and changing competitive landscape.

Perceiving a 'black swan' in his books Taleb introduced the enchanting metaphor to describe significant but rare and 'outlier' – improbable, difficult to predict with traditional methods – phenomena. Hindsight is also included in the black swan concept, that is, the tendency to offer explanations to its occurrence retrospectively.

The retrospective explanation to the 'black swan' phenomenon includes a curious perceptual aspect, although imaginary: retrospection itself is a demonstration of our cognitive skill to envision what might have caused the unexpected phenomenon to occur. Illusory or not but imagination is also based on spanning a perceptual-imaginary architecture that covers the relevant earlier observations, including the black swan. Huge mistakes are then possible because it is a case of inverse problem where backwards calculations or inferences can be erroneous. Relying on that it is afterwards possible to 'perceive' – by historically driven imagination - the processes that had led to the occurrence of the black swan. How else could such phenomena be explained? The question remains then, is it possible to span a relevant perceptual architecture now, for perceiving a black swan approaching and to catch it before it flies away?

12. Participation reveals the firm's perception array and architecture

Organizations vary in how much they involve their personnel, customer-audience and their value network members or partners in reaching for their vision and building it. Firms having their roots in the Nordic countries are known from the participatory organizational culture. However, the underlying thought pattern is the same as elsewhere, namely that company vision is to be shared; unit- and even individual visions should be aligned and by doing so, to secure that the well-defined vision is respected and pursued. Only if something extraordinary or significant happens – in terms of risk management – in the firm or its environment the shared vision can and should be immediately changed or modified. In practice, however, the iteration is accomplished every year and typically no dramatic changes are introduced. Emphasizing the 'shared vision' tends to overshadow the real need for valid organizational perception and because of that, for some time now, many firms have changed their slow and frictional practices. The complexities of the present world, the activities of the global and multi-cultural giants, the directly and indirectly networked environment, the monolithic platforms, and the emerging, extremely dynamic value networks have for some time challenged the straightforward 'shared vision' paradigm and distributed perception is needed.

For example, the connected social media networks – external or internal to firms – and the new information and communication channels have made almost any organizational system practically open and continuously adaptive in nature. Navigating and managing a relatively open system, in a multi-cultural and dynamic network world demands recognition of the relevant value chains that are fast becoming networks. Communication impacts and impulses in marketing and contacting become indirect. Ecosystem and platform ambitions flourish and companies try to find competitive advantages through building them, participating in the existing ones or by conquering them.

Due to market turbulence, firms must become sensitive to changes and become perceptual-attentive systems that span a dynamic observation architecture, guided and directed by its intelligent and multidimensional perception mechanisms. Of course, the mission of a firm remains its foundational force and base but even that can be challenging. Sticking to the traditional vision-strategy cycle is a major risk itself and potential obstacle to organizational progress.

A hilarious and educating article describes how the management of some firms have already learned a double behavior: the strategy life vs. real life: The article "Zorro-management" by professors Mika Pantzar ja Janne Tienari (Kauppalehti 28th November 2013) described their observations on how the local management of multi-national or otherwise centralized, large companies had learned to lead a double life: to obey to and communicate with the headquarters according to the top-down strategy demands and to use the jargon to which they just have to respond by "yes, of course" and "here is our strategy document" and to behave as good company strategists and citizen. But at night – in real life – they put on their Zorro masks and work with real, local company people and try to help them to work, make working life worth living, to use their own thinking and understanding to achieve something good. Not all companies have a brave Zorro to dare this and I doubt if a Zorro ever gets promoted in business and academic Finland.

13. Tools for strategic perception

The hidden assumption in firms is that it is realistic to assume the existence or emergence of a reasonably unanimous audience for the company vision - within in the company. The management feels the pressure for effective communication and produces vision statements that are condensed and easy to understand by everyone. 'Story telling' is motivated by this simple principle – to make the mission, vision and strategy easy for anyone to understand and motivating. Hence, the 'strategy stories' are defined by the weakest links in the firms in how they define the values, objectives and their purpose of existence. Even during the times of AI, it is probably rare to find a strategy formulation that would be complex, inherently adaptive, multi-purpose, dynamic and multi-dimensional in nature – and not easy for everyone to understand but nevertheless motivating to follow.

Instead of emphasizing the coherent vision model in firms, the perception-based strategy view suggests to take it as a fact that a detailed, shared vision is difficult to have, if not impossible and can become a hindrance to the firm. Of course, shared interest in and possibility for opportunity perception is crucial at all levels of any modern firm: you may call it empowerment, delegation, directing attention, motivation, or value-based behavior. A shared ground is needed to guide the orientation toward opportunities, at all scales from the factory floor to the corner rooms of the management.

Figure 8. Time-to-collision neurons activated.

Perhaps, already in the very near future some of the following elements will find their place in the dynamic strategy process of firms having a purpose, motivation and goals:

- spanning an observational architecture
- defining intelligent and purposeful perception
- mining and processing of intention data
- support for opportunity perception
- pursuit of opportunities and
- tuning the feed-back within the observational architecture.

It may be difficult and risky for firms to abruptly change the current strategy systems, especially starting from a historical and well-defined strategy model. The obstacles are many, ranging from strategy-oriented reward systems and power structures to the dominant organizational cultures. I do not have direct data available here but I guess that the speed by which vision statements are today proving wrong, irrelevant or even hazardous, is increasing.

Guidelines for building a purposeful strategy process? Not yet. All animals – alone or as herds – are capable of effective opportunity perception, of purposeful, goal-directed behavior relying on their biologically implemented strategy systems and intelligent perception architectures. With this capability, be they monkey colonies or reindeer herds, they build an internal world model to be used for pursuing their goals and to act with full power when needed.

As a first approximation the concept of 'Firm perception' refers to a functional entity consisting of Perception/observation architecture+ Intelligent perception+Opportunity perception+Opportunity pursuit. Compared to the classic top-down strategy management and implementation process this requires a different organizational approach. I leave it for the reader to consider and evaluate this as a strategic opportunity.

14. A miracle helping us in change – adaptation

Stop the plane! More than ten years ago I was on my way from Helsinki to Stockholm to a workshop on future bio-society. I was frustrated, since at my Institute (Behavioral Sciences) the idea of planning a totally new research program on such an 'esoteric field' – from the local perspective - was not seen as important enough to be funded so I had to pay the travel from my own pocket. This inspired me to spend the 55 minutes on the flight to think about this, wondering why it is so difficult to get (psychology) colleagues and leaders inspired about novel or transformative opportunities and to change the traditional course of actions.

The plane was accelerating and everyone in the cabin could sense the familiar feeling of being forcefully drawn against the back of the seat. Every time on a flight, I enjoy this unusual feeling that makes me thoroughly aware of the immense powers of the jet engines creating a speed high enough to make flying possible. This time, on the plane, during those few seconds, I realized how similar the moments of acceleration are to organizational life under a major change and why change is so often experienced as difficult, scary or both. But there were other acute lessons as well.

Once the plane has reached a critical speed, the pilot and we as the passengers, have no either-or alternative: no returning back, the plane must continue ever faster and fulfill its destiny, without hesitation, and with full force. If it is properly designed and the engineers, mechanics and the pilot have done their job well then the magical powers of the wings, fuselage, and the aerodynamics of the plane are revealed and they will show their marvelous capacities as they are meant to do; they will lift the massive plane and its passengers with grace.

When we face an invitation to accomplish new or revolutionary things and to change our habits or thought patterns it is not the ideas as such that make us worried or resistant, but the requirement to comply to the new forces without which nothing new will happen. Novel ideas will carry us only if we are ready to give them the same chance that the wings are offered by the speeding plane. Neither new ideas nor the plane wings will show their magical powers when the plane does not move or is slow, or the ideas remain as concepts or talk without commitment and forceful action. The magic is revealed only when the change is made to happen with full or at least relevant throttle. Even the best wings will not lift the plane if there is not enough speed to access their sources of the lifting force. The other side of the coin is that also all the faults are revealed at full speed and even before that.

An interesting phenomenon happens when the plane becomes airborne: the moment acceleration is over, when the pressure against the backrest disappears, we adapt to the new peaceful state of mind in a matter of seconds. We don't sense the speed and even though we know it and can read the speed indicators from the tv-screens, we do not feel its presence. The world is stable and predictable again, with no feelings of risk and we continue living our life, life as usual even though we fly at 10 000 meters altitude. Next time you fly, pay attention to this amazing metaphorical transformation and you will understand what it means, in your organization, to put your trust in something or someone whom you do not know personally and in detail, who demands a full commitment from you but who also offers a possibility to a remarkable change and progress. The 'story of the plane' is not enough to assure the passengers, genuine trust is necessary.

Testing 'the final' version first? Surprisingly often major technical and organizational changes are designed and implemented without careful and serious piloting and testing. An example from Finland from some years ago was the renewal of the ticket sales system of the Finnish Railways (VR) and its ict-environment, designed together with a world-leading ict consultancy. The outcome was a nation-wide disaster, when people simply could not get their tickets and it took weeks to repair the situation. The explanation was something like "We did not expect such a crowding in the channels." A nation-wide service.

Another example comes from my own University (and from the whole university system of Finland), where the institute and faculty structure were thoroughly re-designed – without any testing - in the whole higher education system of Finland when also the salary systems and the legal status of the university were totally transformed. Using the plane analogy, it was like a new plane model had been introduced, with a totally new wing design, new fuel system, new service and crew organization but with the absolutely insane change strategy: all planes must be tested at the same time, without piloting, and everywhere with a full load of passengers.

It is amazing to think that some organizational designers can end up doing something like this, and that even the management can bluntly state that "The change is under good control". But the bureaucrats and higher edu management decided to use such a change strategy and to open the organizational throttles, wide open everywhere. The answer to the question "Why did they do this?" is simple: they did not know the change process, risks were not recognized and it was estimated that even if the risks would manifest, the losses could be tolerated – the new wings would carry and they could perhaps be repaired during the flight. It was like the famous movie line of defending the losses that can be called 'collateral damage'. It is scary to wonder where such a gloomy strategy can have its cultural origin. As if this was not enough, a similar strategy was intended for the whole social security and health care system renovation in Finland just recently. Luckily there were enough forces that barely stopped this insane 'pilot' with the whole nation and its well-being.

In my eyes, our institute was accelerating and trying to become airborne, but with all the changes taking place simultaneously, it became clear (to me) that there was a real risk of crash: the worried passengers started an intense conversation while the plane speeded up. Some believed that the problem was in the plane crew and that we should start supporting the crew members who perform best and forget the rest. Some thought that by organizing passenger meetings and by offering convincing instructions to them, it becomes possible to improve the situation. Some suggested that let's put all money on a few competence areas only. Then a plan was made to jump from one plane to another – during the flight, to change the faculty. At the university level, the community of professionals is so multi-dimensional in their competencies that it is impossible to end up with any coherent suggestion of what to do except to offer variable criticism and wail.

There are always organizational aliens like me who think that the problem is in the theory of aerodynamics (what makes an institute fly) and engine design (where the institute gets its power). In an accelerating plane a disagreement in this would create fear and many would be looking for parachutes and I had jumped out early.

Courageous pilots could stop the plane. The wing design of a plane is made to lift the plane with grace and beautiful balance. It is like the motivation of instructors, researchers, professors, and lecturers that will carry them to marvelous achievements. Both the wing design properties and the motivation of the staff in an organization remain invisible until the speed of change is high enough. But then also the faults will be revealed and if the test is conducted with all the planes and all the staff the costs will be tremendous. In the case of our national university system some of the passengers saw the construction failures in the wings but they had no connection with the constructors, pilots, or engineers and they could not mend the situation. The pilots could have stopped then plane, but they did not have the courage to do that - there was no reward for doing that.

I landed safely at Stockholm airport and started developing a concept approach for understanding the determinants of 'future bio-behavior'. As often happens on well-planned journeys, something unexpected took place: I met a brilliant physicist colleague, similarly worried about the changes taking place in our universities, and who on the way back home inspired me to plan and write a story, on "The origins of physics" and "The theory of weak signals" and worrying less about these gloomy organizational events when the plane started accelerating towards Helsinki. They are both now included in this book.

15. Building a future past

Imagine first, how it will feel like to sit at your office desk tomorrow. After this, memorize how it felt last time you sat there. These two mental processes are surprisingly similar.

One concerns a real event and the other one deals with a purely imaginary future. Between the process of perceiving reality and memorizing it, there is something that we have learned to call 'time'. This same 'time' finds its place in our mental worlds when we plan our future. But within these delicate mental processes there hide curious creatures, our imaginary future and past.

Imagine now, how it will feel like, the day after tomorrow to remember how it felt like to sit at your office desk the day before that. The day that we now call 'tomorrow' is in this exercise your 'yesterday' and they are both imaginary, but with a different direction of time. All this is pure imagination generated by the same mental imagery processes and allows us to fly in time, to any direction. Clearly, we can have an imaginary past in our imaginary future. Now the question is, how natural is this for us and is it something that is always linked with our ways of planning for the future? If it is, then preparing for a future must also mean preparing for a new past. Could this planned past be a significant factor in determining how we relate to a planned future, especially to change?

We can imagine remembering something and imagine the time past as happened in these exercises, but it is astonishing that subjectively in these processes there is no difference between memorizing real time and mentally creating purely virtual time that can go forwards or backwards. Somehow it even feels that in our imagination the feeling of time remains the same for both directions.

Preparing for the new past in change. It is as if our memory system acted like a browser with the peculiar feature that it browses our future and the past by the same mechanisms. Why should this matter? I believe it is not only a theoretical phenomenon, but a real mental capacity that we enjoy and which we have learned to use in preparing for our future and the new past.

Problems with introducing change are often linked with the ways people think of their future. Clever change management strategies try to find ways through or around the walls of resistance that people are believed or tend to have, especially in organizational settings. By trying to change the way people think about their future, managers and consultants hope to weaken the resistance and even create energetic acceptance and commitment to the intended change.

What if it is not the thinking about the future alone that is the problem, but the problem of what kind of an implied past the 'change managers' offer? This is rarely, if ever, explicitly considered or expressed in change projects.

Figure 9. My past with an unknown future, relaxing after a hard day of work. Thank you Selim Rentola for the photo and the past.

This may sound extremely theoretical, but think about a single example. Imagine aiming at a higher position at your work or getting a new status for your organizational unit or a project. You know there is a way to do it by keeping your close colleague uninformed about the possibilities that you know of. You have an opportunity to succeed but at a price of mistreating your colleague, perhaps even a friend. In planning and deciding what to do, it is not the future that is the problem, it is the past in that future that you imagine you will create by these clever moves. Because of that imagined future past many but not all will think twice; it is about human strategy and its consequences.

I believe that imagining a future past is a very basic psychological mechanism that is activated in all change situations where our attitude towards change is at test. The way we think about possible futures and imaginable pasts together determine our relationship to the planned change. This is, perhaps, why many of us want to leave their marks on the history even though the visible actions superficially have the nature of 'planning for the future'. We don't talk about future pasts, but future history is not unheard in visioning and dreaming. A lesson to change agents is to think how to build the best achievable past. After all, our past is what we are.

15 SHORT STORIES ON INFRA-STRUCTURE AND MOTIVATION

1. Ethics of infrastructure business

I live in Southern Finland, where we were hit by a major power supply catastrophe on 26th December 2011 (I use the term 'catastrophe' that was avoided by our power companies, Gov authorities, leading print media and radio) that lasted for 60 hrs. We were extremely lucky: it could have been -20 deg Celcius outside but it happened to be nearly the warmest Xmas ever and the damages were not nearly as bad as they could have been. We could survive without breaking water pipes and freezing. Our Governmental bodies were saved from total humiliation and the loss of nation's trust in them.

Figure 1. A winter view in Southern Finland

Unfortunately, our politicians learned nothing from this, it took only a couple of years and they sold our power grid to an international, greedy player who is now using its obtained, practical monopoly here, avoiding taxes and ripping us off by increasing costs in power transmission. Leading politicians just stand by and let us pay, with minor superficial adjustments in national control of this mess. Our lives depend on reliable electricity. This is a warning sign to any nation intending to outsource its major infrastructure and make it lucrative business to unknown players.

The storm cut down a massive amount of power wires and made South Finland look like North Korea, life in a total darkness. Why do I call this experience a 'catastrophe', here where I live and where Helsinki, our capitol with most of its services untouched is only 50 kilometers away? In a global sense, it was a minor problem, but locally and for many citizens it was a symbolic threat of technology misuse, greedy ownership, a source of human stress, and a cause of major economical, work and health related and other losses. In a well-fare state like Finland it was an educational exercise to learn what such a simple design failure reveals about the society and especially of its infrastructure management – and businesses. It was a test of trust we failed. The human aspect of technology was totally forgotten.

In addition to our power supply, this challenge became again acute in Finland when our previous Government wanted to offer our railways, health care, and social security services to open markets. Now there a player selling our precious water. How should we open these for businesses and how could we prevent negative human effects of greedy money making? We should know this exactly. Some are going to make a significant business out of them and we do not know how they will benefit or harm us as citizens. Human use of technology is in the core of all these initiatives, because money can be made by it and it scales up.

In candle light. I started writing a version of this text in 2011, under candle light, listening to the sounds of the approaching chain saw crews – men cutting down the trees that had fallen on power cables that run in the air. You may wonder why on earth are we using air cables in Finland where everyone knows what happens to the power lines in a heavy winter or when trees fall in a storm. I could clearly hear the chain saw sounds but I had no idea when we will have power supply again.

Our fridge was already warm and the deep-frozen lamb, reindeer filet, our delicious wild berries and mushrooms had been spoiled, the water heating system did not work, Internet was down, and the mobile had been down for two days. During writing I could already call my friends and ask for information about the situation, but even that did not help, there was no relevant or accurate process knowledge available from the energy companies. They had the net, but I did not. My mobile was charging in my car outside. We were not trapped like many elderly and sick people were.

More than half a million people (we are only 5,5 million altogether) were left without electricity for one or two days and some like we and our neighbors even for a longer time. Tens of thousands of us live in private houses where it is not possible to pump water without electricity, heating systems do not work without it, mobile and internet connections are dependent on the power supply to the link stations, local net connections are tied to functional wi-fi systems and of course, computers become quickly dead.

Yes, we can buy batteries and could even get converters to turn battery power to 220 V AC to use our mobile and internet devices but the operators had been down because the links had reserve batteries that lasted only for a few hours. Why such a short reserve time? It costs. Power aggregates were immediately sold out. People in old people's houses had been in serious trouble because they did not have reserve power sources, water, functional kitchen and everyday health care so that many of them were evacuated to city areas. Grocery stores suffered significant losses.

The end of the year was approaching and individuals, communities and companies needed to take care of their economic matters and accounting that was not possible because the computer and net-based application systems were down. Sun was up only for 6 hours so that solar panels were of no real use. At home we had candle light which was not enough for reading anything but was a great source of cozy atmosphere for listening to the radio. Luckily we had bought a small chargeable radio from a science fair in San Jose, CA. It has a small solar panel but it also works by manually winding its generator - it was fun. We have a similar flashlight as well so we were not dependent on batteries.

Where was radio? Technology can offer simple human help – if the operators are prepared. We used the winding radio, listening to it and searched for reliable knowledge of our local power supply prognosis. No practical information was available, the news channels focused on national matters as usual and they only talked with general references to locations like "south of Siuntio", "whole Veikkola" (these are both small village –like entities) "wide-scale", but had nothing to say about the situation where we lived and where we could see the total lack of lights and hear the distant sound of an aggregate in the darkness.

Half a million Finns had not been able to watch tv so they had turned to the radio, just like us. What was in the air over the first days? Believe it or not: business as usual, no big deal. After having been without power for two days, on the local radio we could still follow three hours of national ice hockey reporting (!) on line, with special commentators at every game site in Finland but practically no reporter on the sites of this unprecedented catastrophe.

No accurate local news was offered, and the national political and weather reports were broadcasted as usual. No local progress information, only the number of the affected going up and down: on the first day of the catastrophe, we heard that 300 000 households had been without electricity for several hours already, then the estimate decreased and increased and then another storm wave hit Finland and it increased again. The cumulative number of households affected was of the order of 400 000, in different parts of Finland, meaning that about 1 million Finns had been affected.

Our news broadcasting was slow and passive, the operators did not understand their human role and purpose. We were struck by seeing their total blindness for using suitable media technology and even make business of it. The catastrophe would have been a perfect opportunity for the radio to create a significant bondage and build trust with their audiences but they failed to do so. Later I watched a tv-discussion on the power catastrophe on our national channel where one of our ministers, a manager from a major energy company, a leading figure from our ministries and a specialist on emergency affairs participated. Nobody mentioned the word 'radio'.

You would expect that once, when both the Internet and the mobile were down, radio operators would have sharpened up and seen their chance of showing their real human care and relevance. I would have been happy to pay 10€ extra a day for an accurate local radio service where knowledgeable reporters, perhaps only two or three of them, but somewhere around where we live, had acquired accurate information for us and helped us plan our life. Radio could have proven its social potential as well by allowing local people to share their observations, knowledge, and willingness to help. A little human-technology thinking and they've had a new service up in an hour. Nothing like that was available. Decades ago, radio amateurs had this role.

Everything is under control – not. Living through the catastrophe I realized the necessity to build healthy models for national technological infrastructure management and its related businesses. The management of national capital is a mess and a shame in Finland. I imagined such a model would be an essential part of national strategy, but it wasn't, not even close. All the problems we Finns suffered from were not caused by nature only but by ignorant politicians and by the unhealthy business models of our operators and energy companies. If we do not take care of our infrastructures, these and other willing companies will conquer them and we lose what is rightfully ours. This conquering is a most natural thing for companies to do, if they are allowed, because it makes money, kicks out competitors and make customers helpless. Unfortunately, sad examples already exist in Finland and many politicians are ready to launch more of them, in the name of 'free' markets.

The energy companies – and everyone in Finland – have learned over a hundred years that air wires fail when trees fall over them. Knowing this, they have still sold us the idea of a continuous power supply, charged us for that, and we have trusted in this implied promise. The profits have been shared over the years for this privilege they have.

Who pays for correcting mistakes? Imagine that a company sells breast implants made of silicon to a medical center and it is found out that the implants have a fault in their material. It causes serious health problems so that it becomes necessary to remove them from thousands of women. When patient organizations and hospitals contact them they just explain that "Yes, we are very sorry and we are already working on a better version, but of course, we will include the development costs into the price of the new implants that can replace the risky ones." "What about the damage caused by the removal operation? Lost working time? Other material and psychological costs", you may ask. "Sorry, can't help you."

Why should we pay for human-technological ignorance? Firms have made profits by selling cheaply manufactured and dangerous products (power supply that can seriously fail, dangerous implants, stupid AI) and the firms and their managers have been rewarded by their business success in doing this in an efficient way (selling the implant that was cheaper to make, power supply that did not require serious investments into ground wiring, AI that …).

Clearly, the lack of investments in better wiring was good business, but the power supply catastrophe caused damages, including direct losses, like spoiled food in households and shops, extra time and materials devoted on heating, evacuation costs, loss of working time, and travel costs due to lack of communication channels. The spectrum of indirect costs was huge, comparable only to the losses in wartime, including losses in businesses, lost customers due to their problems that were caused by the power failures, and many others. A curious national feature is that we are probably one of the leading nations in the number of illegal strikes, which has educated us to be tolerant to these national disasters and their impacts on everyday life.

These sad experiences made me think about the ethical aspects of infrastructure problems in any nation, locally and globally. The devastating forest fires in California and later in Australia and Brazil come to mind, as well as the terrible consequences of reckless mining industry. It's all about care: any company whose business is based on the use of global, national or local infrastructure must accept the responsibilities involved.

Business from infrastructure brings responsibilities. National infrastructure has fuzzy owners who don't want to pay for the responsibilities and only seldom, the innovators and developers who have invested their passion in developing it can expect to be rewarded for their contributions. As an academic example, at my own university, and in others as well today, for any young researcher, building infrastructure for the university and for common good is a fast lane for a young researcher's career suicide. Ability to plan and build infrastructure such as labs, research tools and software is not measured or rewarded and typically the use of infra brings no value whatsoever to those who built it. My own 'miniature experiences' on this date back to 1970's when programming vision research and speech synthesis systems that were used for dozens of scientific publications, including Nature, but where my name was lagging from all of them, even from the acknowledgements. Nobody offered credit for building this infra. No wonder then that the value of infrastructure has remained dear to me.

When infrastructure is not 'owned' and it is available for productive uses it becomes a target for hungry souls in business, research and everyday life. Society is typically late in realizing the real value of evolving, future infrastructures. Sometimes there are significant indirect effects like the Nordic agreement on mobile communication framework where early adoption of regulated and standardized communication systems encouraged Ericsson and Nokia to invest in right technology and to gain their leading position on cell phone markets.

In Finland, we have not had much choice in trying to survive our winters and hence, the original promise of our leading energy provider was to secure our living in the exceptional conditions of Finnish winter. This is forgotten now and our national power grid is being used for sucking our money from and via it.

When something goes wrong like in the power catastrophe, and there was a risk for major compensations for the damage made, the owners become invisible, national offices and ministries throw the ball around and prove how they have taken care of their own formal responsibilities and nobody reminds us of the history of all this. Whenever a fresh business proposition is offered, candidates pop up and become visible again, lobbyists, ministries and offices pave the way and there is a rush to the market place. That is the moment when we, as citizens, should have our eyes open even when our parliament representatives are blindfolded.

Here are some preliminary principles to start with, for parliaments and ministries to consider in opening any national infrastructure for businesses (for local oligarks, 'olicompanies').

- Ask citizens what they see as essential infrastructure in their life and country, why they feel so, what they worry about it and what they are ready to do for it. Don't use the word 'infrastructure' but talk about water, forest, space, air, lakes, archipelago, roads, …
- Provide a yearly asset document that describes the status of the main national infrastructures that people as a nation and as citizens own and what is their value for people, public services, and firms.
- Declare the ownership of the infrastructure that is under consideration for businesses so that everyone in the country understands who owns it and what rights this ownership provides to the citizens, as its true owners. A good model is the Finnish everyman's right.

Every Finn understands the rights and responsibilities involved. We understand the implications and learn it as a cultural practice, already as children.

- When infrastructure rights are offered, sold or opened for any actor, declare the intended business models for public discussion, make a thorough, open what-if scenario analysis that describes what the owners (we) can gain and what we can lose now and in the potential futures.

- Describe publicly what businesses can be conducted with the rights achieved and to whom they can be sold, transferred or leased in future and how this could happen.

- Describe the national investment history and any present and future plans to keep the infrastructure functional. This will help decision makers to decide about pricing and compensations for damage if needed.

- Make sure you can, as a nation, back up from a bad deal.

It is common knowledge how our forest companies were accused and convicted for their price cartels. Indeed, companies are able and willing to join their strategical forces so why not once create ethically sustainable cartels between energy companies, by sharing the principles of ethical production and distribution of energy? They would easily kick out unethical competitors who would try to break the rules. Other infrastructure businesses could do the same.

2. Sharing without caring is exploitation

Everyman's rights in Finland can surprise many of our international guests who are not used to moving freely in forests, rowing on lakes, fishing, skiing, going ashore on wild islands and enjoying the delicious berries and mushrooms wherever they can be found. In its simplicity (cf.

https://www.visitfinland.com/article/everymans-rights/) our
Everyman's right means: "Act responsible in Finnish nature".

What a wonderful formulation for sharing economy, and
in the world where we want to learn and support sustainable
development and behaviors.

Some time ago, before the first snow in the southern
Finland, visiting the forest here nearby in Siuntio, with my
wife, picking up delicious mushrooms (suppilovahvero in
Finnish, *funnel chanterelle*) for our Sunday risotto, in the
charming, wide forest, just the two of us there, we realized how
the everyman's right is an early predecessor of responsible
sharing economy, a peculiar form of nature-airbnb, an ideal
and free form of it.

We did not know who owns the forest we visited, there are
typically no signs or notes of it, but everyone, just like us, treats
it with respect, enjoys its offerings - berries, mushrooms or just
its peace and beauty. Like most Finns, we never leave any
garbage behind and try to maintain the nature as it is. We know
that someone takes care of this forest - someone we never met
and to whom we feel gratitude and try to behave accordingly.

There is a peculiar global aspect in this extraordinary right:
it is not ours only, but concerns other citizens of the world as
well. It is not dependent on where you live, what you own or
earn and it does not cost you anything. Only net and spinning
rod fishing require permission. Anyone can enjoy nature while
following the simple rules of courtesy, care, and good
behavior: respect the nature, don't spoil, destroy or exploit it,
don't go too near peoples' houses and living, don't disturb,
don't make unethical business of it. You can enjoy simple
fishing without any permission. All Finns learn this code of
conduct as kids – and most Finnish parents and friends want
to pass this wonderful tradition and right to the future
generations.

Everyman's Right is a legally defined code of conduct,
regulation, but unlike in Norway, for example, we have no
specific law to follow. Over time, it has evolved as a cultural
practice, dating back to the early times when the first hunter

tribes had their ways to share hunting grounds and live in the difficult conditions of the north. Today, new forms of adventure sports and games like treasure hunting have found the wild – within the limits of the Everyman's Right.

Sharing and caring economy. Learning to move in nature by obeying these simple principles is not only a joy but also a way to respect and care for something that we own together. Elinor Ostrom would again have a say and give a smile on this.

Underlying this wise nation-wide behavior is something that will be necessary for any future form of sharing economy and sharing of technology: motivation to think of others and leave behind something that is good for those who come after us. Without this motivation sharing is impossible and becomes only selfish exploitation. Growth requires care. Everyman's Right is a wonderful model example of caring & sharing economy.

Luckily Finland is not alone with this and more and more people will be learning this necessary future skill and have a chance to practice it in nature. New technologies relying on human design thinking will continue to emerge and support it, keeping up this amazing system and practice.

16 UNHOLY MARRIAGE

1. University-business collaboration

I have published a 'legacy article' on this topic (University-business-government collaboration: from institutes to platforms and ecosystems. Nyman, 2015) and will not go into details here.

An academic, working with ambitious human technology cannot do it without being in touch with excellent and leading technology firms, partnering with them and organizing various forms of collaboration. There are no fixed models for this and as the conditions for mutual engagement change, continuous innovations are needed.

World of science and knowledge creation transform fast and we don't know the form of the future knowledge forums. What and where are the emerging knowledge sources, how are they accessed, how do we create new knowledge together, how is this knowledge shared, valued, applied, protected, multiplied, made business, what will be the role of AI and ML in this – and how is old knowledge pushed aside, refreshed and replaced by new one? How do we as knowledge creators and our knowledge work environments change in the middle of this evolution? For a curious academic mind, it is impossible to observe this drama as an outsider.

Not so long ago, it was clear for linear thinking that universities should stick to basic research. Some other people or organizations could then become interested in the results – because of the promising profit forecasts – and start commercializing the available basic research knowledge and findings. Accordingly, the academic researcher must not be contaminated by r&d or the 'dirty' business money involved. Indeed, the word 'dirty' is not only evil imagination of mine: it was sadly familiar to a global company leader who cited it in one of the EU University-Business-Forum talks some years ago. The European etymology of this attribute is a mystery to me but it is used to criticize the researchers who work in close connection with firms. In between the lines it carries the message that basic research money is somehow 'clean', through mysterious ways.

At my own department, the war of words was explicit and meant to harm the reputation of our team doing research on the impact of high-quality magazine paper on reader experience and quality perception: our research was called, by some colleagues as 'toilet paper research'. The paper mill M-real Ltd with whom we worked had a known and successful brand in this sensitive, and indeed very human field, although we did not study *that* sensitive human quality perception (our experience-sensitive methods would have worked there, too).

An implicit belief in many argumentations is that the geniuses and masterminds live only in basic research labs. This view has its historical roots, the medieval catholic church as an example, and it is not unusual to separate the history of science from the history of innovations and technology. Today, you are not supposed to start your scientific career in a garage but it is a heroic place for an innovative technologist.

Researchers can be curious and creative creatures and for many of us, the search for novelty and new solutions is more important that the breed of researchers we belong to. This type of behavior will be amplified by the breakthrough of the new generation Internet, open X, and the coming boundary-breaking possibilities for collaboration. Magnificent human and social powers will be released and the question "Is it basic research?" will have no simple meaning.

Why worry? There is a genuine European science neurosis that expresses itself as a fear that basic research will suffer and will lose its significant position in the world of science. Not much worry is devoted to wonder what are the real mechanisms by which - through consult guidance, massive offices, lobbying, courses for bureaucracy, closed networks, and well-prepared and bureaucratically functional applications - big EU and other-money is poured into research projects. I assume it is partly a fear of applied research money, industry interests, power, and entrepreneurs - a fear quite similar to what is entertained by people afraid of immigrants and unfamiliar cultures. In Finland, only some years ago this was expressed by the Academy of Finland in a statement that our science is too much directed by applied research interests and money.

There are opinions about Silicon Valley, its history and its present nature, but even with its current problems related to living, equality and the power of money, it is an unavoidable example, especially to us Europeans, of an ecosystem where basic research, applied research, r&d, business and marketing can live side by side to benefit each other. Unfortunately, it is rare to see or read about models where these two parallel worlds would lead a healthy life by feeding each other.

2.   A fair bond between basic and applied research

Here are my thoughts on the foundations on which healthy future ecosystems for basic and applied research can be built in higher education contexts (see Nyman, 2015, above):

- Cherish and develop an ambitious basic research concept and build an economical and spiritual ground for it. Applied research can make profits and scale fast and its economical and human time constants can be significantly shorter than they are in basic research. Because of this, it is necessary to invent funding and business models that guarantee a sustainable position for basic research.
- Build an economic environment with a fair and ethically sustainable incentive code. This is crucial in integrating basic research and industry/business oriented application work. The challenge of ethics does not concern applied research only.
- Experiment with new forms of ownership where material and immaterial capital values are in balance. Today this is typically not true and anyone with a

slightest material investment can expect significant profits while major immaterial investments by researchers (time, knowledge, experience, network, personal commitment, personal value networks, passion) is treated haphazardly. This is an unsustainable situation and needs to be corrected if we aim at fair organization of basic and applied research to live and prosper together.

- Build social platforms that encourage cultural mobility within the research community. Dominating paradigms become methodologically, economically, and in their governance closed systems that should be monitored and prevent the potential harm they can do.

- Educate the industry and business representatives and their communities on the potential, cultures, and development processes in these new environments.

- Make sure that public sector, industry, and business representatives learn about the existing knowledge and competence potential, working cultures, and development work in the contexts where basic and applied research can meet.

- Secure economic independence by profitable business collaboration. Basic research communities must profit from their collaboration with industrial and business partners. Contrary to the suspicions that universities can become dependent on businesses, it is possible to innovate successful models whereby universities can reach economic independence.

- Help the young generations of students to adopt the multi-dimensional value system that this unavoidable development requires. They are the future managers.

17 ON THE VALUE OF QUALITY

1. Content specificity + academic publishing = difficult equation

Working within the Golden Triangle, we did not immediately brake the sound-barrier of scientific publishing, but nevertheless grew convinced of the scientific value of human-centered, semi-qualitative research methods. The main reason to this insight was content: it is a multi-dimensional human factor and it is not self-evident at all how to relate the content-orientated approach to traditional, narrowly focused and quantitative, basic-psychological research or to the applied segments of it.

Take a simple (some purist academics might see this as naive) example challenge from magazine industry, a high-class fashion magazine like Vogue. It can be (bluntly) considered as a high-quality visual-cognitive-emotional-commercial-cultural-fashion object triggering and serving human experiences with all its variable aspects ranging from aesthetics and style to color spaces, and from creative lay-out to the sales and branding of variable products. Everything of it, from its physical lay-out to the color gamut can be superficially, but accurately quantified, even the contents, but in its essence, it remains a high-class object of interest and meaning, an extremely complex, cultural product and phenomenon. To understand what a magazine means for a reading person, holistic approaches are desperately needed, but they are often outside typical academic realms. Our own academic environment did not see such a problem as worth studying or discussing at all. On the other hand, professionals in magazine publishing seemed to trust on popular and every-day psychological fads. This was strange, since billions of people read and view magazines and in U.S. alone, for example, there are about 8000 magazines. Fresh knowledge would have a tangible value.

Because of the content, fashion magazine psychology is different from the psychology of other high-class magazines although the human-cultural, psychological 'platform' on which all magazines live have their psychological-cultural commonalities or base. To call it only 'reading' is simply banal. In this sense magazines are not different from computer games. Take the National Geographic, for example: even if its production, print and publishing processes were identical with all other magazines, it's role and meaning in the reader's mind would remain a mystery if the content and its psychology were not properly considered; it is very different from Vogue.

It is practically impossible to introduce general, *research based* human guidelines to magazine design that would have practical value, something that the best designers had not already been aware of, because of their design history and special capabilities. If there is something useful to discover in addition to the way the leading creative professionals in the industry think about magazine power and functions, then something new and relevant must be found to make publishers interested. Designers don't typically have extra interest or money to spend in academic research to conduct 'impact research' on their products.

However, if the researcher can show, by data and demonstrations that the publishers could improve what they do, by knowing better their readers, for example, then they can sometimes become interested and as any other ambitious professionals, become curious about how their product works in the reader's mind and what could be the new knowledge that would help them improve and promote their product quality, creativity and to offer delight to their reader-customers and their life. Again, it is difficult, if not impossible to find relevant and current data directly from the available psychological research; the media with all its ramifications evolves fast and so does its audience. Academic research lags behind.

Psychologically orientated media researcher must be careful in using generalizing textbook-psychological concepts and research frameworks in media studies. She must respect magazine contents (or the contents of any other media) in its widest and deepest sense, and not only that, but from the perspective of the reader and her relationship to the content and the magazine brand, to look at the life and culture of the reader with curiosity and interest. This makes magazine (reading) quality a fascinating human research problem. If someone claims that brain recordings have something valuable to offer for magazine readers, it is pure speculation, ignorance, misunderstanding and underestimation of media world, or even worse. Measuring the photometric, color profile, psychophysiological and other subjectively quantified quality of the magazine, its paper, the print, and the lay-out becomes interesting and relevant only with the content and its relation to the reader world and experience, but content and meaning are always first. Then there are the unavoidable advertisers and other media-dependent actors. In this sense, content and quality are inseparable and specific to each case or genre of magazines. The same is true for arts.

2.   How and why study magazines?

Magazines can appear as so everyday objects and 'old school' material that they seem too naive research topics for any serious research. This can be especially so when compared against the modern, progressive digital media with all its possibilities. But think again: with their extremely high visual and design quality and style, cultural-historical background, object-nature, style aspects, the journalistic and editorial skills of the people producing them, and rich contents covered, magazines make a perfect high-quality human object of study. The Golden Triangle approach relies on this view and can contribute to the search for excellent design and ways to offer compelling contents.

When using real products as study objects, it is not possible to manipulate their components freely. You can take parts of a magazine, like texts, articles, photos or adverts to the lab and study them in isolation, but then the reader-magazine relationship becomes distorted and unnatural and the studies become useless.

We conducted our first studies in late 1990s with several genuine look-a-like magazines of different genres and invited a publishing house to design and produce them like real products but with the research aims in mind. We wanted to gain knowledge from our studies on reader quality impressions and the role of paper affecting it. The first test magazines were produced exactly as the real ones but with only 16 repeated pages and *ipsum lorem* and their properties defined by our research interest. The test subjects were people who had real interest in this type of magazines and used to read them. Later we took the same approach with books and packages, with real materials, for example, and in one case with a globally leading fashion magazine who asked for our opinion on some of its design features. I that case, for the research purpose, together with the publisher we created real-like, experimental versions of the fashion magazine. Qualitative and semi-qualitative data and correspondence analysis were used to get results that made reader experiences possible to show so that they could have real meaning for the designers. Of course there were problems, too.

The Golden Triangle method requires high-class material which is as close to real one as possible. I have met comments that this is expensive and complicated. Compared to the potential losses of weak design and material decisions, it is not. However, when conducting such studies one must know why they are run and how the knowledge obtained could be used in publishing practices to contribute to the magazine. The researchers must be genuinely interested in and respect the media and be ready for co-learning with their media partners. Cross-disciplinary team work was a necessity.

3.   From print to mobile phone cameras

Another example of our GT approach comes from mobile phone industry: camera design and manufacturing, especially the measurement of camera image quality. When we joined the project at Nokia we already knew that very high image quality cannot be defined in terms of traditional photometric qualities of camera sensors and optics alone (resolution, MTF, dynamic range of sensors, color space, and many others) – they are technically necessary measures of performance, but they alone do not offer accurate or relevant design guidelines when reaching for very high image quality; there are many subjective and technical, quality-related interdependencies among camera components.

As simple as it may sound, camera image quality is ultimately related to the uses of the camera: an image is nothing if it is not viewed and it does matter what is viewed, by whom and why. It is not a question of usability, which is a significant factor, of course, but instead a matter of *subjective quality*, specific to the content, the viewer and the device used, and to the way photos are observed and used in everyday human, social or professional settings. In this sense, the modern uses of mobile phone cameras, like the 360 deg systems and the future AR and VR, for example, are psychologically significantly different from the use situations of traditional high-end cameras even when their technological components are similar or identical. Their quality considerations are specific to image contents and use situations.

We worked with standard mobile phones and their cameras and camera components. One of the insights from this (starting from 2005 with Nokia) was to consider the mobile phone cameras, as devices for taking what we simply called *everyday photographs*. This may sound like a trivial decision, and indeed it was not at all typical within the industry then, although related standards (e.g. I3A Camera Phone Image Quality Initiative) were emerging. We realized that the quality criteria for the mp cameras must be relevant for everyday photos, that is, to their content and not only to images as signals. At the lab we had improvised discussions on what would be a sufficient number of image contents to be used in our image quality tests so that the measures of camera performance with these contents would cover all relevant use situations. Our first estimations varied: some suggested a dozen different contents and some even 30 or 40 would be needed. My own guess was about 20. In practice, less than a dozen wisely selected content classes seemed sufficient for differentiating between the mobile phone cameras and image processing components and algorithms at that time.

The emerging international standards (ISO, ITU, I3A) later had their own suggestions and guidelines. Today, specific data bases are available for validating the testing and comparison procedures. They consist of mobile phone photos, e.g. CID 2013 Camera Image data base (from our lab) which includes 480 images captured by 79 imaging devices (mobile phones, DSC, DSLR) using six Image Sets and the images have been evaluated by 188 observers. (Virtanen, T. et al "CID2013: a database for evaluating no-reference image quality assessment algorithms", IEEE Transactions on Image Processing, vol. 24, no. 1, pp. 390-402, Jan. 2015). In CID2013 the number of image clusters (contents) is only eight based on studies conducted on thousands of subjects and shown to cover rather well the critical imaging situations needed for revealing camera performance. Indeed, there are several important and widely used image data bases, but I have here mentioned only the one developed in our team.

In summary, the human-centric approach with the Golden Triangle showed its power in quality evaluation and r&d when working with any complex and quality-ambitious media product - a book, magazine, camera, AR, VR, 360 deg imaging system, computer games, and a 2D or 3D movie all of which we have studied and published some of our data.

18 LIFE ON THE EDGES

The following, longish stories are very personal and I first became hesitant to include them here. However, I saw this book as a chance to tell how we, psychologists, have worked with human technology topics and to thank some of my colleagues and friends with whom I have learned what I write about. There are many short stories which show that the work was not linear or easy. I have touched episodes that remind us that thinking and having ideas, or even trying hard does not happen without obstacles. So, I have tortured myself here by recalling some of them. This is also a soft form of a memoir to which I can return to after some years and see what I have later re-understood in it.

1. People matter

I start from relatively recent experiences, from the last 25 years. My team had an unusual academic marriage, starting in 1998 with M-real Ltd paper mill: psychologists in the academia working side by side with engineers and marketing people of the famous paper mill. Our collaboration lived on the open-minded, interacting, and welcoming team of people at the mill, and its network of local and international clients in their value network. It is not a minor aspect for a humanist researcher to feel welcome in such massive industrial spaces and settings, their powerful technological environments, and then of course, the impressive production and management culture. It was a learning lesson to our team's young humanists to learn to live *in* these worlds - the academia and industry - and not only talk about them.

The supporting atmosphere never failed us at M-real Ltd, when we needed to find new and better directions and never-before tested methods for understanding the end users of their paper products, the magazine readers especially - and to do it reliably and fast. The industry representatives welcomed our humanist team early to take a critical look at their most important product quality issues. It was energizing - not the opposite to what can easily happen - to hear the comments from the manager and the engineers: "I think we should be much better and more focused in this ...", "we need new approaches ...", "we have to see the big picture ....", "our customers are not interested in that at all, but ..." as I could often hear from Henrik Damen (now at SAPPI) and Esa Torniainen (at Paptic Ltd making wood-based, sustainable design products to replace e.g. plastic bags), both with M-real then. The inspiring and energizing culture led to ambitious and fast learning but also allowed clever risk-taking. Such a welcoming atmosphere in collaboration can be easily underestimated and forgotten when performance mania and static role constraints – and hurry - get a grip of people. University lab needs more than orders from a factory: collaboration, interaction, and a shared idea of the purpose are crucial success factors. And fun.

Our project was a major, decade-long success, economically, too including reader/user experience research on high-quality magazines, advertising, packaging and print in general, but also digital magazines and books. Later it led to r&d orientated research with e.g. Nokia on mobile phone camera image quality, 3D displays and 2D&3D movies, collaborative & distributed innovation, and even computer games research. You may wonder what has been common in these diverse works: it was the Golden Triangle, in all of them, in one form or another although we did not use that name then. The research topics were not new to us, but the approach was novel and dynamic in most of these fields and even today it is rare in most application areas having a visual nature. On the way, we faced serious obstacles, but mostly not with our industry partners or cients.

Similar methods and approaches as ours are used in other than visual, subjective quality studies and r&d; they can be found in high-quality audio, food sciences, textile industry and in acoustics applying subjective and acoustic-physical methods.

Our key insight in the visual product domain was that when a product or any of its components or features is of very high quality, neither present theories of perception, nor any findings now and in the near future of brain sciences have much to offer when the aim is to understand what goes on in the mind of the observer, customer or user of such high-quality material. Of course, it is necessary to master the relevant visual technologies perfectly in printing, imaging and other relevant technological aspects; they are necessary ingredients in any good measurements and production, but they are not sufficient. We had simply amazing technological wizards as our collaborating partners in industrial scale paper production, printing, digital imaging and publishing.

This may sound odd and surprising to an engineering mindset, but already early we discovered how the higher the image quality of still images, the worse even the best computational algorithms performed in estimating image quality. I have above considered this under the topic of 'Subjective image quality' and of course, the field is advancing fast and better computational and even image generation tools and algorithms are emerging. I expect interesting advances from the use of AI and especially semi-supervised learning approaches and generative adversarial network (with a human component) type of 'interacting AI' approaches.

Writing this personal story, somewhat out of the core of the book, I honor and thank my colleagues and name them, whose collaboration I have enjoyed, and who have been skillful and creative in building innovative ict applications for psychological uses. Such tech-minded people and innovators working within the academia who have not been after a science career, tend to be forgotten. Even their most valuable and useful accomplishments are poorly measured in the present science world, in the formal race for publications. I fully share the thinking that is beautifully described in the bestseller books *Shop class as soulcraft: An Inquiry into the Value of Work by Matthew B. Crawford* and in the book by *Robert Pirsig, Zen and the Art of Motorcycle Maintenance,* my long-time favorite, offering their remarkable insights on perceiving things and 'doing' the world and its objects. I have contributed my share, some of it described in my book *'Perceptions of A Camino'*. Academia seems to quickly forget these forums of 'soulcraft intelligenzia', the creative people, the makers, working with their hands and brains in concert. There is a serious trap in this today.

Human and social scientist, beware of technological development work! I described here earlier, how it is practically a career suicide for a young scientist living under the pressure of the publication race, to invest his or her precious time and competence in building infrastructure for others to use - that is, to exercise practical skills - for a research team, an academic institution or a unit, and to do this for the hungry, career-oriented colleagues. In no time, like in my own field, will he or she be beaten and eaten by the publishing colleagues who have put their time on running the studies on the systems built for them and writing the copy-paste-method sections in the articles. Afterwards, on paper and cv:s it seems that they master the methods as well, when citations are counted. This is increasingly not true but practically nobody cares. It is a strange, silently accepted fraud in scientific publications to put author names on article front pages without explaining exactly, for example, that author N.N. has no idea how the computational analysis tools used in the studies work mathematically, what limitations they have, and how exactly the recordings, for example, led to the measurement data obtained.

Nobody counts the hours it takes to become a competent craftsman. One professor brought (only) bananas - as a reward to me - when I was working hard in tuning his system for experimental use. As far as I know, my name was never mentioned as an author in the papers he published – except for one document I wrote myself about the system I had been building.

The embedded rational rule and incentive of today is: do not invest your time in anything that is meant for general use – unless you have learned to fight for your rights because the systems and organizations don't do it for you. Excellent leaders who take care of ethical principles are needed and can make a difference but my guess is, they are a rare exception. This sounds like paranoid science fiction during the times of Open Source and Open Innovation thinking, but unfortunately, in this case the paranoid can be right. A few enlightened people within the global academic management seem seriously worried about this.

In Silicon Valley, for example, the situation can be slightly different since technically skillful people there have their recognized value and there are extensive markets available within and outside the academia. This is a serious strategic challenge for the miniature science funding clubs in the smallest countries in Europe, the academia in Finland being an excellent example of this. It is not a question of efficiency, it is a matter of creating healthy work places, where any intellectual property, technological included, receives a just position and respect it deserves. I have earlier written about a similar theme in an article *'Infrastructure as a success factor'* in Psykologia 3/2005, in Finnish as it is a local history, a true story on how the present (Finnish) science system in psychology forgets those who have built its house foundations. This happened at my university and I don't know if it's a familiar phenomenon elsewhere, too.

Part of the strange mismatch equation is that technology advances fast, and any solution becomes obsolete, sooner than the copy-cat articles of fashionable research paradigms. Significant citation impacts have time constants of more than about 5-10 years while technology advances with significant time constants of about 3-5 years. There is no Google Scholar or technology-index for showing the power and significance of technological contributors.

Despite this, and not understanding it then, as a beginning researcher and with my enthusiast colleagues, we invested all our passion, time and efforts to design and build research and innovation infrastructure, electronics, sw, hw to fellow psychologists, to the department, and later even for the net of

Psychology Departments in Finland for open use.
Psychological insight was the guiding force in innovating
technology uses, not only technology. This provided us with
the joy of multi-disciplinary, creative and practical 'soulcraft
work'. Of course, we benefitted from it by learning, but as far
as I know, there is no published record of our extensive
contribution.

2.   Intel 8008 - my intellectual turning point

I love to make human-technological things that 'work' and
build infrastructure to make their use possible. More often
than not, I have built infra which I have not had time to use.
This motivational history of doing it in the academia originates
from my childhood electronics hobbies but semi-professionally
it is from the early and mid-1970's when I worked with
computer environments, building software and electronic
interfaces for various, simple laboratory settings. Our first self-
made 'computer' at the Department of General Psychology in
1974, Helsinki, was based on Intel 8008 that my colleague
Pekka Lehtiö (1941-2016), a psychologist as well, had designed
and I started interfacing and programming it. He introduced
the microprocessor to me and after that everything in my
electronic and digital design work and thinking changed.
     This might be fun reading for my young engineering
friends. I used the 8kb core (ferrite) memory of HP2114 as the
test memory for the 8008 and the idea was to build as simple
and clever code as possible (to save memory space and to
make it fast; it had the clock speed less than 1 MHz) for
running a (digital) sinusoidal visual stimulus signal-generator
that Pekka had built, and an adaptive, psychophysical visual-
threshold measuring algorithm I programmed and simulated.
The system was meant to generate sinusoidal, visual test
gratings on a b/w display, with variable parameters for
measuring the human contrast sensitivity function (MTF-like
description of human spatial visual performance) that Fergus
Campbell and John Robson from Cambridge had developed

and introduced. Such systems were not commercially available and very few in Finland were programming microprocessors then. Otherwise I used the HP2114 for running psychophysical method simulations and experiments programmed in Assembly language and Fortran. This might appear as simple and straightforward instrumentation work, but by accomplishing it, for a psychologist, it meant a tremendous philosophical journey in the world of HCI and a way to think about and imagine the potential of computers in psychological research and applications.

I have an amusing story to tell about my first encounter with '8008'. At around 1972-73 I had just finished the design and construction of what I thought was a very clever digital circuitry, using only discrete logic circuits. It run the method of constant stimuli, that is, it scheduled and generated randomly distributed codes of the visual stimuli to be presented to the test subject, recorded her responses (button pushes) and their timing, counted the results and then presented them on a seven-segment display.

To accomplish all this, it used shift registers to generate pseudo-random numbers (I even used random time sampling to feed the seeds to the generator algorithm), it had a simple memory structure for storing and counting the responses, and had accurate and adjustable timing and synchrony. Output was through a fast d/a converter. Any amateur who thinks this is a simple matter can try to design this process by using basic logic functions only. My colleague Seppo Hatakka, a psychologist too, was a proficient discussant when I built the system consisting of about 40 discrete logic chips, all of them nicely hand-wire-wrapped on one board. When the circuit was finished, tested and it worked, I read the specs of Intel 8008; it was clear as a day that such designs and chip jungles will become obsolete and all that and more can be easily programmed for a microprocessor. This created a most unusual feeling, a combination of frustration, inspiration and visionary joy, something that is almost an invariant aspect of the experience we can have when finding a better technology or a new idea to replace the old one, to think anew. Having worked hard with the 'old approach' only amplified the power of the new vision.

Of course, there were the mainframe and mini computers that served as mental models for what the microprocessors could accomplish. Many saw that future computers could now be everywhere. But this model was wrong, and it did not take long for us psychologists to realize *how everywhere* and at the reach of people these processors could be. The word 'ubiquitous' did not exist and neither did 'user experience' or 'personal computer' occur then in the mid-seventies. I believe that in this situation, we could, as psychologists see their future use better than technologists, simply because the idea of 'human behavior' in the psychologist's eye is so much deeper and extensive. This has not changed today. However, a psychologist who does not understand the emerging technologies has a hard time imagining transformational or new ways of using technology; he cannot have much valuable to say about potential HCI futures.

It was a delicious lesson on how an ambitious and new technology works on us: if we can live through the frustration of facing change and the imperative to rethink, a new door opens to us – but it requires serious work and practice, always. After 8008, at around 1977, together with Antti Merisalo, we both built another system based on Z80, the 8080 processor. Antti was a rare psychologist with genuine understanding of electronic lab instrumentation and an inspiring partner in visioning the future of digital technology in human sciences. He introduced operational amplifiers and their numerous uses to me. On the 8080 board I used a fast self-made direct access memory interface for a d/a to drive and synchronize our relatively fast visual stimulus displays. I programmed it in hex by writing the symbolic code on self-made programming and compiling slips.

A compelling single case study of specific dyslexia was run on the 8080 system and then published in Neuropsychologia (Nyman, Laurinen, Hyvärinen, 1982). The article has an important message to the study of reading and vision, but as it easily happens, it has been buried in the masses of single case studies and remained unnoticed. It includes some astonishing findings about the speed of spatial processing in the visual system and a fascinating beginning of a story of 'dyslexia' case cured. The secret behind the fast, visual stimulus generation required in this study was the 8080 with its simple direct memory access (memory cycle stealing) unit I built.

The work with the 8080 environment took me one step closer to real-time operating systems and inspired to think about the organization of multiple parallel tasks in resource-limited and time constrained systems. It prepared me for complex cognitive systems thinking.

The problem of multiple-tasks and limited cognitive resources has remained a massively underestimated topic in the public psychological discourse, although today it is more relevant than ever with the new technology. I believe that, typically, psychologists do not realize the relevance of real-time systems theory in their own fields. They don't know what a real-time operation system is and does, what is its theory, and how it is built. My friend Markku Silen, then at Digital Equipment, invited me to work, every now and then with them and it became possible to learn a lot about the best real-time operating systems at the time in their computers and even become a teacher and consultant on them.

Clifford Nass (1958-2013) at Stanford University studied multi-tasking behavior and found out how heavy multi-taskers are very poor cognitive performers. But even he did not consider seriously the problem of resource-limited, real-time operating system behavior as an explicit model for explaining the human phenomena he had observed. In cognitive psychology, the talk about operating systems (like in the context of working memory) and about interrupts is mostly just talk although formal real-time models have been around at least since late 1960's.

The interfaces used in our primitive computers were not fancy, but working on the edge of advancing technology at the time, was immensely inspiring and we learned early many of the critical human aspects of HCI: building them, made it necessary to think about their core aims, design principles and about the nature of the human interface in general – someone at the lab had to use them and the subjects needed to have systematic ways of 'behaving' with them. Don Norman's work was well known to us and it was indeed a pleasure to tell him this story personally when I visited him in spring 2010 in Palo Alto.

At Helsinki labs we used various, adaptive, psychophysical threshold measurement methods in the vision studies, and it was necessary to imagine and build simple, often changing user interfaces for diverse experimental purposes. Running experiments under simple UIs was an educational experience about the nature of HCI: they were primitive, but we learned to think about their psychology. An extra benefit of this was, that by knowing the best technologies available or about to come to the market it became possible to feed the psychological imagination of even better technologies and their uses. Combined with well-grounded psychological knowledge this stimulated the foresight for the future.

With the fast pace of AI and ML, coming closer to our everyday life and workplaces, there is a significant paradigm-shift taking place in human and social technologies. We need to understand and design systems that engage the best human powers and motivations, that is, our genuine human psychological needs, deeds and resources. It is no longer enough that the design of a device, app or a system has compelling functions and it is user-friendly or the images produced can be manipulated and they do not contain noise and false colors, or that it is possible to update and share personal data easily. A solid human-technological design ground is needed.

Future will bring technologies that enrichen our psychological, human core and soul, nurturing and facilitating what is most valuable in the lives and minds of people and communities. We must learn to master the human-technologically interfaces to our and others' minds. It is not an overstatement to claim that the search for technology-independent psychological phenomena has been launched. We aimed at this this with the Golden Triangle approach, but it is far from perfect and we had very limited foci in our work. Nevertheless, it carried some signs of human-technological future.

Strange enough, there still exists the hidden mismatch between engineers and psychologists: psychologically and empirically grounded work can, in the eyes of technologists, appear as 'soft', expensive or impossible to apply 'in real-life and real devices'. On the other hand, psychological models, e.g. of attention, working and other models of memory, perception – with some notable exceptions - often neglect and dismiss complex, situationally rich, real-life phenomena.

No wonder then that the giants like Facebook, Google and Twitter have become masters of dealing with variable real-life contexts and they continuously design ways to study for them relevant human and social phenomena – without the academic pressures and constraints. Indeed, empirically grounded work can be extremely inspiring to technological innovators, especially when it feeds original, lateral thinking and imagination and remains detached from the dominating hypes. Our work with magazine & packing industry, digital imaging, 3D movies, and gaming support this view. The psychology of technology should evolve faster than is happening today. However, this 'grounding' does not mean that technological solutions could be derived directly from psychological knowledge; visions and imagination are needed and often the best disruptive innovations become evidence-based only post hoc.

Seeing your own history at Intel Museum (if you are old enough). During my trips to Stanford and Palo Alto I sometimes visited the Intel museum which is a specific fun since everything shown there - microprocessors and their applications from the beginning of 1970's - is something I have touched and seen with my own eyes, almost like milestones of personal technical growth, having worked with most of the early models. Analogous to the Intel story at the museum, my interests and work took me from digital circuits and microprocessors to strategic brand management (analogous to "Intel inside" branding), for a while.

Seeing the first processors at the museum reminded me vividly of the first encounter in reading their specs - even without seeing the processor itself then - how it lured me with its 'I can do it' -call, so easy to accept. Looking at the later processors 386/387 and the not-so-inviting pc's, it was clear that the processors quickly lost the power of invitation talk, they became standard and had no transformational value except for their improving speed and performance. The early brand of Intel was natural, born out of the revolutionary potential of Intel processors.

There is another curious and inspiring thing to see at the museum: *Moore's law* - the original publication where it was presented - is shown in a cabinet, behind a glass or plastic window. Anyone eager to fit functions like straight lines to data should see this. The figure in the publication contains four (!) real data points from the years 1962-1965 and a (not a straight) line fitted to them. The 'law' is based on this prediction. It is a serious takeaway lesson and an excellent reminder to us, trying to see to the future of human technology: when fitting a function to the available data points, what matters is what we think and imagine about the function, its underlying phenomena, what it represents, and which phenomena or theory/hypothesis it tries to represent. For a creative and knowledgeable mind, it is perfectly fine to be 'wild' in this, even with scarce evidence. But if we do not know what the function represents, if we have no reason to imagine why it should be a specific function, if we just show correlations, then it's better to stick to the hard limitations of statistics and look at correlations and sums of errors squared. The future remains obscure then.

Strangely enough, some years ago, when I visited there, the first processor displayed was the later 8080, not its predecessor 8008 or even 4004. I wonder why?

The elegance of shadow boxing. In mid-1970's it was clear to me and to my few colleagues in Helsinki that personal computing will be a major development. The Byte magazine, starting in 1975 shared this view and added fuel for the revolutionary thinking. I believe it was the first forum from where I read about Bill Gates activities, mainly adds. It did not look great, but it was; it was more miniature IT concepts than real products and solutions, but a human-technologically imaginative eye could see far.

When I gave an enthusiastic talk in 1976 at the National Psychology Association meeting in Helsinki about the future of computers in psychology (my visions about future laboratory control, stimulus generation, experimental manipulation, simulation, computation, microprocessors), the psychologist audience simply could not understand at all what I was talking about and for a passing moment, I wondered if there was something wrong with my thinking and the story I tried to tell. Later I heard that the talk gave me the life-long (local) reputation as a psychologist who does not understand much of real psychology but is just a poor (perhaps interesting) technologist. I became a technologist in the eyes of the technology-ignorant psychologists.

It was a long way to the everyday use of human technology; multi-disciplinary activities were not abundant then. An exception to this ignorant psychologist audience was Carl Hagfors (1932-2001) from the University of Jyväskylä, who was a skilled designer of skin conductance (GSR) analysis-systems and who understood the value of computers for signal analysis. Once at around 1976 he invited me to his lab to program and test his transient/sustained model of GSR components. He was a curious character, ahead of his time but not much appreciated by the colleagues. Indeed, he did have some funny, even weird ideas, like how to implant warning devices in elgs and reindeers approaching roads or how to program a computer to tell an infinite number and variation of dirty jokes. I believe he had a patent - or was preparing it when we met - for 3D tv.

Technologically, it was already quite late - in the 90's - when I tried to convince the national network of Psychology Departments (Psykonet) to start using a collaboration software platform, Lotus Notes to support their multi-faceted and poorly coordinated activities. The reception was like a replay of the meeting in 1970's: I was supposed to introduce the idea in a telephone conference to Psykonet board of representatives having their meeting outside Helsinki in another University. At the time, I was the busy Dean of the largest Faculty in Finland, and the Head of UH had called a crisis meeting (economy issues), so that I could not travel to the meeting and had to step out from the urgent UH meeting of Deans and wait in my office, on the line in Helsinki. No-one at the Psykonet meeting-end made a connection with me. The mystic explanation I heard from one of the representatives there was that they did not have a long enough telephone wire (!) to connect my line to the local telephone-audio in the meeting. It was perhaps the worst network problem I have encountered since, and the project was postponed by a year. Nobody was worried.

I took the task to plan the system architecture with Antti Hulsi, a devoted cognitive scientists and technologist and its implementation started in the following year. Then I just got into trouble with some influential people there and what I experienced as a malevolent attitude problem so that after one year, I knew not to waste my time and quit leading the network task force. Introducing new, extensive technologies is often a social-historical-inter-personal endeavor, more than a technological challenge and universities are not different from other organizations in this. Of course, there are numerous change management strategies to manage such situations, but when there is no trust, shared goal and purpose, but instead a lack of interest or lack of curiosity or simply blunt malevolent behavior, then it is no use participating. There are all the reasons to expect these challenges to flourish with the now emerging AI and ML at workplaces. On the other hand, spontaneous passion, perception of opportunities, curiosity, inspiration, and collective support makes it possible to fly to Mars.

Channels on Mars: Stars, telescopes and image quality. From 1972, before starting my own lab and getting to know Intel, I worked for a short time in a vision research project at UH and became fascinated about visual neuroscience and developing the measurement of contrast sensitivities of the human visual system. The technological ground for the project was created by Pekka Lehtiö and I spent long hours learning programming and simulation, running the simulations of the threshold algorithms, and programming device drivers and implementing threshold algorithms for psychophysical lab experiments. Photometric calibration of the display systems, programming the drivers for millisecond control of the displays taught many things about visual stimuli, image technologies, 2D signal mathematics and calibration measures. All the earlier knowledge about optical design, astronomy, and telescopes that I had gathered from studying astronomical telescopes with Martti Koskimo, proved both useful and inspiring. Together with the background in amateur astronomy and the passion for computer instrumentation was a natural base to build systems for vision research. As is often the case, cross-disciplinary influences feed creativity.

With Martti Koskimo - with whom we were also the founding members, and among the first blackbelts of the first karate club, Wadokan in Finland - from 1967 on, we had intensive discussions about image quality of astronomical telescopes. Martti is an amazing professional-like amateur astronomer who has excellent knowledge of optical design and computer-guided manufacturing and measuring of optical components. Different telescopes have different anomalies and there are numerous models and methods by which optical corrections can be accomplished and evaluated.

A natural key topic in our discussions in 1970s was, how to optimize image quality for different purposes, like seeing faint stars and star clusters, or seeing the details on the surface of the Moon, Mars or Saturn. We realized that diffraction limit (Rayleigh criteria) is but a relative measure and that what humans see when looking at the surface of Mars, for example, is much more complicated than seeing faint stars. In addition, observing the rills on the surface of the Moon shows how the visual system is not only a set of spatial frequency filters, but it has intelligent, computational skills as shown by the ability to see subtle discontinuities in image details. Sky and Telescope - magazine was almost spiritual nourishment to read and learn about these topics and I still read its Finnish equivalent, the wonderful 'Tähdet ja Avaruus' -magazine I sometimes like to subscribe to my close friends and their children. I wrote three short articles to it in mid 1970's on the topic of 'Physiological optics' offering perceptual-psychological insights to amateur astronomers.

Still today, even the best visual system theories are unable to explain the complex and multi-functional visual processes that every amateur astronomer can experience any night. We imagined various possibilities to correct atmospheric turbulence and to compensate for 'seeing conditions', that is now a reality in adaptive optics. Spatial frequency analysis came to some help through Tom Cornsweet's book on 'Visual perception'. Reading Goodman's book on Fourier optics and Rosenfeld's book on digital image processing, made it clear that complex measures and computational tools are required to characterize the quality of natural/complex optical images - and vision. Later at around 1983, I was lucky to get to know professor Fergus Campbell (1924-1993) who invited me and my colleague Pentti Laurinen to visit him at his Cambridge lab. With John Robson, also from Cambridge, they had originally introduced the spatial frequency approach to the psychophysical study of human vision. This theoretical and practical framework had predecessors like Otto Schade, television image quality pioneer, but Campbell and Robson and their colleagues gave the Contrast Sensitivity Function (CSF) of human vision a clear formulation and introduced the world-wide measurement practices. The concept was inspiring to computer scientists, physiologists and ophthalmologists and I realized that there indeed was a tribe of physiologists-psychologists who shared the same passions with optics and computers as I did.

Over our meetings at Cambridge I got to know Fergus and like a blessing, he became an influential and supporting mentor, the only one I have had during my science career. I still miss him, and enjoy remembering many of his views and remarks that could shine light on the idea of ambitious science and the idea of pure minds working in science. In the middle of the hasty, performance-oriented citation race, I remember his comment to colleagues bragging about their 16-hour working days: *"All we desperately need is a five-minutes break in this continuous stupidity."*

Looking back, at the UH lab and its followers I can return to the vision topic, to our different and fresh approach, which rests on paying respect to what people in real life look at, experience visually and what is relevant for them – like for the astronomer looking at the sky through telescope.

We named the approach 'Interpretation Based Quality', IBQ. It is still somewhat a mystery to me, what the present young generation of image quality researchers see as the most important human image quality challenges and where do these views originate from. Imaging technology has achieved a very high-level performance, creating an illusion that it is now simply a technological matter to make best possible images. However, subjective image quality experience remains a slowly opening mystery. It is possible though, that this qualitative challenge of what can be seen through instruments will remain with the best systems built by man. In fact, even the publicized images from Mars are often technologically tuned (sometimes by hand) so that they offer the information that we, as humans want and love to see. Machines may record unseen things but we are curious and imaginative – we select what to look for and we can close our eyes.

3. Obstacles

I have here earlier told how it is not easy to get people and firms excited and willing to invest their time and money in the best of ideas in human technology. In the following I return to some of these topics shortly, but the motivation is not to bemoan on this, but to demonstrate some of the challenges waiting when moving on the slippery edge of human technology.

Following the news from the leading firms and innovators one is lured to think they are practically sucking every clever human insight into their products, but this is far from the truth, even today. Even the simplest, psychologically grounded ideas and concepts remain extremely difficult, if not impossible to introduce to the dominant firms, platforms and technologies. Why this is so, was one reason to write this book, trying to understand it myself, too.

Why don't firms implement the best psychological insights in their products? The most amazing turn-down experience I've described above was the Nokia case in the year 2000, for which the history – what Apple did - has shown what its scale was. Even simple and straightforward presentations to the firm, to the management and the influential technology staff did not matter. When it is a question of life, it should, but it didn't. This is not infrequent in Finland, but my empirically based guess is, it's not unfamiliar in Silicon Valley either.

Organizational agnosia. Agnosia is a peculiar neurological disorder where the patient can have normal sensory functions, his overall mental processes might work well and there is nothing wrong with his everyday perception and memory, but he is unable to recognize certain specific, complex patterns or objects like faces, some artifacts or even colors. It offers a tempting analogy and a reminder of what I have sometimes experienced in firms and other organizations where I've

378

offered new psychological insights to their services and technologies.

After the year 2000/2001 when I had suggested Nokia that they "*should have an architecturally open structure*" we could follow iPhone launch in 2007 and App Store opening in 2008. There would have been several years to prepare and implement a revolutionary strategy. Of course, there is the possibility that Nokia had been unable to build the extensive and holistic strategy that made Apple the king of mobile phone business. But nobody seemed interested in considering what this 'opening' would mean.

Reviving the recollections now, it is possible that there was a reason to the agnosia, that I cannot know. I think I can remember some Symbian enthusiasm already then – although I knew nothing about it and nobody told me about it. Perhaps they had already stepped on the Symbian train and rushed on the rails but there was no doubt on my mind that they were heading to the end of rails. It was just impossible to know what the competitors would do next and how soon, but I was convinced they would do something of significance. Failing to get good ideas through is a psychological if not personal-ethical test. I never imagined going to a competing firm and try to suggest the same strategy to them. I remained a serious Nokia fan, but an outsider.

Then there is the problem of role expectations. Why would firms listen to a *psychology* professor offering his 'strategically uncomfortable' psychological insights about human technology? In case of Nokia there was the monumental drama Nokia was experiencing: it's turnover in 2001 was 31 bn€ - there was no place for 'loose human talk'. Now after two decades it indeed looks like a case of strategic agnosia, a most dangerous form of it, where the patient – a firm in this case – does not even know that it suffers from this problem. Academia is not free from these problems either.

A psychological case of technology-independence. Sometimes in 2005 or so with my team at University of Helsinki (UH), we tried to participate in a UH pedagogical technology competition, a very human endeavor as we saw it. We were enthusiast about our successful, distributed collaboration model we had developed and worked with for several years, studying and improving it every year. We had learnt how problematic and rare it is to build technology-independent pedagogical models. So, to the competition we introduced our *technology-independent pedagogical model* of building and managing distributed collaboration between university courses, firms and organizations. It was implemented in educational settings, typically at the university level, for 2nd to 4th year students from different fields, from psychology, technology and economics.

We had tested it with several large business and public sector customers benefitting from innovative student work, and it was used for organizing this as distributed collaboration. The model included relevant teaching and learning episodes, in a way that is not grounded to any specific technological platform or to collaboration tools like emails, chat-forums, and knowledge banks. The idea was to secure that at the beginning of each course, we were free to choose any technological architecture and platform. Anyone working on this field knows that it is not at all a trivial matter to do it in technologically feasible manner. As far as we (Jyrki Kaistinen, Jari Lehto, Pentti Marttiin, Jari Takatalo and me) knew, there were no such explicit models available in the literature and it was rather original thinking we presented in the application. The response from the evaluation committee?

"It is impossible to see what this has to do with educational technology. It does not match the requirements for participation."

We were kicked out from the start. They did not even want to hear us. Well, the costs of this loss were not major, only mildly psychological – our hilarious frustration - since we knew the approach had everything to do with any technology, present and future and it had worked extremely well.

It is not rare to hear the argument – I have my bag full of stories on this - that focusing seriously on future-looking and technologically viable human factors and running experiments to test design alternatives (I don't mean focus group studies or living labs which I never used, their context is different) is too expensive. But of course - and I have seen it in real-life media studies, for example - it is possible to run insane, costly experiments that are a waste of money and that the management funding it don't even see it as strange.

If there were sometimes challenges with firms, the work in the Finnish academia was never easier. Conducting applied research within the Golden Triangle in 1990s, did not immediately lead to standard research articles and our citation counts were modest at first. Clearly, the mixed-approach research remains problematic in the present-day academic performance measurement environment. When technology advances fast, as is happening with visual technologies and new media, for example, new design- and use paradigms emerge faster than the academic performance measurement practices can follow. In the long run this leads to serious problems in how to support and maintain this mixed research orientation in the academia.

My own experience from the Institute of Behavioral Sciences and its Faculty (UH) was a unique horror story: the management simply neglected us over twenty years, the ignorant evaluators repeated their totally misplaced 'critical evaluation advice' and finally when we just continued our own extremely successful approach at POEM, they started kicking out our competent and talented people. There are several 'content orientated' local factor behind this as well, but basically it was a question of opposing the applied research direction and its value base in the traditional academia. My guess is that we were not the only ones suffering from this. This situation is not rare outside Finland and it is one of the reasons, in addition to money, the new knowledge creators like Google and Facebook have now their chances to find a strong, if not a leading role in beating the academia in applied research. Innovators may often feel that they are pushing their ideas with a rope and of course, the only healthy solution is to act and move, preferably laterally and not to stop.

Management talk about the importance of users and applications is easy, but professionally, it is a serious and demanding task to know which human aspects are such that they should and could be served well, as soon as technology allows it, and to invest in them early. Often everyone seems to have a say on the human factor matters, from CEO's, CEE's, Business Directors to anyone but only seldom a devoted and experienced professional human specialist is invited. Steve Jobs was different, but his value did not originate from his position - the position was necessary to drive through his transformational ideas. He was indeed a materialized decision maker who decided on human factors, over anything else. Few firms can enjoy from such a use of power (and the pains) in these matters and have a rare combination of competences to lead the firm. A sustainable and economically viable design culture is necessary, where human-technological factors are proactively analyzed, questioned, decided upon, and continuously refreshed during the design process. It is extremely rare to meet technologists who understand the potential business benefits of unusual human solutions. Numbers are difficult to manage in this context.

I believe that rich and imaginatively grounded psychological knowledge is the best way to forecast future technological breakthroughs that concern everyday life. The problem is, how to identify the relevant realms of psychological knowledge and thinking that have this forecasting potential and how to get these ideas through organizational and other barriers?

Our experiences from the reviews on our human technology articles have shown how the reviewers, having an apparently engineering science or industry background, can be blind and reluctant to a thorough empirical and critical psychological testing. They enjoy using ready-made, or off-the-hat type of fashionable and inviting concepts, with a thin or non-existent empirical or human-theoretical support. Strange enough, especially engineers and economists seem to become madly inspired whenever brain studies and physiological recordings, almost in any form, are included in the studies concerning human nature and experiences. Brain recording or physiological recording tricks seems to work like a Trojan horse with the appearance of the trustworthy clinical-white and grey. There is even research on how readers are biased by colorful brain image photographs in scientific articles. A plethora of ill-defined concepts and ideas can be introduced when brain recordings, scanning images, or mappings are used. The psychological content of these stories often just collapses, without anyone noticing it. I have written about this for the Innovation Journalism 7 Conference at Stanford, summer 2010 (Nyman et al., 2010).

4. Healthy workplace makes us bright

We do live in a complex world, both privately and in organizations. Surprises wait for us, be they related to future work, the design of AI at work places and loss of jobs or just unhealthy impacts of social media on individual growth and public behaviors. How to survive disastrous events in organizational life? The answer is simple and it scales up: in the middle of the turbulence and confusion, build a healthy work place and a community around your own work, whether it is your board of directors, your team, or your partners working with you. Don't fight and revenge; we can be strong without a fight; don't' join the circle of destruction; help your young colleagues to continue building a healthy environment. Make it heritable. Trust the self-organizing power of healthy relationships. Trust the positive opportunities of future technology, especially in any of its social forms, and nourish them. Why? Because it makes us bright and creative. Because it gives us ears to hear and eyes to see. Because it is healthy, in a very human sense.

Several years ago I wrote a short column to a journal "Tekniikan näköalat/Visions of technology" of Tekes "Flames of motivation in enterprises" and offered a checklist for the creation of positive flames in a firm or any other organization:

- Does your organization have a valuable aim such as special quality, innovation, recognition, ethical product or a service or other non-quantifiable aim?
- Does the personnel experience that they have been provided with an opportunity to work at the upper limit of their own passionate competence?
- Do the personnel feel that they have been provided with the conditions and resources to excel in their work?
- Do you follow the "no asshole rule" (cf. Robert Sutton from Stanford) in recruiting the management and other workers?
- Are good manners a necessity at your workplace? (cf. Jeffrey Pfeffer, Stanford)?
- Is the management capable and willing to interfere when misbehavior and unjust behavior occur?
- Do at least 3/4 of the personnel feel that the rewards and salaries are fairly determined?
- Do you have time to immerse in other activities besides your core tasks?
- Is your organization free from local 'politics'?

Based on our research and collaboration on management with Marko Parkkinen, CEO and his team at SEEDI Ltd Finland, I would add at least three elements to this:

- Do you have people who are excellent in perceiving opportunities both outside and within the organization?
- Do you have people who can inspire others to participate in development work?
- Do you have people who get things done?

My claim, based on purely subjective, qualitative experiences over the years, is that if you can say "yes" to these, then something good is happening or is about to happen in and to your organization. This is difficult to prove but I believe that even a failure in business or other organizational activity - still having these characteristics - provides better potential and an increased probability for success in the future, the power of resilience. I also believe that any organization, small or large, which is not able to say "yes" to these simple items will break up and loose its social and intellectual capital.

How to get there? Finland today is probably the number one country in *talking* about being the number one country in the world. We are on the top of numerous rankings, extending from equality to national happiness. Curious enough, it seems that this national discourse is not the cause of our undeniable international success like being the best place to live in, having hosted Nokia with its great history, or having top quality basic education system. Instead, having experienced this success, many want to join this conversation and enjoy the borrowed global light of fame. There is a trap hiding for those trusting in the power of talking about and shining under the borrowed lights of success. It has not been difficult to notice the willingness of some – politicians, business leaders, consultants, researchers - to play a role where they imply that our success would somehow be attributed to them.

Today in Finland, a typical recipe offered for achieving any ambitious goals, is to invest in better brains, top-of-the-top scientists, leading businesses and technologies, right substance in education, and top units on any field and by making everything big. We want to buy and build – not to think - us on the top. Our journalists and businessmen are eagerly supporting the build-up of this new belief system. Something crucial has been forgotten in this success: it is not about what we do, what is the aim, and who does it but *how* we start and then do it.

Putting collaboration ethics first. This background on my mind, I was happily surprised when invited to give a talk to young researchers at Aalto University, about my own career as a research leader. After the talk, someone from the audience asked something like "You seem to put an extreme emphasis on the ethics of work, why do you do that and what do you mean?" I realized that I had indeed done that, but had not explained what I mean or why I believe in the importance of strong ethics at work place, even more than I believe in the contributions of the 'best brains'.

So here is a short beginning of an explanation. It is also an explanation to myself. The first thing to do to is take a good look at the mirror and see if the main problem smiles there as Robert Sutton reminds in his hilarious but serious book "The No Asshole Rule". Assuming that I have already done that, I can think about the value of a healthy workplace.

Here are some further ideas about a healthy work place. I'm quite sure that the members of my teams and research group at my university have a lot to say about this, and how well I have been able myself to behave accordingly. Should they indeed comment on that, on some forum, it would reinforce my definition of a healthy work place: team members can disagree, it is valuable, a source of creativity and it is not a conflict to avoid.

- We are different and do apparently same things but mostly for totally different reasons. People are actors with a purpose, not parts of processes, not even process owners, and we don't just follow management's views, visions and orders, however well formulated and wise they may be. These different individual reasons are the main drivers of what we do and a potential source for innovations that can differentiate us from others. This does not happen without a genuine acceptance of these profound differences. Often in organizational studies these reasons or behavior drivers remain invisible. In fact, I wonder if they can ever be fully known or visible; they remain the individual secrets of life and personal motivation. If seriously misunderstood they can become a risk factor at critical moments.
- When people show a true commitment to their work place they deserve uncompromised protection of their

intellectual capital. Their value is not in how much they contribute directly or what it is in detail that they produce, the real value is in their human commitment. It is not only about what they do.

- In the long run, any ingenious invention, innovation or a deed can become totally worthless, or not worth the cost if it is produced by unethical means. The logic of this belief is that unethical behavior has extremely long-term consequences: mistreating your colleagues in career competition, stealing ideas, spoiling the environment, isolating people, preventing others from having merits, keeping silent about information that is against your own interests, lobbying the decision makers to get rid of 'difficult' people who have different opinions, teaching bad manners and allowing false behaviors, revenge, all these maintain unhealthy organizational culture and create an unethical environment which becomes practically hereditary. The negative consequences become extremely difficult if impossible to correct quickly.

- I've been astonished to observe how negative behaviors and behavior styles can carry over generations e.g. in the form of ill-minded critical logic and a will to hurt and oppress people and colleagues intellectually (camouflaged as 'critical thinking') and otherwise. I have been amazed to see this spread over three generations without even a direct link like between a young person (adopting these manners) and the early originator of such bad behaviors. Simply by being a member of a team having historical connection to that kind of earlier behavior has been enough to infect the young, learning person. Someone powerful in the organization can initiate this negative value system, trigger the chain, lure people to adapt to this, to admire him or her, and create an atmosphere difficult to break because it has ecological power in the organizational career and survival race. In academic environments, it is easily misinterpreted as critical thinking or competence, which it is not; it is a destructive use of power by unhealthy individuals. We don't see the real effects immediately, but time, sometimes in decades, can reveal them.

- In 500 years, which is not a long time in human knowledge history, the potential harm of unethical behavior in making innovations today masks its potential benefits. Hence – I believe this is indeed so – no misbehaving genius has such a value that it would be wise to let these disastrous powers run wild: we may win by tens of years but lose by the hundreds. This is one reason why it is so difficult to build peace and non-violence; working backwards is strenuous and often impossible.

- Most of the good work in science and in other fields can directly benefit from a healthy workplace that invites everyone to think, to support trials, facilitate difficult but slow work, to help learning from mistakes and crisis, celebrate a good and fair atmosphere, and reward from finding alternative directions.

- The obtained results, the efforts to get them, and the rewards achieved must be shared in a fair manner, without forgetting those who have made a difference. Succeeding in this provides social and cultural amplification, a huge source of energy, joy and commitment. I can here repeat the saying, the source of which I have forgotten, that we are all on a journey together, whatever we do, in business, science, service, building rockets, cleaning floors, on our journey to solve the problem of the Universe.

- Clever minds move fast and in many a direction, simultaneously. They can be easily jammed by negative control, paradigm guards, and by narrow definitions of what is a 'result'. Results can be something that nourishes everyone in the organization and the environment – or the unknown future.

- A healthy workplace has a character of life-long curiosity which keeps eyes open to different directions. It has the capacity for opportunity perception and opportunity pursuit.

- It is easy to blame others, and risks hide here as well. However, it matters how we talk about ourselves, about our colleagues and the environment. I've heard a scientist talk about his 'enemies', by which he simply meant another research group. This rhetoric paints our own souls with exactly those dark shadows meant to paint the colleagues. Silence can be a tool of aggression as well, a separation of one floor or a corridor in a building can maintain organizational isolation.

Finally, how does this make us bright? I'm sure my bright friends have seen it already.

FINALE

The image quality work at POEM (Psychology of Evolving Media and technology, now followed by Visual Cognition group a University of Helsinki) started already in 1998 and I like to mention the young team Satu Eklund, Marika Koskenkanto (then Raitisto), and Markus Salonen together with Jukka Häkkinen making a significant contribution to our method development. At first it was not possible to publish the extensive experimental work since the funding company M-real felt it offered so much competitive advantage on their market that they kept it company confidential. However, it's as good a sign of success as any reference count. Several presentations do exist on our about 30-40 full-size studies from the first years since the year 2000 concerning visual quality and reading experience of magazines.

We also worked together with M-real Ltd and John Brown Publishing company to produce the international award-winning series of 'M-real magazines' that dealt with 'ambitious' vision, publishing, magazine design and printing. It became a major source of inspiration and was based both on our knowledge on visual perception and the progressive design and publishing ideas from John Brown Publishing people.

Working intensively with Nokia - mobile phone camera image quality and their amazing team - from around 2004 we started publishing the data in Electronic Imaging (SPIE) conferences in California and many of our 'first generation' article references are from there. But there is a weird development - neglect of true content and insights - going on in the science scene in Finland, and perhaps elsewhere as well: scientific journals have been ranked and the young scientists (on my own field, at least) became reluctant to publish in these conference proceedings. This may be computationally motivated from the publishing and cv-career perspective but as a result, the young researchers miss a chance to meet and interact with the members of the best global imaging community, getting together to share, learn and publish their data.

From this narrow mindset-perspective the conference publications often had no reputation value in the evaluations by my ex-department where they were considered as having zero impact (or perhaps even negative as I have felt and seen it). In the reality of the imaging world I believe they introduced novel ideas and useful method approaches and applications, some that have even been partly copied. Indeed, we helped to produce the best mobile phone camera image quality in the world, on our own part at Nokia. During the last few years there have been several interesting spin-offs from this research approach, related to e.g. decision making (cf. the recent work by Tuomas Leisti).

Only a couple of months before these final edits, Jaakko Mattila, a wonderful Finnish artist asked me to look at his works and tell, as a perceptual psychologist, what I 'perceive' in them, and to tell it in his beautiful book "Works on Paper – Watercolours and etchings 2006-2019". I ended up with a short article: "Let there be a mistake – and light!" What could be a better exclamation to end this essay. Mistakes can be a blessing and a start of something, like Jaakko's series of amazing works.

ABOUT THE AUTHOR

Dr. Göte Nyman (born 1947) is a professor of Psychology at University of Helsinki, Finland (UH, emeritus) and has worked in numerous fields extending from basic research on vision and the brain, to human technology, r&d, networking, and organizational and brand development. Currently he is working with IoB related apps helping people and firms in situationally relevant communication and developing concepts for human-centric implementation of AI and ML. He is actively involved with Stanford Peace Innovation lab as a team member and advisor, contributing to their work on promoting peace and non-violence, especially with the help of modern and future technologies. Göte has an extensive history in university management as a Dean, Head of Department and founder of the cognitive science program at UH. He is a long-time member of the Finnish Pattern Recognition Society (Hatutus) and has published about 200 scientific writings and articles. This is his sixth book some of them together with his colleagues. Göte's blog "gotepoem" is at http://gotepoem.wordpress.com/.

www.ingramcontent.com/pod-product-compliance
Lightning Source LLC
Chambersburg PA
CBHW030248290526
45785CB00001B/8